# THE SPECIALIZED AGENCIES AND THE UNITED NATIONS

DOUGLAS WILLIAMS

# The Specialized Agencies and the United Nations

## The System in Crisis

*With a Foreword by*
*Sir Anthony Parsons*

C. HURST & COMPANY, LONDON

*in association with the David Davies Memorial Institute*
*of International Studies, London*

Published in the United Kingdom by
C. Hurst & Co. (Publishers) Ltd.,
38 King Street, London WC2E 8JT
© The David Davies Memorial Institute
of International Studies, 1987
Printed in England on long-life paper
ISBN 1-85065-025-X

# FOREWORD

## by Sir Anthony Parsons

In the early summer of 1984, Mr Curtis Roosevelt, Principal of the Dartington College of Arts and formerly a long-serving official of the United Nations Secretariat, suggested to me that it would be useful to bring together a small group for discussion of aspects of the United Nations which, we considered, had not been adequately studied. We were both thinking among other things of the crisis facing the Specialized Agencies and analogous institutions in what is known as the 'United Nations Family'.

Mr Roosevelt accordingly invited a group of diplomats and officials of different nationalities, all of whom had experience of the United Nations or of other multilateral organisations, to spend a week-end at Dartington and engage in an informal and unattributable discussion of these problems. Our talks ranged far and wide and there was a unanimous feeling at the end that it would be valuable for further work to be put in hand. We accordingly suggested to the David Davies Institute that they might commission a study on the Specialized Agencies. This book is the outcome.

In the two to three years which have passed since our Dartington meeting, the outlook for the United Nations has become even bleaker than it seemed then. Britain has followed the United States out of UNESCO, and the financial crisis caused by cuts in American contributions, Soviet withholding of funds, and failure on the part of other states to pay their dues promptly and in full has severely inhibited the functioning of the principal organs of the United Nations, including the General Assembly. The question now has to be asked – will the system of international order created mainly by the United States in the wake of the Second World War survive as a meaningful instrument in the changed world of the late twentieth/early twenty-first centuries, or will the United Nations be allowed to degenerate into no more than an irrelevant, albeit clamorous talking shop (what T. S. Eliot might have described as 'the loud lament of the disconsolate chimera') with its social and economic functions relegated to being what another poet, Philip Larkin, might have characterised as 'a joyous shot at how things ought to be/Long fallen wide'?

The causes of the malaise in the Agencies are a reflection of the reasons why the United Nations as a whole has become an object of disillusionment and exasperation in the Western world, particularly in the United States. The United Nations was created as a limited body (founding membership restricted to those who had declared war on the Axis powers) of predominantly like-minded states, the Charter being founded on mainly Anglo-Saxon democratic values such as 'the sovereign equality of all its members' (Article 2(1)) and one member one vote (an extension of one person one vote). Today's United Nations is a universal body with more than three times the number of its original membership, comprising states which are very far from being like-minded, many of which have populations no larger than that of an average European or American city. Absence of like-mindedness is not simply a question of differences in political and economic systems and/or patterns of alliances. It is compounded by profound cultural divisions. Moreover, the whole organisation has become obsessed by political and economic problems concerning which the West finds itself in a small and embattled minority, the question of apartheid in South Africa, the Arab/Israeli dispute and the North/South economic 'dialogue' being among the most vivid examples. To add insult to injury, the Soviet Union cynically uses the United Nations as a forum in which to bid for the hearts and minds of the non-aligned majority, posing as the champion of national liberation and anti-(Western) imperialism. Small wonder then that the United States has become impatient with an organisation which, in the view of the present Administration, complicates rather than ameliorates disputes, contains a parliamentary majority bent on pillorying it and, what is hardest to bear, expects the United States to pay up to 25 per cent of the costs of a system in which the largest donor can exercise no more control than the smallest. In the Agencies, UNESCO being a glaring case in point, the situation is further exacerbated by the wide range of autonomy enjoyed by the Directors-General who, buttressed by the non-aligned majority of minimal contributors, are in many cases disposed to ride roughshod over the views of the minority who find themselves in the position of paying the piper without being able to bring any influence to bear on the tune.

Against this background, the trend in the 1980s has been for the major powers to address both political and economic problems bilaterally or in regional or functional groups, thus avoiding the tumult and the shouting of the United Nations, which has been inexorably pushed to the outer margin of events. I am not a starry-eyed idealist, and have had plenty of experience of the worst features of the United Nations. But I still regard this trend as undesirable, even dangerous, in terms of world peace and the improvement of the general condition of the human race. I have had first-hand experience of what the United Nations, and only the United Nations, can do in terms of defusing crises which threatened global confrontation.

I have participated in successful mediation and conciliation initiatives between disputing parties which could only have been carried out by the United Nations. I have seen what the staff of the UN Agencies can do in the field for the poor, the illiterate, the sick, the homeless, refugees and so on. If the exasperated West and the frustrated Non-Aligned would look to the achievements of the past rather than dwelling on the sterilities of the present, they would surely concede that, without the United Nations and its Agencies, the world would be a far worse and more dangerous place even than it now is.

The first step towards reversing the present trend must be for each side to admit that all the fault does not rest with the other; that the majority have been ill-advised to use their voting power and the weight of their rhetoric to try to bully the minority into acquiescence with all their aspirations; and that the minority have been misguided in reacting so negatively to their loss of ability to control an organisation whose rules they themselves formulated. Both sides should appreciate the potential value of what is at stake and move towards an accommodation before it is too late.

It is for all these reasons that I regard this book as a most valuable contribution to the debate about the future of the Specialised Agencies. It addresses all the problems I have mentioned, and many more, with an admirable clarity of analysis and absence of partisanship. Its conclusions are sensible and practicable and should be taken seriously by all those who are more interested in a genuine attempt to rehabilitate the economic and social systems envisaged at the creation of the United Nations than in the ephemeral glories of paper victories and rhetorical extravagances.

# CONTENTS

## *Appendixes*

## TABLES

# PREFACE

## by Mark Allen

The inspiration for this book has been described by Sir Anthony Parsons in his Foreword. Having served both in the United Kingdom Mission to the United Nations (as the Minister for the UN Economic and Social Council from 1968 to 1971) and, following my retirement from the Diplomatic Service, as a member of the UN Joint Inspection Unit (which also serves the Specialized Agencies) from 1978 to 1984, I share the concern of those who met in Dartington to discuss the decline in support for the UN Specialized Agencies.

In the last few years, the outlook for the whole UN System has become – as Sir Anthony Parsons writes – steadily bleaker. Not only have the United States, the United Kingdom and Singapore withdrawn from UNESCO; but in the United Nations itself, the very nub of the System, the financial situation is one of grave emergency. The effect of the withholding of contributions has been compounded by serious misgivings, not only on the part of the major contributors, about the efficiency of the administration, the level of staffing, and the procedures for budgeting and programming. A group of high-level intergovernmental experts appointed by the General Assembly (of which I had the honour of being a member) has recommended, among other things, drastic staff cuts and reorganisations on which, as I write, the General Assembly has yet to reach a decision. And the Secretary-General has ordered severe emergency economy measures. The administrative and financial situation at the United Nations is reflected in many of the Specialized Agencies.

I was therefore very happy to be invited to chair the Study Group assembled by the Director of the David Davies Memorial Institute of International Studies, Miss Sheila Harden, who herself served for a number of years in the United Kingdom Permanent Mission in New York. The other members of the Study Group, all of whom have wide experience in or around the UN System, were;

Mr Roger Barnes, Executive Secretary, International Civil Service Commission, 1975–80;

Mr George Foggon, Director, London Office of the International Labour Organization, 1976–82;

Dr Richard Hoggart, Assistant Director-General of UNESCO, 1970–5;

Mr Arthur Kilgore, researcher and lecturer at the London School of Economics and Richmond College;

Mr Will Mathieson, consultant, United Nations Development Programme, 1976–81;

Dr Davidson Nicol, Executive Director of UNITAR, 1972-82;
Lord Oram, Parliamentary Secretary, Overseas Development Ministry, 1964-9;
Mr Stanley Please, World Bank Director of regional programmes for East Africa, 1972-7, and East Asia and the Pacific, 1978-80;
Mr Curtis Roosevelt, former member of the United Nations Secretariat;
Mr Douglas Williams, former Deputy Secretary, Overseas Development Administration.

Dr Erik Jensen, Director of the London Office of the United Nations, and Mr Roy Mattar, Industrial Adviser, Commonwealth Secretariat, were present as Observers.

We are also very grateful for the help and advice given by the following, none of whom is responsible for the facts or opinions contained in the book: Mr Kenneth Dadzie, who attended early meetings of the Group in a personal capacity while he was High Commissioner for Ghana in London; Mr K. B. Asante; Mr W. H. Dodd; Mr Henrik Geer; Mr Philip Hayes; Mr Peter Lai; Mr K. D. Luke; Dr William Mashler; Dr K. H. Reich; Mr John Sanders, and a number of officials in Whitehall, the UN Secretariat and elsewhere.

At an early stage in our proceedings the Group decided that one member should be chosen to write the study and Mr Douglas Williams, who had provided a detailed outline for our initial discussion, was unanimously chosen to undertake this task. The Group met on several occasions in 1985 and 1986, discussing the various chapters, and the text gradually took shape, all of it written by Mr Williams except where otherwise indicated. It would be impossible to exaggerate the debt which the Group owes to him for his diligent research and his creative writing done over many months and many versions of the draft.

Finally, I should like to thank the Director for assembling the Group in the first place and for piloting it through many months of work, and to express our appreciation to Miss Mary Unwin for all her hard work on the editorial side and to Miss Esme Allen for typing successive drafts of the manuscript.

This book cannot be more than one contribution to the debate which is taking place in many countries about the United Nations and its System, especially in the light of its recent financial crisis. As a contribution to debate, therefore, the Group submits it to all who are concerned about the future of an historic institution. It is also the Group's hope that the book will help to dispel some misconceptions about the United Nations and that it may constitute a source of information, not always easily available, on the way the System works - or doesn't.

# AUTHOR'S PREFACE

## *Frictions of the Past and Prospects for the Future*

In the mid-1980s the United Nations 'System'[1] of · Specialized
Agencies established after the Second World War was undergoing
severe strain, which in one case – that of UNESCO – resulted in the
withdrawal of the United States, the United Kingdom and
Singapore. The main sources of this strain are twofold. First, the
developing countries feel that the Agencies of the United Nations
have proved inadequate both in the major task of stimulating and
organising the changes they seek in international economic arrangements (changes commonly summed up in the demand for a New
International Economic Order) and in the more practical enterprise
of providing them efficiently with the technical and financial
resources they need. The second source of strain, and the one now
posing the biggest threat to the future of the System, is the view of
some Western governments that the Agencies have been misused to
promote debates on issues outside, or only marginally related to,
their proper function. In particular, Western governments (notably
the United States) feel that the Agencies have been used to mount a
sustained attack on the market-oriented economic policies which
Western governments espouse, as well as upon some of their political
objectives and their social philosophies.

The conflicts are however taking place at various levels. Some
involve clashes of opinion on major political issues. Some involve
differing philosophies about the right way to secure economic
development and world prosperity. Some involve differences of
opinion over the functional performance of the Agencies, including
their administration, staffing and finance; and these issues, though
more mundane, have over time produced as much exasperation as
differences of opinion on major political issues or major economic
policies. The result of these strains has been to threaten the operation
of some Agencies more than others, but in the process the United
Nations System as a whole, as it evolved in the 1950s and 1960s, has
been weakened. Indeed, some consider that in consequence the
processes of international co-operation built up after 1945 are now
in danger of disruption – though this opinion is probably unduly
alarmist.

To understand how the present situation has arisen, it is necessary
to know something of the previous history of these Agencies and of

1 For a definition of the 'System', see Chapter II.

the System as a whole. On a number of grounds the System should be retained and improved rather than abolished or replaced, partly because in certain functional areas individual Specialized Agencies have made themselves almost indispensable to member states; in other areas the process of international co-operation which they have organised renders services to some member states which are of great importance to their welfare and development, and which could only with difficulty be provided in some other way. In addition, despite the fact that in recent years some of the Specialized Agencies have become arenas for confrontation, this is not true of most of them. Despite the many difficulties of the present and the short-comings of the past, the UN System as a whole has made an important contribution to promoting international prosperity and the organisation of peaceful change. There are ways in which it could be improved and proposals follow on how this should be done.

# ABBREVIATIONS

| | |
|---|---|
| ACABQ | Advisory Committee on Administrative and Budgetary Questions |
| ACAST | Advisory Committee on the Application of Science and Technology |
| ACC | Advisory Committee on Co-ordination |
| ASEAN | Association of South East Asian Nations |
| CDP | Committee on Development Planning |
| CGIAR | Consultative Group on International Agricultural Research |
| CPC | Committee for Programme Co-ordination |
| DAC | Development Assistance Committee (OECD) |
| ECA | Economic Commission for Africa |
| ECE | Economic Commission for Europe |
| ECLA | Economic Commission for Latin America |
| ECOSOC | Economic and Social Council |
| ECPC | Enlarged Committee for Programme Co-ordination |
| ECWA | Economic Commission for Western Asia |
| EEC | European Economic Community |
| EFTA | European Free Trade Area. |
| ESCAP | Economic and Social Commission for Asia and the Pacific |
| FAO | Food and Agriculture Organisation |
| GATT | General Agreement on Tariffs and Trade |
| IAEA | International Atomic Energy Agency |
| IBRD | International Bank for Reconstruction and Development |
| ICAO | International Civil Aviation Organisation |
| IDA | International Development Association |
| IFAD | International Fund for Agricultural Development |
| IFC | International Finance Corporation |
| ILO | International Labour Organisation |
| IMF | International Monetary Fund |
| IMO | International Maritime Organisation |
| ITU | International Telecommunication Union |
| JIU | Joint Inspection Unit |
| NAM | Non-Aligned Movement |
| NIEO | New International Economic Order |
| OAS | Organisation of American States |
| OAU | Organisation of African Unity |
| OPE | Office for Project Execution (UNDP) |
| OPEC | Organisation of Petroleum Exporting Countries |
| OECD | Organisation for Economic Co-operation and Development |
| OEOA | Office for Emergency Operations in Africa |
| SDR | Special Drawing Rights |
| UNCTAD | UN Conference on Trade and Development |
| UNDP | UN Development Programme |
| UNDRO | Office of the UN Disaster Relief Co-ordinator |

| | |
|---|---|
| UNEP | UN Environment Programme |
| UNESCO | UN Educational, Scientific and Cultural Organisation |
| UNFPA | UN Fund for Population Activities |
| UNFSSTD | UN Financing System for Science and Technology for Development |
| UNHCR | UN High Commissioner for Refugees |
| UNICEF | UN Children's Fund |
| UNIDO | UN Industrial Development Organisation |
| UNITAR | UN Institute for Training and Research |
| UPU | Universal Postal Union |
| UNRWA | UN Relief and Works Agency for Palestine Refugees |
| WFP | World Food Programme |
| WHO | World Health Organisation |
| WIPO | World Intellectual Property Organisation |
| WMO | World Meteorological Organisation |

# PART ONE: THE PAST

# CHAPTER I

## THE SPECIALIZED AGENCY SYSTEM: HISTORY AND POLITICAL BACKGROUND

The idea underlying the UN Specialized Agencies is older than the United Nations itself by some eighty years. The present organisations dealing with telecommunications, meteorology and postal services are the direct successors of organisations created in 1865, 1873 and 1875 respectively. Those early organisations had little political purpose but grew out of technical necessity in an age of growing communications by rail and sea. Some, indeed, started as private rather than government initiatives. They did, however, have two features which have become common to all their successors: they acted as clearing houses of information in their speciality and they promoted internationally standardised regulation (often including legislation) where necessary. Only later, after 1945, was a third function added: that of providing techical assistance in their specialist fields to countries in need of it.

The year 1919 saw the birth of a different kind of organisation which had and still has overt political, economic and – above all – social objectives. This was the International Labour Organisation (ILO). The preamble to its constitution contains two important statements which go beyond the merely technical. The first is that 'the failure of any nation to adopt humane conditions of labour is an obstacle to other nations which desire to improve the conditions in their own countries.' In other words, conditions of labour must to some degree be standardised in order to ensure international competitivity. The second is that 'conditions of labour exist involving such injustice, hardship and privation to large numbers of people as to produce unrest so great that the peace and harmony of the world are imperilled.' This was the most sweeping piece of political analysis in the constitution of any Specialized Agency until the arrival of the United Nations Educational Scientific and Cultural Organisation (UNESCO) in 1946, with its declaration that 'since wars begin in the minds of men, it is in the minds of men that the defences of peace must be constructed.' Both declarations gave encouragement to some of the later political excursions of other Specialized Agencies whose purposes were more clearly 'functional'.

In the years of the League of Nations, there was no growth in the number of Specialized Agencies, even though, through bodies such as the Health Organisation or bureaux dealing with narcotics, there was some expansion of activity in the social field. Instead, for most of its life the League and its principal organs concentrated mainly on political issues, and more particularly on issues important to the handful of sovereign nation states existing at that time, especially the avoidance of a second World War.

The failure of that effort had two results. The first was intellectual, epitomised in Mitrany and his Chatham House pamphlet of 1943.[1] This enunciated the theory that a major contribution could be made to world peace by the spread of a functional rather than a political approach to international relations, i.e. nations should devote more attention to working together on solving certain practical problems of a technical character – especially problems which cut across political frontiers – and spend less time in political debate. The second result stemmed from the failure between the Wars to deal internationally with certain major economic problems and from the political consequences which followed, combined with an awareness of the need after the War to organise the task of reconstruction. This led first to the creation, between 1944 and 1948, of three international institutions, all counted now among the UN Specialized Agencies though different from most of them in many respects, which have continued to play an important role in international economic affairs. Indeed, two of them have a great influence on the world economy. They have also – unlike some of the other organisations founded after the War – remained predominantly under the control of their founders, the industrialised market economy countries of the West. The first of these is the International Monetary Fund (IMF), designed to remove the international monetary instability and exchange restrictions which had bedevilled international trade and payments between the Wars. The second is the International Bank for Reconstruction and Development (IBRD), originally designed to finance reconstruction after the ravages of the War but ultimately transformed into a development bank largely for the benefit of the Third World, and given two adjuncts, the International Development Association (IDA) and the

---

1 David Mitrany, *A Working Peace System*, Oxford University Press for the R.I.I.A, 1943. Mitrany provides an account of his own intellectual coming of age and the evolution of his functionalist thought in Part I of *The Functional Theory of Politics*, London: Martin Robertson, 1975.

International Finance Corporation (IFC). The third is the General Agreement on Tariffs and Trade (GATT) which is designed to regulate international trade and to foster the negotiation of trade agreements and the removal of trade barriers.[2]

It was partly the needs arising from reconstruction and partly certain technical considerations which led to the growth of the other Specialized Agencies after the War. Thus the Food and Agriculture Organisation (FAO) had a reconstruction role in that it was in part an attempt, through international co-operation, to remedy the general food shortages of the post-war years. Similarly, the World Health Organisation (WHO) was designed partly to use international action to remove certain threats to world health arising from War conditions which had no regard to political frontiers. Even UNESCO could be regarded as having a reconstruction role, i.e. that of restructuring the minds of men after the ravages of fascism and militarism. Because of their reconstruction role, these three organisations had a social as well as a purely functional purpose, just as the ILO had already. Together they became known as the 'Big Four' among the Specialized Agencies. Other organisations, such as the International Atomic Energy Agency (IAEA), the International Civil Aviation Organisation (ICAO), the International Maritime Organisation (IMO), and the World Intellectual Property Organisation (WIPO), created later, were more the consequence of technical changes affecting the whole world which called for international regulation; therefore, in type, they were more like the organisations which date from before 1914; but all, once reconstruction was over, developed largely into agencies for the exchange of information, international standardisation and the provision of technical assistance.

One new element appeared in 1945 which had begun to emerge between 1919 and 1939, but which had never fully developed. The Covenant of the League, in Article 24, had provided in 1919 that 'there shall be placed under the direction of the League all international bureaux . . . and all committees for the regulation of matters of international interest.' By 1939 plans were afoot to establish a central committee for economic and social questions 'to direct and supervise' the work of the League in this area. Significantly, one of the underlying purposes was to create 'a worldwide co-operative system held together by a network of controls between government departments (other than Foreign Offices), professional

---

2 As will be explained later, GATT is not technically a Specialized Agency but is treated as such *de facto*.

organisations and individual experts' (Zimmern).[3] Partly in pursuance of these ideas, Chapter X of the UN Charter established the Economic and Social Council (ECOSOC). By this device – and to an extent which (as will be described later) has proved limited in practice – the UN System was inaugurated and ECOSOC given a limited measure of supervision over the autonomous Specialized Agencies.

There is no universal agreement on what constitutes the UN System, but for the purposes of this study the term will be used to describe broadly all that complex of organisations, institutions, funds and programmes, operating under the aegis of the United Nations which deal with economic and social questions (it will be described in more detail in Chapter II). At its heart there are now, in 1986, nineteen intergovernmental agencies (the 'Specialized Agencies'). Their work is much influenced by the resources made available to them not only by member governments but also by the fifteen Organs and Programmes Related to·ECOSOC, supported (for the most part) by the voluntary contributions of member governments of the United Nations.

The main elements of this System were *in situ* by 1960, although it has been much elaborated since that date, especially by the addition of new funds and programmes. By 1960 thirteen of the present nineteen Agencies had already been set up and were performing useful work of a functional character in a way which, up to that time, was mostly politically uncontentious. Indeed, before 1960 the chief political threats to the System came from the United States with Senator McCarthy's attacks on the UN Secretariat and attacks from such bodies as the American Legion on organisations like UNESCO for encouraging 'internationalism' and similar 'un-American activities'.

## The effect of decolonisation

A major change came over the System and the Specialized Agencies after 1960. It reflected the change in the United Nations as a whole

---

3 Zimmern outlines his conception of the League of Nations as a system of co-operation in *The League of Nations and the Rule of Law*, London: Macmillan, 1939. Interestingly, Zimmern asks the question: why had the League managed to survive the major shocks to its system since 1931, e.g. the Manchurian Crisis and the Italo-Ethiopian Crisis, without folding? He concluded that the League had become so important for other forms of co-operation that the demise of its machinery for political co-operation was insufficient reason for member states to consider scrapping an organisation they had come to rely on in economic and social matters. Zimmern's optimism may have proved to be misplaced, but questions about political disputes and the survivability of the UN System seem increasingly pertinent.

following the break-up of the British, French, Dutch and Belgian Empires and the advent of a host of new countries with colonial pasts, geographically situated in the tropics and sub-tropics (with all the ecological problems that that implies), many of them short of the administrative skills necessary to run a modern state and desperately anxious to match their political independence with rapid economic progress. The change had many manifestations. First, it shifted the political balance in the General Assembly itself. Secondly, since the new countries were short of administrative and technical skills, and because by 1960 the post-war reconstruction tasks of many of the Specialized Agencies were virtually complete, a new role was found for the Agencies: that of trying to remedy the administrative and technical deficiencies of the new countries by supervising programmes of technical assistance. New funds, the more important of which merged in 1965 into the UN Development Programme (UNDP), were established for this purpose. Finally, the change was big enough to shift the emphasis of debate throughout the UN System to one of concentrating on the political, economic and social concerns of the Third World, as much as on political relations between longer established nation states, which had dominated both the League of Nations and the first fifteen years of the United Nations.

## The political background

To appreciate the full impact of this change on the United Nations and on the Specialized Agencies, it is necessary to understand that it was in part a subordinate aspect of a wider change that has been coming over international relations for most of this century, much of it antedating the foundation of the United Nations and extending well outside it. This change has been summarized as 'The Revolt Against the West'. It has had several phases which have, in varying degrees, at times affected the work of the Specialized Agencies and have played their part in leading up to the present strained relations.[4]

The first phase, which was well into its stride between the two World Wars, was what Professor Bull called 'the struggle for equal sovereignty'. The concept underlies the idea of 'one nation one vote' which was adopted by the founders of the United Nations as the basis of UN procedures and budgeting (see Chapters VI and VII). As will be shown later, it is now a powerful barrier against reforms which might make the processes of decision-taking accord more

4 See Hedley Bull and Alan Watson, *The Expansion of International Society*, Oxford: Clarendon Press, 1984, especially Professor Bull's chapter 'The Revolt Against the West'.

exactly with the realities of power and (unless certain US initiatives in the 1985 Kassebaum amendment bear fruit) it will remain so.

The second major phase was the direction of the anti-colonial revolution. The strongest element in this was opposition to the European colonial powers and to their domination of certain indigenous peoples mostly in Asia, Africa, the Caribbean and the Pacific. The movement was, however, joined originally by the successor states to the Spanish and British empires on the American continent, even though their situation was very different from that of the newly independent countries in Asia and Africa in that their ruling majorities had historically profited greatly from suppressing and exploiting their own indigenous inhabitants. The United States, however, was not permitted to remain within the movement because it was too obviously identified with Western Europe (and *vice versa*) in many aspects of its policy, especially in the post-war period. However, changing patterns in the world economy produced, in the 1980s, some crumbling of the 'anti-colonial' solidarity which had dominated many of the debates within the UN System over the previous quarter of a century. Charges of 'neo-colonialism' (mostly in the sense of economic domination), especially against the United States, gave anti-colonialism some new stimulus for a time, but it may be running out of steam.

The third phase has been the campaign for racial equality, otherwise known as 'the struggle against white supremacism', which was prompted initially by the Anti-Apartheid Movement. Its most publicised effect in the United Nations and the Agencies has been the ostracism of South Africa and that country's exclusion or withdrawal from a number of United Nations organisations (see the Annex to Chapter V). It is doubtful whether any Specialized Agency except UNESCO, if it acted strictly within its terms of reference, could take much action directly relevant to this topic, although several have tried. Its most marked impact within the Agencies (South Africa apart) has probably been on staffing policies (see Chapter XI), and in this context it will remain a factor to be reckoned with.

The fourth phase has been the most important for the work of most Specialized Agencies. This has been the struggle for what the developing countries consider 'economic justice'. It started as a protest against various forms of international economic exploitation, but it culminated in demands for an internationally organised redistribution of wealth, embodied in the proposals for a New International Economic Order. In the case of UNESCO there has been a fifth phase. This has been the struggle for 'cultural liberation': in effect, a repudiation or a questioning of 'Western values', especially in regard to human rights. Linked with this has been a seemingly contradictory demand for the free transfer of Western technology. Both these last phases have had an impact on the work of the Agencies and on the relationship between developing countries and the West which will be examined in more detail later.

## The Soviet role

Many of the effects of the arrival of new countries were reinforced by the decision of the Soviet Union to participate more actively in UN economic activities following the death of Stalin in 1953. Indeed, it then joined some of the Agencies for the first time, although there are some, notably the FAO, that it has never joined. It was particularly successful for a time in heightening the 'international class war' interpretation of relations between developed and developing countries, with the West as the rich and the developing countries as the 'proletariat'. This theory of exploitation had obvious appeal to many of the leaders of Third World countries whose anti-colonialism had been nourished by Marxist interpretations of history and economics. It fitted in well with Leninist theories that 'capitalism, colonialism and imperialism' were the causes of the imbalance between the developed and developing countries. It also offered an explanation for the poor economic performance of some of the newly independent countries in the immediate post-independence period.

## The Non-Aligned Movement (NAM)

But whatever the attractions of Marxist economic theory, the great majority of the recently emancipated countries were from the outset suspicious of power blocs and reluctant to become politically involved in the Cold War. They favoured the policies of neutralism and 'peaceful co-existence' first enunciated at the Afro-Asian Conference in Bandung in 1955, which subsequently inspired the establishment in 1961 of the Non-Aligned Movement (NAM), the largest and most influential Third World organisation.[5] It operates primarily through Summit Conferences at which policies are co-ordinated and resolutions adopted; some of the latter will later be tabled at the United Nations on behalf of the NAM. Since NAM Summit agendas include most of the items discussed in the various organs of the United Nations, NAM resolutions influence the content (and often the actual wording) of the resolutions or

5. In 1985 it had a membership of 101.

amendments sponsored by individual Third World countries in United Nations fora even when these are not officially sponsored by the NAM. The NAM's tendency – at least in the eyes of Western governments – was originally considered to be anti-Western and anti-market economy, and (through Cuba's membership) more 'non-aligned' with the West than with the Soviet bloc. In the 1980s, however, it has shown signs of becoming more even-handed and has also been critical of the Soviet bloc.

## Developments after 1960

The effect of all these changes was that most of the organisations of the United Nations, even those whose primary function according to their constitution was technical and regulatory, became to some extent arenas for debate, or sometimes confrontation, between the market economy North and the less developed South. As it went on, the nature of this debate became strongly influenced by events in the ex-colonies in the years following independence, and especially by what many considered their disappointing economic performance.

In 1960 there had been, especially in the United States, a certain optimism about the future of post-colonial states. Their poverty and administrative weaknesses were popularly attributed to colonial exploitation; once this was removed it was believed that their progress would be rapid. Some believed that the economic problems of the new states could be solved simply by the import of capital – especially capital provided on 'soft' terms by the World Bank and similar institutions – and by technical assistance provided through the Specialized Agencies, reinforced by flows of bilateral assistance supplied largely by the governments of the market economy countries. Major structural change in the world economic system established by Bretton Woods was not contemplated. The development strategies encouraged by the United Nations, and indeed the accepted wisdom of the time, were based upon the building up of capital infrastructure through projects financed by imported capital (much of it on concessional terms) and by externally provided technical assistance in the forms of visiting experts, consultants and feasibility studies. These strategies also came to be based in many countries upon uneconomic attempts to industrialise, often using imported materials with out-of-date technology protected by high tariffs – an approach later stimulated by misapplications of certain theories that became current in the UN Conference on Trade and Development (UNCTAD), after 1964.

By 1970 (the end of President Kennedy's first Development Decade), although the Bretton Woods institutions had been remarkably successful as far as developed countries were concerned, these strategies manifestly had had only a limited effect on the prosperity of many developing countries, especially on that of the poorest sections of their populations. The failure was due to a number of factors – among others to poor harvests, growing populations, administrative incompetence and political instability as well as inappropriate domestic policies, all reinforced early in the 1970s by the oil crisis, which seriously weakened the already poor foreign exchange position of the non-oil producers. In the view of many of the developing countries, however, the failure was due to one cause only: the refusal of the developed countries to transfer resources to them on a big enough scale, and to Western maintenance of international economic structures designed primarily for their own benefit and embodied in the Bretton Woods institutions of 1945.

Again, this approach to the debate has been much reinforced by the activities of UNCTAD.[6] This organisation was established mainly in response to the difficulties of poor countries in using the machinery of GATT to secure markets in Western countries, but also in response to a theory of international economic relations, known as the Prebisch/Singer thesis, which held that in the world as organised up till then 'economic forces worked to the secular disadvantage of the poorer countries (identified as the exporters of primary commodities) and to the advantage of the more advanced industrial countries (identified as the exporters of manufactures).' In the jargon of the debate, this was known as the 'centre-periphery model'. Moreover, it was argued, this trend would continue 'in the absence of countervailing policies and measures' implemented by *governments* and the Agencies.

The thesis had two features relevant to the present work and to the situation facing us at the time of writing. First, the remedies it proposed for the ailments it had diagnosed were to be provided by government action internationally agreed upon, and not by market forces. It therefore tended to reinforce the *dirigisme* in economic affairs already favoured by many governments, whether on Keynesian or Marxist grounds. Secondly, many UNCTAD recommendations would mean the surrender by one group of countries – the major industrialised countries – of important economic advantages and assets and their deliberate transfer to the developing countries; at least, this was the view taken of it from the outset by the developed countries (even though UNCTAD itself and

6 For a good and more sympathetic account of UNCTAD than is given here see *UNCTAD: the first twenty years*, published in *IDS Bulletin*, vol.15, No.3, of July 1984, especially articles in Part I and an article by Alasdair McIntyre in Part III.

its Secretary-General claimed that its basic philosophy was one of compromise and co-operation and not one of confrontation and conflict). Clearly there would be no chance of doing this by the normal processes of international negotiation and bargaining practised up till that time, which generally involved the exchange of concessions from which all hoped to benefit, (e.g. the exchange of tariff concessions as carried out under the GATT). It was a situation fairly new in international affairs in which the weaker side was a permanent '*demandeur*' to the disadvantage of the stronger – at least in the short term, although all were supposed to benefit eventually. Moreover, the organisation of business in UNCTAD recognised this fact right from the outset by providing a basis in its constitution[7] for negotiations between countries by Groups – the most prominent of which have come to be Group B (representing the developed industrialised countries) and the 'Group of 77' (representing the developing countries), with the 'socialist' countries as a separate group encouraging the demand for concessions from Group B, while not being prepared to make any themselves. These divisions tended to spread to the Specialized Agencies, together with their many concomitants, especially caucusing and concentration on the minutiae of resolutions which could have little or no practical effect, rather than negotiating on the substance of issues.

The successes of UNCTAD in negotiating major structural change in the world's economic system have so far not been commensurate with the six major conferences it has held or the numerous committees run under its auspices. (The Generalised Scheme of Preferences is its major achievement.) The last UNCTAD in 1983 was held by many participants to be a failure[8] although, ironically enough, some *developed* countries considered it a comparative success.

This comparative failure of UNCTAD led first, in the second half of the 1970s, to a change of battleground rather than of tactics on the part of the developing countries. They switched their attention to the General Assembly as a forum for pressing their demands while also

---

7 The legal basis for the group system in UNCTAD is contained in UNGA Resolution 1995, 1964. For a text of Resolution 1995 (XIX) see A.G. Moss and H. Winton (comp.), *A New International Economic Order: Selected Documents, 1945–1975*, vol.II, New York: UNITAR, 1976, p. 836.

8 The US President's report to Congress on UN affairs for 1983 stated on pp.113–14. 'UNCTAD VI closed to mixed reviews. The Group of 77 (comprising most of the developing countries) characterised the Conference as having achieved "minimal results" . . . The US believes that one important accomplishment was simply the avoidance of total breakdown, given the degree of difference on so many issues.'

stepping up efforts to press them simultaneously in various forms in the Specialized Agencies. These efforts culminated in the Sixth UN Special Session of 1974 which adopted the Declaration and Programme of Action for the Establishment of a New International Economic Order.[9] This was a consolidated statement of all the Group of 77's demands in trade, commodities, aid, industrialisation, the transfer of technology and similar matters. The Declaration was 'accepted' by the developed countries only with many reservations. Indeed at the Seventh UN Special Session held in 1975 the US representative declared flatly: 'The United States could not and did not accept any implication that the World was now embarked on the establishment of a so-called new international economic order.' He added for good measure that the United States did not accept similar related documents such as the Charter of Economic Rights and Duties of States or the Lima Declaration either.[10] Other developed countries shared this lack of enthusiasm though less explicitly. Consequently, the effect of the Declaration on the real world of economic relations was even smaller than that of the resolutions of UNCTAD. Nevertheless for a time it had a great attraction for the other organs of the United Nations, notably the Specialized Agencies. It is obviously the direct ancestor of UNESCO's New International Information Order. In addition, it has influenced resolutions on a wide range of matters, some obviously directly related to it, such as the transfer of technology resolutions of the United Nations Industrial Development Organisation (UNIDO), or the programmes of agricultural research discussed in the Food and Agriculture Organisation (FAO), as well as others more remote such as the allocation of frequencies through the International Telecommunications Union (ITU). Constant harping on it has given representatives of Third World countries many paper victories in resolutions, but it has been a potent source of irritation in the West; moreover, its effect in the real world has been comparatively slight. Lastly, failure to make progress on these resolutions has aggravated the disillusion of many developing countries with the United Nations as a whole and the Specialized Agencies in particular.

9 For texts of the Declaration and Programme of Action on the Establishment of a New International Economic Order (Resolutions 3201 (S-VI) and 3202 (S-VI) as well as other documents pertaining to the NIEO see Moss and Winton (comp.), *A New International Economic Order: Selected Documents 1945-1975*, 2 vols, (New York: UNITAR, 1976); see also Karl Sauvant (comp.), *The Third World Without Superpowers*, 2nd series, *The Collected Documents of the Group of 77*, vols. V and VI, New York: Oceana Publications, 1982.

10 See Annex II to Cmnd 6308 (London: HMSO).

Another major issue which has affected relations between the West and the Specialized Agencies since 1960 has been that of their alleged 'politicisation'. This matter will be examined in more detail in Chapter V; but by way of introduction, it was this ostensibly which led to the withdrawal of the United States from the ILO in 1977 and played a prominent part in the US and UK withdrawals from UNESCO in 1984 and 1985. The charge against the ILO as formulated by Dr Kissinger in 1975 was that it had 'become increasingly and excessively involved in political issues which are quite beyond the competence and mandate of the organisation. . . . Questions involving relations between States and proclamations of economic principles', he argued, 'should be left to the UN and the other international agencies where their consideration is more relevant to those organisations' responsibilities.' Apart from questions related to the New International Economic Order, the main issues to fall into this category were: first, Chinese representation; secondly, the Arab-Israeli question, and thirdly, apartheid, race relations and liberation movements. Some countries showed considerable ingenuity in the Specialized Agencies in introducing resolutions relating to these subjects which were nevertheless more or less within the terms of reference of the organisations concerned.

The net effect on the real world of all this ingenuity in drafting resolutions has been comparatively slight but its effect in distracting the Specialized Agencies and the governing bodies from their functional tasks has sometimes been greater (though not as great as some Western commentators have alleged). So has its effect on increasing the irritation of the governments of some Western countries (notably that of the United States) with those of developing countries, since most of these resolutions have in one way or another been directed – like the resolutions of UNCTAD – against the policies of governments of the West. The result has been a weakening of Western support, especially US support, for the multilateral approach generally.

After 1980 the situation was worsened by changes in the political complexion of many important Western governments, particularly those of the United States and Britain. The general move by these governments in their domestic policies away from *dirigisme* and towards allegedly free market solutions reinforced opposition to the kind of collective action favoured in UN and Specialized Agency resolutions. It encouraged a trend away from multilateralism and towards bilateralism and regionalism (as in the EEC). This trend showed itself after 1980 even in those organisations which were firmly under Western control, and which up till that moment had enjoyed some favour from Western Governments – including the United States which had played a prominent part in their foundation.

Its most serious manifestation – and one which has had particularly unhappy results for many developing countries – was in the three major economic Specialized Agencies: the IMF, the IBRD and the GATT – the Bretton Woods Institutions. The examples of this trend were numerous. In the IMF, after the tussle over the 1983 replenishment of quotas, the United States refused to countenance another replenishment before 1989, thereby (in the opinion of many observers) increasing the balance of payments problems of many developing countries and decreasing the resources available to the IMF to assist them in their adjustment policies. Both the United States and the United Kingdom have shown hostility to the creation of more Special Drawing Rights (SDRs) and the share of SDRs in world liquidity has now declined to insignificance. (Mr Lawson, the British Chancellor of the Exchequer, even said that SDRs are an outdated concept.) The Compensatory Finance Facility has been 'deliberalized' (by reducing the amounts which members might draw against 'quotas' to finance export shortfalls) and the Extended Finance Facility discontinued. Above all, Western governments – notably the United States – appear in effect to have rejected the kind of international surveillance and co-ordination of balance of payments policies established under the Bretton Woods arrangments after the War, which were so successful in doubling the rate of growth of international trade between 1945 and 1970. (The US budget deficit is the most obvious example of this change in attitude.) As a result of all these moves, the resources available to the IMF in 1985 covered only 5 per cent of world trade, whereas in 1950 they covered 15 per cent.

Similar examples are to be seen in the World Bank family of institutions. The most notorious relates to the 1984 replenishment of the IDA where US opposition imposed a replenishment of only $US 9 billion instead of the $US 16 billion which the IDA had sought in order to maintain its level of lending to the poorest countries of the Third World. There has also been failure to secure fresh supplementary financing: as a result of opposition from Germany and Japan as well as from the United States, the proposal for a Special Fund for Africa faced many difficulties before its final creation. There have been similar failures with regard to the GATT. At the GATT ministerial meeting of November 1982, there was a failure to agree even on a standstill in the imposition of new trade barriers, and since then the GATT has shown itself incapable of dealing with agricultural protectionism in Europe and elsewhere. In 1985 there was even talk in the United States of going it alone in trade matters (in conjunction with a few like-minded countries). On the matter of the Bank itself, there has been an unwillingness to agree to a general capital increase, with the result that there is now a serious danger of a fall in net IBRD lending in 1986 and 1987 for the first time in the Bank's history.

Though none of these moves in itself is lethal to the system of economic co-operation and international supervision established after the Second World War, taken together they are a grave attack on its foundations. They are symptomatic of a general shift towards a shorter-term and more inward-looking approach to the assessment of national interest worldwide. The economic difficulties had global causes, but if the past is any guide, the refusal to attempt global solutions, will seriously exacerbate the world economic recession now facing all countries. Worst of all, the reluctance by the developed countries to support the Bretton Woods institutions indicates a declining willingness to seek international solutions through the existing machinery to the problems of world recession let alone the longer term problems of world development.

The Specialized Agencies were originally established as organisations with a mainly functional purpose to act as international clearing houses of information in their speciality and as a means of advancing international standardisation in certain subjects of international concern. After 1950 they all – though some more than others – acquired technical assistance functions mainly in respect of Third World countries.

Under its Charter the UN was given certain responsibilities in the economic and social fields, especially that of promoting 'solutions of international, economic, social, health and related problems and international cultural and educational co-operation'. The General Assembly discharges these functions in a general way through the Economic and Social Council (ECOSOC). ECOSOC has two broad roles. The first is that of stimulating the activities of Specialized Agencies and certain non-governmental organisations in directions within its sphere of competence. The second is that of exercising a general supervision over them. By virtue of these provisions the UN Agencies were deemed to constitute a 'System' for the purpose of dealing with a range of international economic and social problems.

In the minds of those who established this System between 1945 and 1956, mainly the Western powers, there was a clear distinction between 'functional' questions dealt with by the Agencies and the more 'political' questions dealt with by the General Assembly. Only the constitutions of ILO and UNESCO appeared to leave room for doubt on this score. The advent of a large number of new countries after 1955, however, with a different view of the history of the previous 150 years from that of the founding fathers of the United Nations, and with many large demands in the economic and social spheres which could be met (if at all) only as a result of 'political' pressures, changed all that. In consequence 'political' issues – or at least economic and social demands which could be met only by a change in the 'political will' of the Western powers – intruded more and more into the debates of the Specialized Agencies. Moreover, by 1985 the economic and social philosophies on which many of these demands were based were less acceptable to a number of Western governments (especially the United States) than they had been at any time since the United Nations was founded. This has produced very great strains, even leading in some quarters to a repudiation of multilateralism and a rejection of the virtues of international co-operation.[11]

This situation is unlikely to change in the near future on either side. On the one hand, the easy assumptions about centrally organised and internationally directed state planning which predominated before 1980 may never obtain the same degree of acceptance again. On the other hand, the need for 'adjustments' in international economic arrangements is likely to persist. Furthermore, some forms of international co-operation and direction, as exemplified in some of the Specialized Agencies, are now a functional necessity; others, as experience has shown, are functionally desirable. Moreover, quite apart from the desirability of international co-operation as an end in itself, some elements of a UN System are desirable on functional grounds to secure the best use of the resources provided for the Agencies and to co-ordinate their activities.

The remedy for the present situation is, as far as is humanly possible, to lay less emphasis on the political differences, serious though these are (especially in UNESCO), and to concentrate more on functional efficiency and on real negotiation. This can serve the common interest of all parties, in North and South alike, and even East and West. To achieve it, however, requires many changes of attitude in all camps. What these are will emerge in later Chapters.

---

11 For a British statement of this more extreme point of view see D. Bandow, *Unquestioned Allegiance*, London: Adam Smith Institute, 1986.

# CHAPTER II

# THE CONSTITUTIONS OF THE AGENCIES AND THEIR CONSEQUENCES FOR THE U.N. SYSTEM

As was briefly explained in the last Chapter, there is no universally accepted definition of the United Nations 'System'. However, this study is intended to deal with that complex of organisations, institutions, funds and programmes established under the United Nations, which deal with economic, social and technical questions through the exchange of information, the setting of standards and the promotion of development. It will not deal, except incidentally and to a limited extent in Chapter XVII, with organisations whose primary concern is with emergencies and relief, such as the United Nations Relief and Works agency (UNRWA) or the Office of the United Nations Disaster Relief Co-ordinator (UNDRO).

Within this System there were, in January 1986, nineteen inter-governmental Agencies (if the World Bank trio are counted as one) which are usually referred to as 'Specialized Agencies', although *de jure* only seventeen of them are full Specialized Agencies under the terms of Chapters IX or X of the Charter. (A full list is given in Table 1 of Annex, p.24). The Agencies are autonomous but report to the United Nations General Assembly through the Economic and Social Council. Each deals with a defined functional sector of activity, such as health, agriculture, education or labour. In addition, there are fifteen organs and programmes related to ECOSOC (Table 2 of Annex) some of which fund some UN activities by using the Specialized Agencies as 'executive Agencies' for projects or programmes; they undertake other activities in the economic and social fields direct. Finally, there are a number of what are usually described as 'Special Bodies' of the UN most of which are of only marginal importance to the Specialized Agencies (Annex, Table 3). Most of the organisations shown in all three Tables are represented on a UN Committee known as the Administrative Committee on Co-ordination (ACC) whose role is described in greater detail in Chapter IX below.

1  The best short compendium of information on this subject in English is called the *United Nations Handbook*, published annually by the New Zealand Ministry of Foreign Affairs, obtainable abroad from New Zealand Government offices. Another useful background book is Giuseppi Schiavari, *International Organisations – A Dictionary and Directory*, London: Macmillan, 1983.

## The constitutional origin of the UN System in the UN Charter

The whole System has its origin in Chapter IX of the UN Charter, particularly in Articles 55–57. Under Article 55 the UN is pledged to promote among its members

(*a*) Higher standards of living, full employment, and conditions of economic and social progress and development;
(*b*) Solutions of international economic, social, health and related problems; and international cultural and educational co-operation;

Under Article 56,

All Members pledge themselves to take joint and separate action in co-operation with the Organisation for the achievement of the purposes set forth in Article 55.

These two Articles constitute a broad description of the purposes of the Specialized Agencies (and the other inter-governmental organisations) set out in Table 1 of the Annex, as well as of the organs and programmes listed in Table 2.

## The Specialized Agencies as a group

Article 57 of the UN Charter further decrees: 'The various specialized agencies established by intergovernmental agreement and having wide international responsibilities, as defined in their basic instruments, in economic, social, cultural, educational, health and related fields,' shall be brought into relationship with the UN by virtue of agreements with the Economic and Social Council as prescribed in Article 63 of the Charter.

The terms of such agreements differ from Agency to Agency, but under most of them the Agencies undertake to submit regular reports to ECOSOC, to enact similar staff rules, to send representatives to each others' meetings and to exchange information. Apart from these activities, they are not in any sense under ECOSOC jurisdiction or control. They are in fact highly independent and autonomous (with consequences to be described later). Further, although most Specialized Agencies agree to consider recommendations made by the UN General Assembly, they are not bound by them. It is one of the structural weaknesses of the System that the most important group of technical agencies within it – the Specialized Agencies – constitutionally lacks effective co-ordination in the sense of any centralised control or direction. At best all they have is a measure of administrative co-ordination (Chapter IX). One important consequence of this structural weakness is that attempts to reform the System from the top downwards, which have been numerous in the past forty years, have usually failed or been only very partially successful.

## *The constitutional format of the Specialized Agencies and their finances*

Although every Specialized Agency has its own constitution depending in part on the nature of its functions, for our present purpose it is their common features which are important. Most have a governing body representative of all the member states of the organisation, usually described as an Assembly or a Conference; it generally meets at intervals of two or more years. Equally, they all have an executive body, generally known as the Council or the Board, which is responsible for supervising the general execution of policy between sessions of the governing body. Finally, there is what is in practice the most important of all – the executive staff consisting of the permanent secretariat and the Executive Head, variously known as Secretary-General or Director-General. The Executive Heads are usually appointed for at least four years (sometimes six), after election by the governing body, and generally their appointments are renewable for at least one term and sometimes, in practice, for more.

The financial resources of the Agencies come mainly from three sources. First are the assessed budgets which set the contribution each member state has to make in order to retain its membership (although in practice many are often in arrears); these are broadly related to capacity to pay. Secondly, there are the programmes and organs listed in Table 2 of the Annex which are mainly supported by the voluntary contributions of UN member states, and which use, and pay, the Specialized Agencies to execute various programmes or projects. The most important of these is the UNDP. Finally, there are limited voluntary contributions which some member states make to particular Agencies and which can play an important role in some instances, though not a major one. (This is discussed in more detail in Chapter VII.)

## *The sources of strain within the UN System*

Some of the sources of strain within the UN System have their origin in political circumstances which lie outside the United Nations itself. Of these, some were referred to in the preceding Chapter; others will be examined in more detail in Chapter V below. Many others, however, spring internally from the structure of the System and of the Agencies within it.

In this context, and even more in the context of any possible reforms, the main factor to be borne in mind is the autonomous character of the Agencies and the fact that each has its own constitution, its own responsibility for appointing staff (including the election of its own Executive Head) and its own independent sources of funds in the assessed contributions of its members which cover most of its 'core' budget. With the United Nations itself, the Agencies have only a treaty relationship by virtue of their agreements with ECOSOC. This feature of the System was deliberate on the part of those who set it up in 1945. The tendency of the League of Nations had been to centralise its functional agencies. The United Nations deliberately tried to bestow upon them a marked degree of independence which would then encourage them to show initiative in their particular sectors.[2] As is usually the case when new institutions are created, nobody foresaw the areas in which frictions would subsequently develop. They were, however, three: the question of finance, the question of administration and staffing, and the question of co-ordination. All these matters will be examined in more detail in later parts of this book, but a brief outline of them now will be useful to an understanding of the rest of Part One.

## *Finances*

The finances of the Specialized Agencies almost since their creation have been a steady source of friction between them and other parts of the United Nations but even more between them and those governments (both Western and the Soviet bloc) who have to provide most of their funds. The difficulties arise mostly from the fact that those who pay the piper cannot call the tune. As already mentioned, the Specialized Agencies derive the major part of their funds from, first, the assessed contributions of their members. Because these are generally fixed for each member as a percentage of the budget in the General Conference of the organisation concerned and are based roughly on a country's capacity to pay, most member states pay less than 0.01 per cent of the budget, the bulk of which is paid by the Western governments (usually up to 5 per cent in Britain's case, often as much as 25 per cent in the case of the United States), with sizeable contributions coming also from the Soviet bloc. (See Appendix A for scale of budgets and the allocation of contributions in the main Specialized Agencies). The budget itself – both its scale and the types of expenditure – is fixed by the General Conference on the basis of one member state, one vote. A powerful source of donor discontent with the Agencies arises from the fact that donors' control of expenditure – and of the

2 Generally, but with some notable exceptions, the Agencies have not been distinguished innovators in their sectors.

programmes to which that expenditure relates – is not proportionate to their contributions to revenue.

The second part of the funding is from other Agencies or from Programmes within the UN System, notably from the UNDP for technical assistance projects, and, increasingly in the recent past, from the World Bank and similar institutions whose primary purpose is not technical assistance but capital investment. Most of this money is for particular projects or programmes, although a proportion of the expenditure on each project (currently 13 per cent of the cost of each) goes towards the 'core' budgets of the Agencies, i.e. in effect for the cost to the Agency of administering it. This limitation, although it offers some control on activities undertaken by the Agencies, also causes friction *between* them as they compete with each other for the limited funds of the UNDP and of other organs or programmes with funds to spend.

This second part of the funding has also played a major role in one other aspect of the System. Beginning with the Jackson reforms of 1969–70, an attempt was made to secure the channelling of most voluntary funds through the UNDP and then to use this concentration of resources to enforce the 'co-ordination' of the Specialized Agencies. From the outset, they resisted this attack on their autonomy. Thus the budgetary question became related to two others which have caused problems within the UN System and have used up much diplomatic effort, especially among the donors – namely, that of administration and that of co-ordination and programming.

## *Administration and staffing*

The administrative problems of the Specialized Agencies have over the years received much attention both from the United Nations itself and from member governments. They – or certain aspects of them – have been the subject of a number of formal investigations, as described in Chapter IV. A number of institutions within the System have been set up to improve co-ordination and performance between the Agencies across the board. Important among these are the Advisory Committee on Administrative and Budgetary Questions (ACABQ), the Administrative Committee on Co-ordination (ACC) and the Joint Inspection Unit (JIU). Finally, since the reforms of 1977 following Resolution 32/197, there has been a Director-General for Development and International Economic Co-operation with responsibility for 'exercising overall co-ordination within the system in order to ensure a multi-disciplinary approach to the problems of development on a system-wide basis'.

This is not the place to examine all the intricacies of this saga over the years, although some will be further elucidated in later Chapters. They will doubtless continue to take up much diplomatic and administrative time in the future. Reference must be made, however, to two aspects of the question which require special consideration and need to be borne in mind from the outset.

*The Executive Heads (Directors-General and Secretaries-General).* The first aspect is the position of the Executive Heads of the Specialized Agencies. They are extremely independent, and their powers have often been compared with those of feudal barons, owing only such allegiance to their United Nations king as they choose to give, with domains – as Jackson put it in 1968 – 'the equivalent of principalities, free from any centralised control'.

Often they are individuals of strong personality around whom legends accumulate – at least in their organisations. Indeed, it is essential that they should be if the concerns of their Agency are to receive proper international attention. Each one is *elected* to his office by the governing body of his organisation. To secure election he needs not only the support of a majority of governments but also some support across the international political spectrum if he can possibly get it. He therefore wants to show some kind of sympathy with the aspirations of all the groups of governments operating in the organisation, but more especially with those who control the majority of the votes rather than with those who supply the major part of the funds.

Once he has been elected, his attitudes and policies can be much influenced by his aspirations for his own future which, if he does not take steps to safeguard it, can be bleak. An Executive Head is unlikely to be an administrator who can look for a future career in either the international civil service or his home service once his appointment ends. Therefore he probably wants at least a second term and even further extensions if he can get them. He may want to move to higher things in the UN System (e.g. to become Secretary-General, as is often alleged of the more powerful of them) although few have succeeded in this aim. He may be looking for political office in his own country (in this some have succeeded). It is thus in his interest to gain and retain as much support – or at least the minimum of opposition – in as many quarters as possible. In some Specialized Agencies this has been a frequent source of friction between the Head of an Agency and the major donor governments. Personalities also often play an important part: for example, the readiness of M. Maheu when he was Director-General of UNESCO to accept resolutions which commanded Third World support, regardless of how much they outraged the Americans, was alleged by US officials to be due as much to anti-Americanism as to his desire to demonstrate his fanatical belief in the virtues of the organisation (a belief which the Americans – especially in the age of Senator McCarthy – were not inclined to share).

The greatest single source of the strain that has developed in the UN System lies in the fact that the Executive Heads, by the very nature of the way they achieve and retain office, are likely to be both highly political animals and to be mainly concerned with their majority support in votes (rather than in finance). They are unlikely to be primarily concerned with the technical efficiency of their organisation and its performance in its functional field and even less with the views of donor governments who carry so small a percentage of the votes.

*Staffing.* The second aspect is that of the appointment of the staff – a question examined in more detail in Chapter XI. The constitutions of Specialized Agencies mostly provide that staff 'shall be appointed by the Director-General under regulations approved by the Governing Body'. As Richard Hoggart has shown,[3] the Director-General's role in hiring and firing is usually more important than the regulations; in the hands of a martinet, it can be a dangerous power capable of damaging the effectiveness of an officer even in his technical field. The constitutions also provide that 'so far as possible with due regard to the efficiency of the work of the Organisation, the Director-General shall select persons of different nationalities'. In practice the reference to 'different nationalities' has over the years tended to receive more attention than the qualification about 'efficiency', leading in some instances to a deterioration in the quality of the work – even on technical subjects. This in turn has produced dissatisfaction even in the recipient countries with the quality of the technical advice they have been receiving – a dissatisfaction tempered however, by the prospects it has also offered of administrative employment for some of their nationals.

Finally, the constitutions provide that 'the responsibilities of the Director-General and his staff shall be exclusively international in character', and they 'shall not seek or receive instructions from any government or from any authority external to the Organisation'. Moreover, 'each Member of the Organisation undertakes to respect the exclusively international character of the Director-General and

3  R. Hoggart, *An Idea and its Servants: UNESCO from Within*, London: Chatto & Windus, 1978 (see especially pp. 148–59). This book conveys better than any other what it is like to work inside a major Specialized Agency, not least from the picture it provides of M. Maheu.

his staff and not to seek to influence them in the discharge of their responsibilities.' Like so much else in the original provisions of the Specialized Agencies, these are very Anglo-Saxon concepts, which have never been accepted, even in principle, by the Soviet Union and the East European States (see Chapter XI). Over the years the force of these provisions has been steadily weakened, and breaches are now the rule. Such breaches render little service to the functional success of Specialized Agencies, however 'realistic' it may be to turn a blind eye to them. It would be to the advantage of all member states who want to see the quality of the work of the Agencies improved, to try and ensure that these provisions are better observed in the future than they have been in the recent past.

## Co-ordination

The questions of finance and administration have in the past been closely related to the question of co-ordination. Some of the institutional expressions of this concern (e.g. in the ACC and the ACABQ), have already been referred to, as well as the unsuccessful attempts to enforce co-ordination through the financial sanctions of the UNDP. The problem will be examined further in later chapters. The intention has been to restrain inter-agency rivalry, especially in the competition for funds from such sources as the UNDP and the World Bank, and to secure more co-operation between the Agencies in promoting development in Third World countries. The Jackson Report of 1969 tried to solve the problem by making the UNDP a co-ordinator of the Agencies, both centrally and through its resident representatives in the field, and by using its central funding capacity as an instrument for this purpose. As shown in Chapter XV, its success in this has been very limited: the Executive Heads would not accept a role for the UNDP beyond being *primus inter pares*.

A parallel attempt, under JIU auspices, through the Bertrand Report of 1969 which considered the question of programming and co-ordination throughout the whole United Nations System, seems to have produce better results. It recommended the introduction of systems of programme budgetting throughout the United Nations System, which now gives forecasts of expenditure for as long as six years ahead and relates them to the programmes and activities to be undertaken; it has to some extent provided a basis of comparison between Agencies. It was hoped that it might enable a co-ordinating body such as ECOSOC to spot duplication between Agencies and even to orchestrate the activities and the priorities of the Agencies in the whole development effort; but these reforms have been only partly successful for reasons which are amplified below.

Efforts at improvement have continued over the years and are continuing. They culminated in a comprehensive General Assembly Resolution on the Restructuring of the Economic and Social Sectors of the UN System (A/Res/32/197) of 1977. Nevertheless, the Agencies still compete for funds and jealously guard their autonomy. In the process they often divert attention from the real issues of international development and from their own proper functional role in promoting it. Nevertheless, their work in securing international cooperation in the economic and social fields has been important in their special sectors and much of it has been beneficial. Moreover, in these sectors some of the Agencies have acquired a body of specialized knowledge in some areas which is unparalleled; this has been the case even in organisations like UNESCO whose general reputation for administrative competence is not high and which have been riven by political contention. The next Chapter attempts a brief catalogue of some of the successes and failures.

ANNEX

## ORGANISATIONS FORMING THE UNITED NATIONS SYSTEM

### Table 1

*Inter-governmental Agencies*

| | |
|---|---|
| FAO | Food and Agriculture Organisation |
| GATT | General Agreement on Tarriffs and Trade |
| ITC | International Trade Centre |
| IAEA | International Atomic Energy Agency |
| ICAO | International Civil Aviation Organisation |
| IFAD | International Fund for Agricultural Development |
| ILO | International Labour Organisation |
| IMO | International Maritime Organisation |
| IMF | International Monetary Fund |
| ITU | International Telecommunication Union |
| UNESCO | UN Educational, Scientific and Cultural Organisation |
| UNIDO | UN Industrial Development Organisation |
| UPOV | International Union for the Protection of New Varieties of Plants |
| UPU | Universal Postal Union |
| WHO | World Health Organisation |
| WIPO | World Intellectual Property Organisation |
| WMO | World Meteorological Organisation |
| WTO | World Tourism Organisation |

*World Bank Group*

| | |
|---|---|
| IBRD | International Bank for Reconstruction and Development |
| IDA | International Development Association |
| IFC | International Finance Corporation |

# Table 2

*Organs and Programmes Related to ECOSOC*

| | |
|---|---|
| UNHCR | UN High Commissioner for Refugees |
| UNICEF | UN Children's Fund |
| UNCTAD | UN Conference on Trade and Development |
| UNDP | UN Development Programme |
| WFP | World Food Programme |
| WFC | World Food Council |
| UNCDF | UN Capital Development Fund |
| UNEP | UN Environment Programme |
| UNFPA | UN Fund for Population Activities |
| UNFDAC | UN Fund for Drug Abuse Control |
| UNSF | UN Special Fund |
| UN Special Fund for Land-Locked Developing Countries | |
| INCB | International Narcotics Control Board |
| ACC | Administrative Committee on Co-ordination |
| UNRISD | UN Research Institute for Social Development |

# Table 3

*Special Bodies of the United Nations*

| | |
|---|---|
| INSTRAW | UN International Research and Training Institute for the Advancement of Women |
| UNITAR | UN Institute for Training and Research |
| UNRWA | UN Relief and Works Agency for Palestine Refugees in the Near East |
| UNU | UN University |
| UNV | UN Volunteers |
| UNDRO | Office of the UN Disaster Relief Co-ordinator |
| UNIDIR | UN Institute for Disarmament Research |

# CHAPTER III

# THE OPERATIONS OF THE U.N. SYSTEM

A study such as this cannot give an adequate account of the operations of all the organisations which make up the UN System. Some of their main features, more particularly those which are of general importance or which have proved contentious, will be described later in this Chapter;[1] but before doing so there are some general points which, in addition to those already mentioned, should be borne in mind.

The first point is that the Specialized Agencies differ from one another in the extent to which their functional operations – as opposed to wider political considerations[2] – dominate the rest. Even leaving aside the big three economic Agencies (the IMF, the IBRD and the GATT), functional considerations are clearly dominant and are likely to remain so in such organisations as the World Meteorological Organisation (WMO) or the Universal Postal Union (UPU). In others, such as the International Telecommunication Union (ITU), although functional concerns are dominant, some of these concerns are themselves politically charged (e.g. in the ITU because of the use of radio frequencies for propaganda broadcasts).

Secondly, many of these organisations are as important to developed as to developing countries, especially in their roles as standard setters and sources of information. Equally, they are sometimes as important to governments in their purely domestic activities as in their international activities (e.g. weather forecasts and the activities of the WMO are important to farmers as well as to airline pilots); and many of the domestic activities of all governments could not now take place without the international regulation as well as the information provided by some of these Specialized Agencies. Indeed, at least six Specialized Agencies discharge functions in areas

---

1 In Britain, published material about the operations of the UN Agencies from year to year is not readily available, and in recent years press reporting has been poor. In the United States, the President's Report to Congress on *US Participation in the UN*, published annually up to 1983, gave an excellent conspectus, but unfortunately it seems to have been discontinued. If any government could match New Zealand's publication of a handbook of the UN by publishing an independent review annually of each Agency's activity, it would render a great public service. UN publications are too 'diplomatic' to be useful.

2 In the context of the Specialized Agencies the word 'political' has a number of different connotations, some of which are discussed in Chapter V.

in which some international regulation is essential to the running of the modern world (viz. WHO, ICAO, UPU, ITU, WMO, IMO). For this reason alone, governments can hardly have a uniform policy towards all Specialized Agencies as a class (except perhaps on budgetary and administrative issues); no government could afford to withdraw *en bloc* from them all, however annoyed it might become with the activities of some of them.[3] Furthermore, if this is so, some elements of the System – i.e. of UN supervision of the Agencies – have to be retained.

Moreover, even from many of those such as the FAO and the WHO, whose concerns by their very nature are primarily with the problems of tropical countries, no Western government could now withdraw without losing the possibility of influencing important aspects of economic and social policy worldwide. This is true also of some of the activities of UNESCO, as representations within the United States and the United Kingdom against withdrawal emphasised. (Indeed, the United States and the United Kingdom will remain members of the semi-autonomous International Oceanographic Commission after withdrawal from UNESCO, although the same is not true of the International Hydrological Programme.)

Because of the way it operates, the ILO is a special case – but one which (despite the US withdrawal of 1977) makes it almost as important to developed industrialised countries as it is to developing countries. This arises from the fact that the ILO by virtue of its constitution can on some issues take 'collective decisions of a quasi-legislative character' for creating and defining international labour standards, encouraging the adoption of these standards by all member states and for supervising their application. Through that and other features of its constitution and operations, the ILO has played an important role in improving international standards in labour conditions which the governments of all countries, including especially those of developed industrialised countries, have an interest in seeing applied universally, because their application implies 'economic costs' which can affect the international competitive position of those who apply them. The same is probably true of what may later become a Specialized Agency – the UN Environment Programme (UNEP) – because of the economic cost of anti-pollution measures.

Another functional distinction which arises within the Specialized

---

3 Indeed, this does not appear to be the intention of the critics of the System. E.g. see Douglas Bandow, *Unquestioned Allegiance*, London: Adam Smith Institute, 1986, pp. 28–9, where a more selective approach, assessing each Agency in turn, is suggested.

Agencies as a group is that three of them, by virtue of their Articles of Association, have real resources under their control or within the scope of their bargaining and negotiating powers. The three are the World Bank with its bankable funds to invest, the IMF with its gold and currency reserves to spend on currency stabilisation, and the GATT with its power to supervise the exchange of tariff concessions among its members. Each of these, however, is substantially under the control of the states which provide the resources, and their points of friction *in the past* have been mainly with the developing countries and not with the West, though with a breakdown in the consensus on economic policy which prevailed up to 1970 this has been changing in the 1980s.

This is not true to the same extent of another institution which, although not itself a Specialized Agency, is an important source of the Agencies' funds – namely the UNDP. Even if it is supported by voluntary, not assessed, contributions from member governments, most of its money comes from the industrialised countries represented in the OECD, who therefore retain a measure of effective control, which is more discreetly exercised in the UNDP than in the Bretton Woods institutions. As long as the major donors remain dominant in these latter organisations they are unlikely to want to withdraw from any of them unless the cost (which in the case of the UNDP and the World Bank often has to be borne at the expense of bilateral aid programmes) becomes too great; or unless on ideological grounds they come to reject altogether notions of international co-operation in the fields of tariffs, balance of payments adjustments, and development banking (as appeared at one time to be happening in some quarters in the Reagan Administration).

In the discharge of their functional responsibilities the Specialized Agencies have been, on balance, a success individually. Some of the things they have done have been essential to the running of the modern world. In their functional operations their weakness has sometimes been an excess of caution and a lack of originality in some important instances (e.g. the FAO and the development of new techniques of agricultural research on problems of tropical crops in the early 1960s which is examined in Chapter XIII). Many of their staff have been motivated by high international ideals, but some – and in recent years, it is alleged, an increasing number – have been of indifferent quality. Nevertheless, operationally the Agencies have been reasonably successful, although because of weaknesses in their system of evaluation it is hard to demonstrate how successful. Contrary to the beliefs of Mitrany however, the functional approach has done little so far to lessen political tensions (though there have been cases, for example in some of the disease

eradication programmes of the WHO, where the importance of a
subject has caused political considerations to be ignored). Rather,
the intrusion of politics has tended to weaken the effectiveness of the
functional approach.

Despite the successes of the individual Agencies within the System
however, what is not so clear is whether the System as such – i.e. the
loose grouping of all these organisations under ECOSOC responsible to the General Assembly – has contributed much to their
success, and, if so, what it has contributed; or indeed whether
grouping them together in any way (i.e. whether or not under
ECOSOC) serves a useful purpose. Certainly since 1945 many international organisations, some of them outside the UN System altogether (especially regional organisations), have been created and
operated successfully without the benefit of the UN's supervision.[4]
A few have been voluntary organisations but many have been intergovernmental. Moreover, especially over the last twenty-five years,
a great deal of international effort in the United Nations has been
expended in trying to systematise the System – that is, in trying to
orchestrate all these diverse activities of the UN 'family' and make
them work towards some common ends.[5] Success has been limited;
this subject will be examined in more detail later.

First, however, it is necessary to look more closely at some of the
main organisation which make up the system. Any classification of
them is bound to be somewhat arbitrary, but for the purposes of this
Chapter they will be considered in four groups:

(*a*)  *The Big Four*, consisting of UNESCO, the FAO, the WHO and
the ILO, which in January 1986 became the *Big Five* when the UN
Industrial Development Organisation (UNIDO) became a proper
Specialized Agency. The distinguishing features of these organisations *for our purposes in this book* are that, although they deal with
specific functional sectors, their functions impinge so widely on the
economic and social life of most states (all of which have domestic
policies on health, education, agriculture and labour), that many of
their activities cannot but be 'political'; in that sense they are almost
bound to be a source of friction from time to time between states of
differing social and economic philosophies. This fact has frequently
tempted some of them to be more 'political' than was necessary to
the fulfilment of their functional purpose. In this they can be

---

4  The number is now approaching 300.

5  This is the process described in para. 5 of the Annex to Resolution 32/197 as being
   'to ensure the over-all co-ordination of the activities of the organisations in the
   United Nations system and to that end, the implementation of the priorities
   established by the General Assembly for the system as a whole'.

distinguished from the more narrowly technical organisations described in the next category.

(*b*) *The technical organisations.* These are the organisations whose primary purpose is to establish rules or standards which will enable certain specialized services of member states to co-operate internationally so as to perform a more effective technical function domestically. The main ones are the ITU, the UPU, the IMO, the WMO, ICAO, WIPO, the IAEA and some activities of the WHO. It has not always been possible to exclude from them disputatious political issues, but at the end of the day most states have regarded the technical advantages of membership as paramount and have lived with any political strains.

(*c*) *The 'economic' or 'Bretton Woods' institutions.* Until 1977 these consisted of the IMF, the IBRD and its two offshoots (the IDA and the IFC), and the GATT. In 1977, however, they were joined by a fourth organisation, the International Fund for Agricultural Development (IFAD), financed in part by OPEC money (and with a governing council which reflected this fact). IFAD operates on principles which are substantially the same as those of the IBRD but it is confined to making concessional loans in the agricultural sector.

(*d*) *The organs and programmes related to ECOSOC.* These are the bodies listed in Table 2 of the Annex to Chapter II. In this Chapter, however, comments will be confined mainly to those whose activities are related to the organisations identified at (*a*), (*b*) and (*c*) above.

## The traditional Big Four (UNESCO, FAO, WHO, ILO) and the new Fifth (UNIDO).

*UNESCO.* The United Nations Educational, Scientific and Cultural Organisation came into being on 4 November 1946. Its purpose is described in its Constitution as 'to contribute to peace and security by promoting collaboration among the nations through education, science and culture in order to further universal respect for justice, for the rule of law and for the human rights and fundamental freedoms which are affirmed for the peoples of the World, without distinction of race, sex, language or religion, by the Charter of the United Nations'. Its mandate is clearly very broad, and opinions on how it should be discharged have always differed widely. Its ensuing troubles have been very well publicised, particularly in the period since 1984, though often tendentiously and with little analysis of the background, and they led to the withdrawals from the organisation of the United States and Britain. (They may also have contributed to the withdrawal of Singapore, although this is not clear.)

The organisation has always operated through running a number of major programmes. The percentage of expenditure on each programme is a reasonable guide to its relative importance in the total activities of UNESCO. By far the largest is its educational programme (which in 1984 took up nearly 37% of its budget).[6] The main aims of this programme are to promote equality in educational opportunity, to combat illiteracy, improve the quality of education, and foster international understanding. In addition, the programme focuses on a number of special issues such as improving the status of women, promoting human rights, controlling drug abuse and developing physical education. The education programme has also usually contained elements which some governments regard as contentious, notably supporting the education of the youth of national liberation movements[7] and promoting education in disarmament issues and education 'related to the collective rights of peoples'. A number of Western governments besides those of the United States and the United Kingdom took exception to such education on the ground that it tended to sacrifice individual rights to the interests of governments.

The second major programme which in recent years has taken up about 30 per cent of the programme budget is in the natural sciences. Here UNESCO has sought to promote international scientific co-operation, through programmes such as the International Hydrological Programme (IHP); the International Geological Correlation Programme (IGCP); the International Oceanographic Commission (IOC); the Integrated Global Ocean Service System (IGOSS); the Programme studying oceanography in the Western Pacific and a number of other programmes concerned with 'Man and the Biosphere'. Some of these programmes overlap with programmes being run elsewhere in the UN System by such bodies as UNEP, the WMO, the WHO and others; thus UNESCO has a reputation for trespassing on the preserves of others, as well as for taking credit for successful programmes for which others are chiefly responsible.

The third major area of UNESCO activities (about 11%) is that of culture, especially sponsoring programmes to strengthen 'cultural identity, creativity and cultural development', including matters concerned with the protection of the world's cultural heritage; and for preventing the illicit import/export and transfer of cultural property. These programmes have undoubtedly stimulated

---

6 The percentages which follow all relate to 1984; but they have remained fairly constant this decade.

7 E.g. the UN Institute for Namibia in Lusaka.

co-operation and exchange in the cultural field worldwide even across the Iron Curtain and have done something to encourage freedom of expression and creativity.

UNESCO's fourth major programme (12%) relates to the social sciences on which, in the opinion of many observers, UNESCO bit off more than it could chew with its limited resources. The aim was to develop social science facilities in Asia and Africa as well as to strengthen the role of social research as an instrument of development planning. The results have been scrappy. Under this programme, attempts to give 'peoples' rights' predominance over 'human rights' have occasioned much criticism in the West.

The fifth programme, while representing only 7 per cent of UNESCO's budget, is the one which has secured for UNESCO most of its adverse publicity in the West. This is the programme studying communications. Included in it is an attempt to establish a 'New World Information and Communications Order' (NWICO). It is this proposal which, combined with accusations (many of them made by members of UNESCO's own staff) of administrative incompetence and financial extravagence,[8] led to the US decision to withdraw from UNESCO and was a factor in the British withdrawal. Of more long-term importance are activities for the development of communications, one of the objectives of which is to offer practical assistance to the countries of the developing world in building up their communications. UNESCO has also made a useful contribution to international arrangements concerning copyright (though this is a major concern of WIPO and again has led to accusations against UNESCO of 'trespassing').

*FAO*  The Food and Agriculture Organisation was founded in 1946. It is one of the largest of the UN Specialized Agencies, and it has tried to give international support to national programmes designed to increase the effectiveness of agriculture, forestry and fisheries. Its prime objective is to bring about sustained global improvements in nutritional levels, food security and rural incomes, especially for the disadvantaged, through increasing rural productivity. In its fisheries activities its major aim has been to promote the management and the best use of the world's fishery resources, especially both the marine

8  Particularly the charge that 60% of its budget is spent in headquarters administration, leaving only 40% for field operation, although the dividing line between headquarters and field staff is perhaps even more difficult to draw in UNESCO than in other Agencies.

and inland fisheries of developing countries. Historically, forestry has been the smallest of the FAO's major programmes, but in view of the desperate shortage of fuel, even for ordinary domestic purposes, in many developing countries, this is acquiring greater importance. Indeed the FAO is now helping many countries to meet the evergrowing demand for forestry products, while simultaneously ensuring environmental balance and stability against the increasing encroachments of agriculture on forestry lands.

In pursuit of its objectives, the FAO, through its Committee on World Food Security, has produced a number of proposals for action at national, regional and world levels to promote food security by increasing and stabilising supplies and improving distribution. Some of these proposals have proved controversial. The FAO has also provided the International Agricultural Guidelines (IAG) to promote a more balanced growth in agricultural production, to improve food distribution and to secure a rising share for developing countries in expanded agricultural trade. These guidelines, too, have proved contentious, partly because some member governments feel that the FAO proposals impinge upon the responsibilities of other international organisations, especially those concerned with trade in agricultural products.

The FAO has also initiated proposals dealing with plant genetic resources. These, too, have proved contentious. At present these genetic resources are collected, processed and disseminated by the International Board for Plant Genetic Research (IBPGR), which works very closely with the Consultative Group for International Agricultural Research (described further in Chapter XIII). The present system has come under attack because some Third World countries (mostly in Latin America) think it gives too much control of plant genetic material to laboratories in developed countries and to transnational corporations. The FAO has established the Commission on Plant Genetic Resources to deal with the matter.

In addition, the FAO has been active in the international effort to assist African countries affected by drought and grave food shortages and in this it has worked closely, though sometimes less than harmoniously, with its offshoot, the World Food Programme, which uses food aid for social and economic development and emergency relief. Although, therefore, the work of the FAO has not been disturbed by discussion of extraneous political issues, some of the work it has done within its mandate has proved politically contentious. Its present Director-General has also come under criticism (especially from the US Administration) for empire-building, extravagance and decisions made contrary to the wishes of the main donors. A more serious criticism is that he has frequently encouraged policies which might be popular with the majority of member states' governments but which were not best designed to encourage agricultural productivity. Usually such projects involved major expenditure on capital works.

*WHO.* The World Health Organisation came into existence in 1948 and has proved one of the most valuable of the UN Agencies, despite occasional, and indeed at times acute, turbulence in debates on subjects ranging from the medical consequences of nuclear war to the use of breast-milk substitutes.

Its objective is set out in the first Article of its Constitution as 'the attainment by all peoples of the highest possible level of health'. It has six regional offices to supervise its operations (an unusual feature in the organisation of a Specialized Agency), but also provides worldwide technical expertise from its Headquarters. Apart from its Governing Body (i.e. the World Health Assembly which elects its 32-member board), it is advised by a number of expert committees, scientific groups and consultative meetings on particular subjects and it also organises seminars, technical meetings and training courses for the education of health personnel in all categories. The main thrust of its activities in recent years has been towards promoting national, regional and global strategies for the attainment of its main target, namely 'health for all by the year 2000'; or 'the attainment by all citizens of the World of a level of health that will permit them to lead a socially and economically productive life'.

The WHO's many programmes of particular value have fallen into four broad categories. The first has been directed to establishing health infrastructures to provide primary health care services to the majority of the world's population. The second is programmes designed to immunise all the world's children against six of the major childhood diseases. The third, whose major achievement to date has been the eradication of smallpox, is directed to controlling and eradicating the main tropical diseases. Finally there is a programme designed to develop and organise the manpower and technology needed for disease prevention and control.

The WHO is generally accepted now as one of the success stories of the UN System, thanks in part to its present Director-General (now in his third term of office). Its annual budget worldwide was US $990 million in the biennium 1984–5, made up of regular contributions from member states, assessed under the usual scale of assessments [9] and from voluntary contributions from member states, other

9 See Chapter VII for further comment on WHO finances.

UN Agencies and non-governmental organisations. (This is less than the British government's expenditure in any one of four of the fifteen regions on the National Health Service in England.) Its beneficial effect on the health and welfare of humanity has been enormous.

*ILO.* The International Labour Organisation, established in 1919 by virtue of the Treaty of Versailles, is one of the oldest of the Specialized Agencies. Its purpose as defined in its Constitution is 'by international actions to improve living conditions, raise living standards and promote productive employment'. It has a unique tripartite Constitution, which gives voting rights not only to representatives of governments but also to representatives of employers and workers. Originally part of the League of Nations, it was recognised as a Specialized Agency of the UN in 1946.

The ILO differs from other Specialized Agencies in another important respect besides its tripartite composition. It has responsibility for the formulation of international standards for the protection and improvement of labour and working conditions. These take the form of International Labour Conventions and Recommendations which the member states are required to submit to their competent national legislatures within 12–18 months to consider for ratification. Once a member state has ratified a Convention it is bound to bring its domestic laws and practice into conformity with the terms of that Convention [10] and to report periodically to the ILO on how the Convention is being applied. These reports are examined by an independent high–level Committee of Experts which reports its findings to the annual ILO Conference. By the end of 1985 the International Labour Conference had adopted 161 Conventions. (There is no requirement to *ratify* recommendations.)

The ILO runs wide-ranging programmes of technical assistance to developing countries, financed by the UNDP as well as by funds in trust. They cover issues such as the promotion of employment, development of human resources, vocational training, small industries, rural development, co-operatives, social security and industrial safety and hygiene. One of its major efforts since 1969 has been the World Employment Programme aimed at stimulating national and international effort to increase the volume of productive employment, and the fulfilment of 'basic needs'. Associated with this activity is the ILO's International Centre for advanced Technical and Vocational Training in Turin. The ILO's 'in house'

10 It is British policy not to ratify *until* its domestic legislation conforms with the necessary Convention.

research is reinforced by the work of the International Institute for Labour Studies located in Geneva.

In the face of many difficulties, but on the whole successfully, the ILO has been a powerful force since the 1920s for raising and maintaining the living and working standards of workers round the world. It was largely due to the ILO's influence that the Development Strategy for the United Nations Second Development Decade (1970–80) firmly linked economic development with social development: 'The ultimate objective of development must be to bring about sustained improvement in the well-being of the individual.' Inevitably, however, dealing with the social problems which lie within its portfolio, its activities are controversial from time to time; this aspect is referred to again in Chapter V.

*UNIDO.* In January 1986 the 'Big Four' were joined by a fifth Specialized Agency, the United Nations Industrial Development Organisation, which came formally into existence when eighty states had deposited the necessary instruments of ratification. UNIDO was first established as 'an autonomous organisation within the UN' by General Assembly Resolution 2152 of 1966 and has operated as such since then financed from the UN budget. Its broad purpose was to do for the industrial development of developing countries what the FAO was doing for their agricultural development. It has worked in the past through a modest programme of technical assistance (amounting to $87.1 million in 1984) on developing new technologies (ranging from 'laser welding to rural blacksmithing'), carrying out studies and research, and conducting seminars and meetings on such things as new industrial techniques, new sources of energy and other measures to raise the industrial capacity of developing countries. Its success to date could generously be described as 'modest', partly because it is doubtful whether the nature of the subject lends itself to action by an international bureaucracy. Much of the time of meetings in recent years has been taken up with discussion of the conversion of the organisation into a Specialized Agency rather than with the problems of the industrialisation of Third World countries. Its field work in the future as an autonomous Specialized Agency will probably be much the same as in the past, but its constitution has some interesting features which will be referred to later (especially in Chapter VI).

## *The Principal Technical Organisations (UPU, ITU, IMO, WMO, ICAO, WIPO, IAEA)*

*UPU.* The Universal Postal Union was originally established in

1875. Its aim is to 'promote the organisation and improvement of world postal services and to promote in this sphere the development of international collaboration'. For this purpose the members of the UPU have agreed to be considered as a single 'postal territory' for the reciprocal exchange of correspondence. It has performed an essential function in organising the growth of world postal services.

*ITU*. The International Telecommunication Union came into existence in 1934, replacing an earlier organisation founded in 1865. Its main tasks are to allocate radio frequencies and maintain a register of radio frequency assignments. It also seeks to establish the lowest possible rates for an efficient telecommunications service compatible with financial viability, to promote measures for the safety of life through telecommunications and to make studies and researches for the benefit of its members. It performs an essential international service, though because of the importance to governments of the matters with which it deals (especially radio frequencies), its conferences are the scenes of hard bargaining from time to time and occasionally attract public attention.

*IMO*. The International Maritime Organisation started in 1959. It has its headquarters in London – the only UN Agency to do so. Its functions are to facilitate co-operation among governments on technical matters affecting merchant shipping, including safety at sea, the control of marine pollution and the abolition of discriminatory and restrictive practices affecting merchant shipping. It has been reasonably successful in achieving its objectives.

*WMO*. The World Meteorological Association, established in 1951, replaced the International Meteorology Organisation set up in 1873. Its functions are to secure co-operation worldwide in the establishment of a network of meteorology stations, to organise hydrological and other geophysical observations relating to meteorology, to promote systems for the rapid exchange of meteorological information, to promote standardisation of weather observation in their publications, to further the application of meteorology to aviation, shipping, agriculture, etc., to promote activities in operational hydrology, to encourage research and training and to promote the World Weather Watch (which is indeed now its basic programme). Its international role is of growing importance in monitoring the world's weather and improving the competence of meteorology both to assist communications and to forecast extreme weather conditions likely to lead to natural disasters, as well as in the collection of meteorological data of great importance in many large-scale development projects. (This data is sadly lacking in many developing countries – an omission which has been seriously underestimated in the past as a factor in poor development planning, especially in Africa.) The WMO has also run an ambitious and successful programme of technical assistance to help developing countries participate more fully in its work.

*ICAO.* The International Civil Aviation Organisation was established by a Convention which came into force in April 1947. Its functions are to assist international civil aviation by establishing common technical standards for the safety and efficiency of air navigation and by promoting simpler procedures at borders. It has developed regulatory plans for ground facilities and services in international flying and it disseminates air transport statistics and studies of aviation economics. It also prepares studies on the development of legal procedures relating to air matters. It plays an essential role in modern air communications and in securing the necessary international agreements on these matters.

*WIPO.* The World Intellectual Property Organisation was established in 1970 and became a Specialized Agency in 1974. Its purpose is to promote the protection of intellectual property throughout the world. Its operations have two elements. The first is the protection of copyrights in literary and artistic works which are subject to the Berne Convention of 1886. The second is the protection of industrial property (i.e. patents on inventions, trade marks and industrial designs) which are covered by the Paris Convention on Industrial Property signed in 1883. Membership of WIPO is open to any state which is a member of the Paris or Berne Unions, or is a member of the United Nations or is invited to join by WIPO. It has enjoyed some success in updating existing treaties and in securing their ratification.

*IAEA.* The International Atomic Energy Authority was set up in 1957 'to seek to accelerate and enlarge the contribution of atomic energy to peace, health and prosperity throughout the World'. Strictly speaking, it is not a Specialized Agency, but an 'independent intergovernmental organisation under the aegis of the UN'. It is responsible for ensuring that advice provided by it or at its request is not used in such a way as to further any military purpose. It is authorised to assist research on atomic energy for peaceful purposes throughout the world, to act as an intermediary in the supply of materials and services etc; to foster exchanges of scientific and technical information; to arrange the training of scientists and to administer safeguards and establish safety standards. It has a special role in the implementation of the Non-Proliferation Treaty. It has also produced a number of feasibility studies for nuclear power plants and has done useful work on their siting, safety and reliability standards. Its value to the world was well illustrated in May 1986 by its work in the aftermath of the Chernobyl disaster in the Soviet Union. With full Soviet co-operation, it acted as a clearing house of information and as a centre for mobilising international expertise in dealing with the consequences of the accident.

## The 'Economic' or 'Bretton Woods' institutions

*IMF*. The articles of agreement establishing the International Monetary Fund were drawn up in 1944 before the UN Charter had been drafted. It came into being on 27 December 1945 and began its operation in March 1947, and not till November 1947 were its relations with the United Nations defined in an agreement of mutual co-operation. Its purposes are to promote international monetary co-operation, to facilitate the expansion of international trade, to promote exchange rate stability, to assist in the establishment of a multilateral system of payments and the elimination of foreign exchange restrictions and to assist members through a temporary provision of finance to correct maladjustments in their balance of payments. Its resources come from the quotas which members pay, partly in gold and convertible foreign currency when they join the Fund. Members' voting power is also related to these quotas. In addition, since the amendment to the Fund's articles in July 1969 which created a new financial resource known as Special Drawing Rights (SDRs), the Fund and its members have also had a quantity of SDRs at their disposal.

In March 1984 the total resources available to the Fund were SDR 89.24 billion (the equivalent of US\$ 95 billion). In addition, the Fund has acquired extra resources by borrowing additional money from some of its members, e.g. in 1962 it borrowed US\$ 6 billion from 10 Western countries under the General Arrangement to Borrow (GAB), an amount which in 1983 was enlarged to SDR 17 billion (US\$ 18.946 billion). The Fund has also borrowed additional resources from the Saudi Arabian Monetary Agency (SAMA).

Members may draw from the general resources of the Fund under credit tranches related to their quotas. When they draw upon these funds, members are subject to certain obligations relating to their domestic internal finances and commercial policies which may affect their balance of payments or their exchange rate. This is a provision which in recent years has involved the IMF in much political controversy as, in the interest of securing short term balance of payment adjustment in a number of developing countries, they have insisted upon changes in domestic economic policy which some countries found politically difficult to tolerate. The growth of the problem of international indebtedness has also highlighted the activities of the IMF and has made their policies a politically contentious issue in the countries carrying a large burden of international debt, especially those in Latin America, the Caribbean and Africa. In the view of some observers, the importance of the IMF in the late 1980s in the processes of world economic adjustment may be declining as compared with that of the IBRD.

*IBRD*. The articles of the International Bank for Reconstruction and Development were drafted at the Bretton Woods Conference in July 1944 and the Bank began its operations in June 1946. Its purpose was to assist in the flow of capital for productive purposes, originally to assist in the reconstruction of countries after the Second World War, but latterly, and primarily, to promote development in developing countries. The Bank raises its capital from subscriptions of member countries, the sales of its own securities, sales of part of its loans on private capital markets, repayment of previous loans and net earnings. By June 1984 the subscribed capital of the Bank amounted to US$56.011 billion; by then the Bank had made over 2,400 loans to 104 member countries totalling US$101.565 billion.

In addition, the IBRD has two important subsidiaries. The first, the International Development Association (IDA), was initially financed by subscriptions from members proportional to their subscription to the capital stock of the IBRD, but since 1960 its running resources have been financed by a series of replenishments provided mostly by the world's richer countries, who are members of OECD. The purpose of the IDA is to make loans to the less developed countries on far more concessionary terms than those of conventional loans such as are provided by the IBRD (in fact they are substantially interest-free with a long grace and amortisation period). By March 1984 the IDA had extended development credits to the value of US$29.1 billion. The main difficulty for the IDA in the 1980s has been caused by US resistance to securing a level of further resources for it which most governments judge necessary to sustain the current level of development in the poorer countries of the world.

The second affiliate of the IBRD is the International Finance Corporation (IFC). It operates in the private sector in developing countries to stimulate the growth of productive private enterprise.

Its resources are derived from a paid-in capital which in June 1984 amounted to US$544.2 million subscribed by 125 countries, together with its earnings by previous investments amounting to US$230.1 million. The IFC makes investments in the form of subscriptions to the share capital of privately owned companies or long-term loans, or both, and will help either to finance new investments or to assist established businesses to expand. By June 1984 it had provided investments amounting to US$6.216 billion, and it also sold loans and equity to other investors amounting to US$3.471 billion.

*GATT.* The General Agreement on Tariffs and Trade was not intended to be the major multilateral forum concerned with post-war international trade. In 1948 the charter for a comprehensive International Trade Organisation (ITO) which if it had come into force would probably have been a proper Specialized Agency, was agreed upon in Havana. But when in 1950 US President Harry Truman, in the face of certain defeat at the hands of Congress, withdrew the Havana Charter from consideration by the Senate for ratification, the ambitious ITO scheme died a quiet death. As a result the GATT. which was negotiated in 1947 as an interim agreement to take advantage of the President's tariff cutting authority before it expired and to capitalize on the rapidly dissipating spirit of wartime co-operation, became the central, if modest, international agency dealing with trade matters. Its identity as an international organisation began to be strengthened as early as 1951 when an Intersessional Committee was set up to consider restrictive trade measures and to ballot Contracting Parties on these issues when they were not in session. The Intersessional Committee was replaced by a Council of Representatives with enhanced powers in 1960. Although GATT co-operates with the United Nations, its origin as an intergovernmental agreement negotiated outside the aegis of the United Nations and with no formal affiliation to that body means that it is not, strictly speaking, a part of the System. In considering what follows in this book about the United Nations and commercial policy issues it should be borne in mind that GATT had been intended to form a part of a bigger Charter containing sections covering economic development, full employment, international investments, international commodity arrangements and restrictive business practices. These would have been supervised by the ITO. Other governments besides that of the United States, however, proved unwilling to ratify the Havana Charter, and therefore the ITO has never come into existence.

The GATT, therefore, although treated *de facto* as a Specialized Agency, is a multilateral trade treaty embodying reciprocal regulations and objectives with four fundamental elements. The first is that trade should be conducted on the basis of non-discrimination. The second is that protection should be afforded to domestic industries through the Customs Tariff and not through other measures (eg. import quotas, other than for safeguarding balance of payments). Thirdly, the contracting parties undertake to consult about tariff changes with a view to avoiding damage to the trading interests of other contracting parties. Fourthly, the GATT provides a framework for negotiations for the reduction of tariffs and other barriers to trade and a structure for embodying results of such changes in a legal instrument. The GATT and its Secretariat has been responsible for a number of important trade regulations, including the adjustments to international programmes following the formation of the European Community. The comprehensive Kennedy Round concluded in June 1967 aimed to remove the trade barriers in both agricultural and industrial commodities; and the Tokyo Round of multilateral trade negotiations concluded in November 1979 with a number of agreements and arrangements on matters other than tariffs, such as technical barriers to trade, import licensing procedures, government procurement, beef and dairy products and the interpretation of various important articles of the GATT (Articles VI, VII, XVI and XXIII).

The GATT was a beneficial influence in stimulating world trade between 1950 and 1970. Growing protectionism since then has posed a threat to its operations. Moreover, it has not proved a satisfactory instrument for promoting the special interests of developing countries (especially poorer ones) in international trade and this was a factor in the subsequent creation of UNCTAD. However, it remains an important influence on world economic arrangements.

*IFAD.* The International Fund for Agricultural Development [11] was established in 1977. It had its origin in the World Food Conference of 1974. Its purpose is to finance programmes and projects designed to improve food production systems especially in the poorest countries and to improve the life of the rural poor. It operates much like other international finance institutions making loans for development projects except that these are exclusively related to agriculture. Moreover, IFAD has developed new methods of using other institutions to evaluate and execute projects. It derives just over half of its funds from the OECD countries but just under half comes

11 The best single short account of IFAD is an article by John Andrews King in *Development Policy Review* for May 1985 (vol. 3, no. 1), entitled 'The International Fund for Agricultural Development: The First Six Years'.

from the OPEC countries – the extent to which it could tap these new funds was in fact the main justification for its creation. Its weighted voting arrangements reflect this funding. Participating countries are divided into three categories – the OECD countries, the OPEC countries and other developing countries – so that any two categories voting together can out-vote the third. During its first six years IFAD financed 135 projects to a value of $US1.580 billion in some 80 different countries. Its methods of operation were generally considered very successful and often innovatory. In the mid-1980s, however, there were problems about the replenishment of IFAD because of a difference of opinion between the OECD and the OPEC countries about further funding. These were resolved in January 1986 when OECD countries agreed to contribute US$ 276 million and OPEC US$ 184 million to a further three year replenishment. IFAD also appealed for a further US$ 300 million for a Special Fund for Africa.

## Some organs and programmes related to ECOSOC

To understand the operation of the System, it is necessary at this stage to say more about some – but not all of the Organisations, Programmes and Funds referred to in Table 2 of the Annex to Chapter II. Unlike the Specialized Agencies, these Funds and Programmes are not financed by assessed contributions from governments nor are they autonomous in the way that Specialized Agencies are. All are established by General Assembly or ECOSOC Resolutions. Some, like UNCTAD, are paid for from the UN budget. Others are supported by voluntary contributions from donors (both governmental and non-governmental). Their role in financing activities of the Specialized Agencies or in some cases acting as channels for funds from Specialized Agencies will be examined in more detail in Chapter VII.

For the purpose of understanding the System, however, and the operations of the Specialized Agencies, we list the most important of these Organs, Funds and Programmes:

*UNCTAD*. The United Nations Conference on Trade and Development was established by ECOSOC Resolution 917 of 1962 and Resolution 963 of 1963 endorsed by a Resolution of the General Assembly. Its main functions are to promote international trade, particularly between countries at different stages of development, with a view to accelerating the economic growth of developing countries. It is also responsible for formulating principles and implementing policies on international trade and related problems of international development. It is supposed to review and facilitate the co-ordination of other institutions within the UN System in the field of international trade and related problems of economic development. (Co-ordination is discussed more fully in Chapter IX.) It is also responsible for international action 'for the negotiation and adoption of multilateral legal instruments in the field of trade' and acts as a centre for the harmonisation of trade and related development policy of governments and regional economic groups.

The Conference is directly responsible to the UN General Assembly and its expenses form part of the regular UN budget. Under its constitution, the 167 members of UNCTAD are divided for electoral purposes into 4 lists. List A consists of the African and Asian states and Yugolavia (95 members); List B of Western Europe and other states with 'market' economies, including the United States (30 members); List C of Latin America (32 members); and List D of Eastern Europe (10 members). Since Lists A and C normally vote together, they have become known as the 'Group of 77' (although the Group now has 127 members). The Conference works through its committees dealing with commodities, manufactures, shipping, the transfer of technology, co-operation among developing countries, and invisibles and financing related trade. In addition a number of *ad hoc* bodies have been established under UNCTAD auspices, particularly dealing with transnationals and the Integrated Programme for Commodities. In general UNCTAD is a body whose activities have been warmly espoused by developing countries, but viewed with little enthusiasm by developed ones, especially the United States.

*UNDP.* The United Nations Development Programme is the main single instrument of the United Nations for providing technical assistance to developing countries and it still plays a major role in the operations of the System though not as central as many once hoped. Its finances are derived primarily from the voluntary contributions by the governments of participating states, pledged at annual 'pledging' conferences. Its objective is to assist developing countries to accelerate their economic and social development by financing schemes of technical assistance and most of the projects funded by the UNDP are executed by the Specialized Agencies and Programmes within the UN System, who compete vigorously for their share of this cake. In 1984 voluntary contributions to the UNDP amounted to $705 million. This compares with its total expenditure in 1983 of $751 million. Indeed one of the difficulties that the Specialized Agencies have faced in recent years is that the funds of the UNDP have shown a tendency to decline (this aspect will be further examined in Chapters VII and XV). The UNDP also administers a number of special funds including the UN Capital Development Fund, the UN Special Fund for Landlocked Developing Countries, the Financing System for Science and Technology for Development, the UN Fund for Population Activities, the UN Revolving Fund for Natural Resource Exploration and the Interim Energy Account. Of these funds the only one which has received sizeable contributions from the Western donors is the UN Fund for Population Activities and it has had some success in its operations.

*WFP*. The World Food Programme is a joint UN/FAO Programme established by Parallel Resolutions of the General Assembly and the FAO Conference in 1961. It runs the Food Aid Programmes designed to meet emergency food needs and to implement food for work programmes as an aid to economic and social development. Pledges are made in the form of commodities, cash or services and the pledging target for 1985/6 was US$1.35 billion. Food aid as a form of aid rather than of emergency relief has many critics,[12] and the operations of the World Food Programme and its relationships with other Agencies (especially the FAO) have given rise to many difficulties, despite some of its success stories.

*UNICEF*. The United Nations Childrens Emergency Fund was established by the General Assembly by Resolution 57 (1) of 1946 originally to provide emergency assistance to children in war-ravaged countries. It was placed on a permanent footing in 1953 and charged with giving assistance to children especially in developing countries. In the main it has been highly successful, and has a good reputation, though a few of its programmes and the strong personality of its energetic Director, have brought it into conflict with other Agencies, notably the WHO. It is supported by contributions from governments and from private individuals (including the sale of Christmas cards). In 1983 (a fairly typical year) UNICEF received $US59 million from private individuals and $US184 million from 108 governments' voluntary contributions. Of the $US246 million that UNICEF expended in 1983 on projects in 113 countries, 27.6% was spent on projects for clean water and sanitation; 23.7% on basic child health; 16.4% on formal and non-formal education; 7.8% on child nutrition; 7.2% on social welfare services for children and 5.4% on emergency relief. It has worked closely with the WHO,

12 A good introduction to this subject is provided by Christopher Stevens, *Food Aid and the Developing World*, London: ODI, 1979.

though sometimes less than harmoniously, on programmes to control diarrhoeal diseases (in 1983 it produced 45 million packets of oral re-hydration salts) and has had a hand in nutrition programmes in 94,600 villages and communities throughout the developing world.[13] Because of its non-political character UNICEF has been able to fulfil its mandate all over the world, including in areas of very great political turmoil such as the Lebanon. In addition, it produces each year a list of worthwhile projects which it has no resources to pay for but which are listed as 'noted projects' in its annual catalogue. These projects are implemented if donors contribute additional funds for a special project.

*UNEP.* The United Nations Environment Programme was established by the General Assembly by Resolution 2997/27 of 1972. Its purpose is to promote international co-operation in the environmental field and recommend policies to this end. It also has responsibility for providing general policy guidance on environmental problems within the UN System. It is financed by a voluntary fund which is used to pay for programmes of regional and global environment monitoring, and for the extension of information designed to develop forms of economic growth compatible with sound environmental management.

It can thus be seen that the UN System covers an enormous range of activity in the economic and social spheres around the world. Operationally it is organised on a sectoral basis, sometimes with the boundaries of the sectors imperfectly defined. The quality of its performance differs widely from one part of the System to another. Almost inevitably it is highly bureaucratic and, over time, abuses have crept in. The need for reforms, either wholesale or piecemeal, to make the different parts of the System work more harmoniously together, has been increasingly felt since 1960. The next Chapter will briefly outline the features of the main attempts at reform to date.

13  UNICEF produces a good annual report, copies of which can be obtained from UNICEF national offices.

CHAPTER IV[1]

# PAST ATTEMPTS AT REFORM: JACKSON AND AFTER

Many of the difficulties described above in Chapter I were clear by the mid-1960s, and led to various attempts to carry out reform. There are valuable lessons for the future to be learned from these attempts.

The first major attempt was the so-called 'Jackson Report'.[2] This was the work of a team of experts led by Sir Robert Jackson[3] and commissioned by the Governing Council of the UNDP to make 'a study of the capacity of the system to handle the resources made available by the UNDP, first at their 1968 level, and second, if doubled over the next five years'. Doubts and misgivings had been widely expressed about the ability of the system to digest and administer large quantities of aid, and it was the general hope that the Capacity Study would lead to serious re-thinking and far-reaching organisational reforms.

The Report, however, went further than this. It outspokenly analysed the shortcomings of the System and much of it is as pertinent today as in 1969. It also made considerable proposals for reform. By no means all of these proposals have been put into effect (those which have been implemented have mostly concerned the United Nations and its subordinate bodies, as distinct from the Agencies) but even those that were not implemented were a major element in the re-thinking that went on during the 1970s and later. One important reason for the non-implementation of some of the Jackson proposals was that the hoped-for doubling of the amounts of aid made available through the UNDP, on which many of his recommendations were predicated, has not materialized. These resources now amount to less than half the total made available within the System. Thus one of the assumptions on which the work of the Jackson team was based proved, in fact, unreal. But for the future the relevance of the quantity of resources to the prospects for reform must be noted.

1 Most of the material for this Chapter was contributed by Mr Mark Allen, a member of the UN Joint Inspection Unit, 1978–1984.
2 *Study of the Capacity of the United Nations Development System,* Geneva: UN, 1969.
3 Sir Robert Jackson is an Australian who, after a long career dealing with development questions, was made Special Consultant to the Administrator of UNDP in 1963. He had previously been Chairman of Ghana's Development Commission.

47

Some useful administrative proposals of the Jackson Report were implemented almost immediately, by the 25th Session of the General Assembly in 1970: the system of country programming on the basis of indicative planning figures provided by the UNDP, some reorganisation of UNDP Headquarters and the abolition of any remaining distinctions between the old Technical Assistance and Special Fund programmes. Some others, such as the institution of a post of Director-General for Technical Assistance and the modification of the old Department of Economic and Social Affairs, have come about in the course of time. Others, such as the practice of programme budgeting and the harmonisation of accounting systems and cycles, have also been implemented as a result of pressure from other sources such as the Joint Inspection Unit. But neither the Jackson Report nor other factors have gone far to shake what the Report identifies as the underlying reason for the system not working with full effectiveness in the 1960s, namely 'the great inertia of this elaborate administrative machine'. The machine is not essentially more manageable, in the strict sense of the term, nor less inert, today than it was in 1969.

The Report states that the inertia of the system derives from three main factors. The first is that officials are so busy with day-to-day business that they have no time to introduce reform. The second is the factor of Agency independence. Third is the lack of co-ordination in the governments of member states.

The first factor is universal, and it is as true – and as unacceptable – in the case of the UN System as with any governmental or business organisation.

The second factor is fundamental. In the middle/late 1940s, the 'Founding Fathers' of the system decided that the system should be polycentric, with connected but essentially separate organisations responsible for political matters (the UN), health matters (the WHO), labour matters (the ILO), and so on. The dangers and disadvantages of having one monolithic organisation were considered to outweigh the dangers and disadvantages of having a dispersed network. So the various Specialized Agencies were set up as separate institutions, each with its own membership, intergovernmental institutions, budget, staff, Executive Head – and policies. There is, in fact, no policy centre for development in the System in the words used in the Jackson Report, no central 'brain'. The Founding Fathers did, it is true, envisage that ECOSOC would play some kind of supervisory or co-ordinating role, as laid down in the Charter; but they did not envisage that the Agencies would be formally accountable to ECOSOC, nor that their secretariats would be formally accountable to the Secretary-General of the United Nations. There is no way in which the Agencies can be obliged to adopt policies laid down by the United Nations, be they matters of development policy, administration or financial methods. The Founding Fathers may well have been right in the deliberate choice they made, but there is no doubt that the organisation – or disorganisation – of the System is an almost insurmountable obstacle to attempts to impose change from the top. The Jackson Report thought that this might be possible, through the UNDP's financial control; but this has not come about, and the UNDP comparatively is financially weaker now than when the Report was written.

The Capacity Study did put forward some proposals aimed at mitigating the dispersal of power in the System. It recommended that the UNDP should become the 'hub' of the System's development work, that ECOSOC should be strengthened and should become a 'one-world parliament', that a Development Resources Panel of the ACC should harmonize developmental policies under the UNDP Administrator, that a System-wide computerised information system in the development field should be developed and that a combined United Nations Development Service should come into being. None of this has happened. The Report also pointed to the lack of internal co-ordination within the governments of member states as one of the main factors contributing to the inertia of the system. It was and still is a common occurrence that the delegations of member states in the intergovernmental organs of the Specialized Agencies support policies or decisions that contradict the views expressed by the delegation of the same states at other Agencies of the United Nations. The reason for this is that, in many capitals, instructions to the delegations to the various organisations of the System are not centrally co-ordinated. This makes it all too easy for the Executive Heads to form their own power-bases in the technical departments in capitals and to mobilise their support against unwelcome outside influences. The only remedy for this is the improvement of internal co-ordination in member capitals – something easier said than achieved, but nevertheless essential if the System is to be improved.

## Later developments

Since the time of the Jackson Report there have been three notable and very different attempts at reform in various quarters: the United States' withdrawal from the ILO in 1977, the Restructuring resolution adopted at the General Assembly Session of the same year, and the withdrawal of the United States from UNESCO in 1984, followed by that of the United Kingdom and, for different reasons,

Singapore. The first and third of these represent attempts to bring about changes in individual Specialized Agencies. The second was another attempt to bring about change in the UN System as a whole.

*The United States' withdrawal from the ILO.* This move by the United States was motivated by dissatisfaction with the policies, not the administration, of the organisation. It was also much influenced by certain domestic factors within the United States, particularly within the US labour movement.[4] In announcing, first, its intention (in 1975) and later its decision (in 1977) to withdraw, the United States expressed its concern over a number of trends that were, in its view, weakening the ability of the ILO to carry out its basic mission. These included policy issues such as the erosion of the principle of tripartite representation, selective application of human rights especially in relation to freedom of association, disregard of due process in examining alleged violations of human rights, and the increasing politicisation of the organisation outside the scope of its mandate, as well as budgetary and administration issues. In February 1980 the United States stated that sufficient progress had been made in reversing the trends to justify it re-entering the ILO.

On the administrative side, the withdrawal of the United States had the immediate effect of reducing the funds available by 25%, that being the proportion of the budget which the United States had been bearing. An appeal by the Director-General of the ILO brought forth supplementary donations which reduced the shortfall to just under 20%, but the administrative consequences were serious. There was a sharp reduction of expenditure throughout the programme, accompanied by a salutary reconsideration of priorities, and a reduction of nearly 10% in headquarters professional staff. It is generally agreed that the ILO is now a much 'tighter ship' than it was before the United States withdrew. This experience may be relevant to the likely consequences of the Kassebaum amendment of 1985 (see Chapter VIII).

The episode seems to show that a country of the political and financial importance of the United States can single-handedly bring about changes both of policy and administration by exercising the power of the purse. Whether smaller countries, or less drastic

---

4  What is said here and later about US withdrawal from the ILO does not purport to be a full analysis of this episode. There is a much fuller account in Walter Galenson's book *The International Labour Organisation*, University of Wisconsin Press, 1981, which is well worth reading by anyone interested in the Specialized Agencies.

methods, could enforce similar changes may be doubted. Some other major countries, notably France and the Soviet Union, have in the past reduced their budget contributions to the UN or its Agencies in respect of decisions or policies of which they disapproved, for instance the military operations in Korea and the Congo; but these measures, which were not accompanied by political acts of withdrawal, did not cause sufficient financial embarrassment to bring about any changes of policy.

*The Restructuring Resolution of December 1977 (resolution 32/197).* This Resolution, made at the UN General Assembly Session of 1977, was a major attempt to reorganise the UN System in its economic and social sectors. It resulted from the continuing dissatisfaction on the part of member states – principally Third World countries, but the Resolution was adopted by consensus – with the unsatisfactory degree of responsiveness by the System to measures and proclamations such as the Second Development Decade and the Programme of Action on the Establishment of a New International Economic Order. The lack of progress on the lines recommended by the Jackson Report was another element in the situation.

The recommendations and decisions of the Resolution were on much the same lines as those of the Jackson Report, in that they sought to achieve greater co-ordination of the system, under UN leadership, and to reorganise those parts of the UN Secretariat that were under direct UN control. Broadly, the reorganisation of the UN Secretariat has gone further and been more effective than the attempts to impose greater co-ordination and leadership by the United Nations on the System.

The attempt to bring about greater co-ordination under UN leadership was expressed in the following main proposals. First, ECOSOC was called on to revitalise its debates and its methods of working. Secondly, 'country co-ordinators', normally the local UNDP resident representative, would co-ordinate the developmental activities of the System in developing countries. Thirdly, a UNDP country programme would be used as the 'frame of reference' for System activities in each country. Fourthly, an office of Director-General for Development and International Economic Co-operation was created at UN headquarters to provide 'effective leadership to the system in development' and to 'exercise overall co-ordination within the system in order to ensure a multidisciplinary approach to the problems of development on a system-wide basis'. And finally, the Administrative Committee for Co-ordination would be reorganised and be responsible for inter-Agency co-ordination in matters of development.

This ambitious plan encountered the same obstacles as those identified in the Jackson Report eight years earlier. Governmental and bureaucratic inertia have prevented ECOSOC from revitalising itself, and the UN System still has no central development 'brain'. The establishment of country co-ordinators has made some progress, but only in individual developing countries, and depending very much on the degree of willing co-operation afforded by often independent-minded Agency representatives and on the extent to which the UNDP representative can become personally acceptable to them. The country programme has been accepted as the frame of reference for their activities in each country by UN System organisa-tions, but this has not prevented the Agencies from trying to 'sell' pet projects to governments; developing country governments have their own development policies and priorities, and in most cases their own development plans and programmes, which provide their own frames of reference, in which UN System aid forms only a compara-tively small part. The Director-General for Development has so far been unable to bring about any degree of leadership, thanks to the internal politics of the System, though some progress has been made with inter-Agency co-ordination. There is little evidence to suggest that the reorganised ACC is more effective than it was, least of all in the sphere of development policy. The representation of individual Agencies in developing countries, which even in 1969 the Jackson Report considered excessive, and which the Restructuring Resolu-tion tried to discourage through the institution of country co-ordinators, has grown from 8,300 staff members in 402 offices in some 90 countries in 1973, to 12,000 staff members in 612 offices in 130 countries in 1983. This could probably have been checked, if not eliminated, by better intra-governmental co-ordination in the capitals of member states.

It can now be said that the impulse which led to the adoption of the Restructuring Resolution in 1977 – preceded as it was by two years of work by a special Committee of the Whole set up by the General Assembly – has faded away. The developmental scene has changed, the problems of the later 1980s are not those of 1977, and the dele-gates and officials have moved on. What were in the beginning annual reviews of progress in the implementation of the Resolution have become triennial reviews, and at the last such, in 1984, all that happened was that the General Assembly took note of various reports by the Secretary-General and the Joint Inspection Unit and referred a draft resolution on the work of ECOSOC to the Assembly Session of 1987.

*The United States' withdrawal from UNESCO.* At the end of 1984 the United States, after having given due warning of its intentions, withdrew from UNESCO, motivated by dissatisfaction not only, as in the case of the ILO, with the policies of the organisation, but also with its Director-General's administration, which it considered inefficient and extravagant. The United States received a good deal of support from some Western countries (including the Federal Republic of Germany and Japan); none of them followed suit in withdrawing until the United Kingdom did so at the end of 1985 after expressing dissatisfaction with the reforms made up till that date. It remains to be seen what will be the outcome of this attempt to bring about political and administrative change in a Specialized Agency, but the prospects are favourable, at any rate on the administrative side, if only because the organisation has no hope of replacing the missing 25% US contribution to the budget.

Two conclusions emerge. The first is that it is much easier to bring about change in one organisation, whether it be a Specialized Agency or the United Nations itself, than over the System as a whole. When only one organisation is concerned, the power of the purse, if not used to excess, is at least as great as the power of the vote or the resolution. The United States would never have obtained resolutions in the ILO, or in UNESCO, condemning the practices to which it objected; but the withdrawal of 25% of the budget is a powerful weapon.

The second conclusion is that the road to System-wide change lies through capitals. Governments created the polycentric system, and the only way it can be modified is by governmental action in all the Agencies individually, as well as at the United Nations itself. This emerges quite clearly from the history of the Restructuring Resolution. The Resolution appeared to most of the Agency Secretariats as an attempt by New York[5] to impose policies and practices on the Agencies, in defiance of the various constitutions which made them accountable to their own inter-governmental organs. The creation of the post of Director-General for Development also seemed like an attempt to downgrade the Agency Heads, who are elected or appointed by governments, whereas the Director-General for Development is appointed by the Secretary-General of the United Nations. Two additional factors strengthened the resistance of the Agencies: first, the UN Secretariat had no great reputation for efficiency or internal co-ordination, and the Agencies were not

5 I.e. a conspiracy of UN officials, ECOSOC, Second Committee delegates and the UN 'establishment' as a whole.

attracted by the idea of being 'co-ordinated' by an organisation less 'co-ordinated' than themselves; second, the substantial fall in UNDP funds from about 1977 onwards reduced the 'clout' of the centre in the System (for instance, UNDP funds accounted for almost 80% of the FAO's programme in 1973 and only 40% in 1983) and drove the Agencies to go out and look for funds for themselves, thus enabling them to maintain their programmes and to reduce further their dependence on the centre. It would have required inter-governmental moves, including debates and formal resolutions, in all the Agencies to change this attitude, and no attempt to do this was made. The Resolution was adopted in New York, reinforced in New York (a Resolution of 1979 urged the Agencies to 'offer' the Director-General their 'full and effective co-operation and assistance'), and its execution was supervised in New York, all to little effect.

How far a more co-ordinated System would be to the general advantage should perhaps be considered. To the extent, for instance, that some of the Agencies have avoided contamination by political issues prominent in debates in New York and have been able to stick to their technical lasts, polycentrism has been beneficial, and there will always be room for differences of approach and method. There can in any case be no question of scrapping all the Agency constitutions and starting again from scratch. It is a question of degree. But until countries can so organise themselves that all their representatives take the same line throughout the System, the scope for general reform seems to be small indeed. Many of these matters are examined further in later Chapters.

# PART TWO: THE PRESENT

# CHAPTER V

## 'POLITICISATION' AND THE SPECIALIZED AGENCIES[1]

### The nature of the charges

As was pointed out in Chapter I, the charge of 'politicisation' in the Specialized Agencies can take many forms, but for the purposes of this book it was most appropriately formulated by Dr Kissinger in his letter to the Director-General of the ILO of 6 November 1975 when he announced the United States' intention to withdraw from that organisation – notice which took effect on 5 November 1977. Dr Kissinger wrote: 'In recent years the ILO has become increasingly and excessively involved in political issues which are quite beyond the competence and mandate of the Organisation. . . . Questions involving relations between States and proclamations of economic principles should be left to the United Nations and other Agencies where their consideration is relevant to those Organisations' responsibilities.'

The objection is thus not to 'politicisation' *per se*. Indeed that would scarcely be possible; all the subjects dealt with by the Specialized Agencies, and indeed the setting up of the Specialized Agencies themselves, are matters which involve government choices and government decisions; by virtue of that fact alone they are 'political'. Moreover, even among the range of matters within the competence of a particular Specialized Agency, many call for decisions which affect many national interests; some indeed involve a conflict of interests either within countries or between countries; many involve genuine conflicts of political philosophy between 'socialists' and 'liberals'. All such decisions are, by their very nature and to varying degrees, 'political', even though they may relate to responsibilities which are clearly functional. It is, therefore, not possible for a Specialized Agency, however narrowly it interprets its mandate and whatever technical criteria it applies to its decisions, to avoid being 'political' at some time or another.

---

1 For a valuable analysis of this subject see Victor Yves Ghebali, 'The Politicization of the UN Specialized Agencies: A Preliminary Analysis', *Millennium*, vol. 14, no. 3.

This point has been generally accepted by all countries involved with Specialized Agencies. The charge, however, as set out in Dr Kissinger's letter to the ILO (in so far as it relates to this issue), is in effect fourfold. The first is that of becoming involved in political issues *'which are clearly beyond their competence and mandate'*. The second is that of attempting to deal with *questions involving 'the relations between States' or 'economic relations for which the UN itself, or some other international Organisation other than the Specialized Agency, is responsible'*. The third charge is that of *'selective concentration' on certain political issues*. (The issues within this last category which have arisen from time to time include human rights, colonialism and disarmament.) The fourth charge levelled by Dr Kissinger was that of *'disregard of due process'*, i.e. the condemnation of a state by Resolution without giving it an opportunity to be heard in its own defence. (In the past this has applied particularly to Israel and South Africa.)

## The issues

The issues which are featured in these charges of 'politicisation' since the 1960s have been varied. More of them have involved North/South than East/West relationships, although till recently the East has shown a greater capacity to exploit them than has the West – a situation which, largely owing to developments in Afghanistan and Poland, may be changing. They are also issues on which developing countries have succeeded in maintaining a remarkable collective solidarity even when their individual interests were not affected, partly as a means of securing a trade-off in votes.

Some of these issues are almost parochial and a number of them have become so routine as to attract little attention even within the organisations where they are raised. In this category are those issues raised in 'Credential' discussions such as Latin America's objections to Britain's right to speak for the Falkland Islands or Gibraltar. Frontier issues of various kinds often feature. Far more serious in its consequences for many years was the maintenance of the Chiang Kai-shek Government in Taiwan as representing 'China' until the People's Republic of China succeeded to the seat in 1971 (i.e. twenty-two years after the Communists came to power in mainland China). This left a serious mark on both the United Nations and its Specialized Agencies because it led to a large gap in their universality and was also considered by an increasing number of UN members to be unjust. Also in the parochial category are the steady attacks on the Soviet Union by China in the general debates of some organisations (e.g. UNESCO and UNIDO) involving charges of 'hegemonism'; but these have left some mark in that they have manifestly annoyed the Soviets and have taken up an amount of Conference time with arguments on how they should be recorded.

However, most of the issues which have featured in charges of 'politicisation' have related to important questions in international affairs of real and long-standing concern to a number of governments. They are also distinguished by being issues which have been discussed in the appropriate fora of the United Nations but on which resolutions passed in such fora have signally failed to make any real impact. Their importation into the proceedings of the Specialized Agencies and other UN bodies is a measure of the long-standing frustration which the participants feel at their failure to make any progress in dealing with them in the proper place, or places. The tactic of raising them in bodies which constitutionally have only a marginal responsibility for dealing with them, or with some aspect of them, has, in most instances, made little impact on any government's approach to any of them, the one exception being the expulsion or withdrawal of South Africa from a number of UN Organisations.[2]

The major issues which have been raised in the 'politicisation' process are as follows:

*The Arab states and Israel.* This issue is the one which probably arouses the sharpest reactions in the United States. With a little ingenuity, it – or some aspect of it – can be raised in most UN fora in ways which are more or less within their 'competence and mandate', even though the organisation concerned is generally powerless to do anything about it. The 1974 ILO Resolution which led to the US withdrawal in 1975 was a good example. It first declared that any occupation of territory was aggression or a violation of human and trade union rights. It then went on to condemn Israel for violation of trade union freedom in its occupied territories and finally called on the governing body and the Director-General of the ILO to use all the means at their disposal to end this violation and guarantee freedom and dignity to the Arab workers concerned. More notorious and persistent, however, have been various Resolutions at UNESCO, ostensibly concerned with archaeology in Jerusalem, in which the proposers also managed to attack the 'occupying power'. The WHO has been invoked to express concern at the poor health of the inhabitants of the

2 A note summarising the position with regard to South Africa as at January 1986 is appended at the end of this Chapter.

occupied Arab territories, to condemn inhuman practices in Israeli prisons, to call for the abandonment of the policy of establishing settlements in occupied territories, and to persuade Israel not to change the legal status of the medical practitioners in such territories. The occupation of Arab territories has been repeatedly raised in the Security Council with all five permanent members expressing concern; and it is there, not in the WHO, that it can be competently discussed.

*Apartheid/race/liberation movements.* The main target of the Resolutions under this heading has, of course, been South Africa. In many ways, from the points of view of its promoters, these have been the most successful of all 'politicisation' Resolutions. They produced a walkout by South Africa from the FAO in 1964, and her later exclusion or withdrawal from various other UN Agencies. They are selective in the sense that other countries besides South Africa practise various forms of discrimination against minorities and majorities without incurring similar international odium, although no other state has an official policy of racial discrimination embodied in legislation on this scale.

The issue of apartheid is of particular concern to the African states, which account for 42 votes in the United Nations. It is also something on which many other countries can show solidarity at little or no material sacrifice to themselves; and it is the ideal topic for the Eastern bloc, since it can be used to embarrass the United States internationally and domestically, as well as those Western powers with large investments in South Africa.

Like the Israeli settlements in occupied territory, apartheid has been repeatedly condemned in the political forums of the UN. In the 1970s it was even possible to arrange a marriage between this and the Arab-Israeli question by certain resolutions which equated Zionism and racialism. Aid to liberation movements is a more complicated area, since it involves not only Resolutions but action on the flow of resources from certain UN bodies (such as the UNDP or the World Food Programme) to organisations which are not just non-governmental but are positively anti-governmental. Up to the time of writing, however, these resolutions have caused fewer complications to the UN organisations concerned than might have been expected.

*Human rights.* The problem of human rights as discussed within UN bodies is twofold, first to define what they are, and secondly to decide their relevance to the topic under discussion or to the Agency concerned. That the United Nations as a whole is constitutionally concerned with human rights is beyond question. Article 1 of the Charter includes among the four main purposes of the UN that of 'encouraging respect for human rights and for fundamental freedoms'. Chapter IX of the Charter which covers economic and social questions (the very Chapter from which the Specialized Agencies derive their role) contains Article 55 which specifically enjoins the United Nations to 'promote . . . universal respect for, and observance of, human rights and fundamental freedoms for all without distinction as to race, sex, language or religion'. These provisions were later supplemented by the Universal Declaration of Human Rights of 1948. This was subsequently elaborated in two international Covenants, one on Economic, Social and Cultural Rights and the other on Civil and Political Rights, signed in 1966, both of which, following the necessary ratifications, entered into force in 1977. Both have been ratified by Britain and the Soviet Union and signed by the United States. *Prima facie*, therefore, considerable progress has been made since the Charter was signed in defining human rights. Furthermore, the Constitution of UNESCO states that one of its purposes is 'to further universal respect for justice, for the rule of law *and for human rights and fundamental freedoms* [emphasis added] which are affirmed to the peoples of the World without distinction of race, sex, language or religion, by the Charter of the United Nations'.

The ILO's obligation to seek 'to improve the working and living conditions through adoption by international legal Covenants and recommendations stating minimum standards in such fields as wages, hours of work and conditions for employment and social security' also constitute a mandate, and moreover one of particular relevance to implementing the Covenant on Economic and Social Rights.

Discussions of human rights, however, have not been confined to those two institutions, nor to the Third Committee of the UN General Assembly, the Human Rights Commission, the Human Rights Committee, or the Sub-Committee on Discrimination and Minorities (all bodies properly constituted under the Charter to deal with them), but have spread to other fora of the United Nations. Despite the definitions in the Covenants, they have also given rise to sharp differences of opinion between the governments of liberal democratic states and those who have a more totalitarian style of government, whether of the left or the right; and especially between those governments which insist that human rights are primarily individual rights and those who insist that they are 'people's' rights, or that, in the interests of 'development', economic and social rights must take precedence over civil rights.

Discussions on human rights issues have hitherto not had quite the same effect on Agencies other than UNESCO and the ILO as have some of the other issues which fall into the 'politicisation' category. Those, however, who have insisted on the primacy of economic and social rights as against individual rights have succeeded best in the process of 'selective concentration'; they have, on a selective basis, imported some of these issues into the work of the Agencies primarily responsible for economic development, such as the FAO or even the IBRD, and of Agencies dealing with social welfare, such as the WHO. Originally, these issues were raised with some success by governments espousing a collectivist point of view to the detriment of those of a more liberal democratic persuasion. Latterly, however, (as will be explained more fully in the note on the ILO below) some of them have begun to cause more embarrassment to governments within the Eastern bloc, and they have done so with Third World support.

*Peace and disarmament and related issues.* Constitutionally, the proper forums for disarmament questions are the General Assembly itself, the Committee on Disarmament (which the General Assembly established by Resolution 1722 of 1961), and the Disarmament Commission in Geneva (which the General Assembly established in its present form by Resolution 502 of 11 January 1952). A number of Specialized Agencies, however, have sought to discuss various aspects of disarmament and the removal of the causes of war; some of these will be described in the sections on the particular Agencies later in this chapter. The difficulties in these discussions arise from the fact that the Eastern bloc, supported by many governments of the Third World, try to use them to draft resolutions oriented towards Soviet views on disarmament as well as on the wider issues subsumed in the word 'peace'. On these issues also, however, some of the Eastern bloc's ready-made majorities of previous years appear to be diminishing. The practical effect of these discussions on the work of most Agencies has been comparatively slight.

*Rich versus Poor: The NIEO and other economic issues.* This is a major question affecting in varying degrees the work of most of the UN Specialized Agencies. Dr Kissinger's letter, referred to above, argued that 'proclamations of economic principles should be left to the UN and agencies where their consideration is relevant to those Organisations' responsibilities.' The position at the moment, however, is that the United Nations, by virtue of General Assembly

Resolutions 3201(S-VI) and 3202(S-VI) dealing with the New International Economic Order (NIEO), and others on Economic Rights and Duties of States,[3] has set out a number of economic principles which are certainly relevant to the work of particular Specialized Agencies. Nevertheless, they are also in varying degrees unacceptable to some of the most powerful members of the United Nations. If they were implemented literally, the present distribution of the world's economic resources would be radically altered with very great political consequences, both domestically and internationally. These are all issues on which, typically, groups of countries have a voting power in the United Nations which far exceeds their economic power. These groups are frustrated at failing to get satisfaction on most of these issues, even though they have pursued them first in the bodies whose constitutional responsibility they are. Their determination to raise them, or some aspects of them, in the Specialized Agencies is a measure of their failure to get substantial structural change in the world's economy through the machinery of UNCTAD or GATT or by General Assembly resolutions. Despite the extreme unlikelihood of the exact prescriptions set out in UN resolutions on the NIEO being accepted, the fact remains that until some greater consensus can be reached on these economic issues, the proper discharge of their functional responsibilities by the Specialized Agencies will be made more difficult, partly by the sense of grievance of many member states, but also by lack of resources – and, more important, by lack of real international agreement on the policies to be pursued and on whether the world economy should be restructured on lines set out in the General Assembly resolutions (see Chapter XII).

## Examples of effects of 'politicisation' on the work of some Specialized Agencies

The impact of 'politicisation' discussions has been more serious in some Agencies than in others. To get some idea of how serious, it is necessary to summarise some of the major discussions of recent years where they have affected the work of particular Agencies.

*FAO.* Discussion of political topics in recent years has not made much impact on the work of the FAO, perhaps because the FAO's general debates have been largely preoccupied with World food security, and with discussion of international guidelines for

---

3 The Charter of Economic Rights and Duties of States is set out in Resolution 3281 of 1974. GA Resolution 3362(S-VII) of 1972 is also relevant.

agricultural adjustment, advice on problems of more balanced growth of agricultural production, the African food crisis and the relationship between the FAO and the World Food Programme. All of these are – or can be – highly political topics in the sense that they can raise complex issues calling for difficult choices by governments, and also fierce political argument; but they are clearly all relevant to the work of the FAO and therefore it cannot be argued that discussion of them is unconstitutional and 'beyond the competence and mandate of the Organisation'.

Another factor may be that the Soviet Union has never joined the FAO (although Bulgaria, Czechoslovakia, Hungary, Poland and Romania have done so), allegedly because of unwillingness to reveal details of its agricultural production. A more likely factor is that most governments are represented at the FAO by delegates with a direct concern for agriculture and natural resource development who are more resistant to attempts to distract them by debates on extraneous political issues than less expert representatives would be.

*UNESCO.* Partly by virtue of its constitution with its mandate 'to remove the causes of war from the minds of man' and 'to remove ignorance, suspicion and mistrust between the peoples of the world', to 'establish clear principles of dignity, equality and mutual respect' and to 'educate humanity for justice, liberty and peace', UNESCO has always been the most 'political' of the UN Agencies; the extent to which its discussions are beyond its mandate is always debatable. Many of its more political activities have in recent years been widely reported, most notably because of its attempts to introduce a New World Information and Communications Order (NWICO). The press coverage these attempts have received probably reflects their relevance to the activities of the 'media', rather than their importance to the work of UNESCO. In the course of its general conference debates on these issues, several resolutions which were, in the opinion of Western governments, 'potentially harmful to the free flow of information' have been carried and others which (again in the eyes of Western governments) could lead to state censorship have gained acceptance (e.g. a study on the 'dissemination of false and distorted information' referring to Western media and a study on the collective 'right' to communicate).

There have also been disputatious discussions on human rights in which UNESCO has been at pains to adopt language which distinguishes 'collective rights' from the traditional rights pertaining to individuals, to the detriment of the latter. Moreover UNESCO has always shown a proclivity for developing programmes which many considered were more properly the responsibility of other Specialized Agencies within the UN System. One of several recent examples was its attempt to involve itself in the establishment of a code of conduct for transnational corporations (an attempt defeated by Western members) which was more properly the responsibility of the Commission on Transnational Corporations. UNESCO has also demonstrated a proclivity for dealing with broad issues about which it could do little, instead of with concrete issues which many saw as its proper task. For example, its budget of 1984/5 provided US$1 million for speculative studies on disarmament and only US$30,000 for literacy campaigns among refugees.

*WHO.* At the beginning of the 1983 Session the Director-General, Dr Mahler, made a strong appeal to the WHO Assembly against raising 'political' issues in a way which made a considerable impression. He said: 'If we allow ourselves to be lured astray into fields beyond our constitutional competence I am afraid we will find ourselves in those very minefields that we have been trying to avoid in the interest first and foremost of the health of the deprived peoples living in the Third World. None of us would want to blow up our Organisation nor would we want to lose the tremendous prestige we have gained as an Organisation of 160 member states, able to co-operate with one another for the health of people everywhere without distinction of race, religion, political beliefs, social or economic development – indeed, what our very Constitution demands of us.' Nevertheless some political issues have in recent years intruded into WHO debates. One of these has been 'the effects of nuclear war on health and health services'. This was the subject of an experts' report, the conclusion of which was that 'nuclear weapons constitute the greatest immediate threat to the health and welfare of mankind.' At the instigation of India and Cuba, this report was endorsed, despite a US argument that 'the question of how to deal with the prevention of nuclear conflict was undoubtedly a political question that has been dealt with by political officers and by political bodies constituted specially for the purpose'; and that the role of the WHO was 'to deal with specific questions of health, finding new and better approaches to disease, to malnutrition and to the improvement of human wellbeing'. The WHO, it was argued, can 'have no serious impact on primary prevention of nuclear conflict'.

The second issue, concerning Israel, has become almost traditional in the WHO, with the Assembly undertaking a review of 'health conditions in the occupied territories of Israel'. Usually this is preceded by an effort to deny the credentials of the Israeli delegation, or to suspend Israel's voting rights or programme services. In

1983, 43 countries joined in co-sponsoring a strongly worded Resolution condemning Israel for launching 'a ferocious war' against Lebanon.

The third set of issues relates to Southern Africa and includes resolutions accusing South Africa of using military attacks to destabilize the governments of border states and calling for SWAPO to be recognised as 'the sole legal representative' of the Namibian people.

*WMO.* In the World Meteorological Organisation the main political issue which has arisen so far was a discussion in the 1983 Congress as to whether, in accordance with a UN General Assembly Resolution, full membership should be granted to Namibia. This Resolution was opposed by the United States and a number of other countries on the grounds that 'the Convention of scientific organisations are not to be amended for political purposes'.

*ICAO.* Political issues normally have little or no effect on the work of ICAO. Following the shooting down of a Korean Airlines aircraft – KAL 007 – off Sakhalin Island on 1 September 1983, however, ICAO became involved in an issue which, though highly political, was undoubtedly within its mandate. Its Council passed a Resolution 'deeply deploring the destruction of an aircraft in commercial international service resulting in the loss of 269 innocent lives', and directed its Secretary-General to institute an investigation to determine the technical aspects of the flight and the route of the aircraft. This Resolution and other discussions at the Congress were subsequently endorsed by the ICAO Assembly in September 1984. As a result, new regulations were drawn up and agreed by all, including the Soviet Union, for civilian flights near militarily sensitive areas.

*ITU.* Since the ITU is concerned with the allocation of radio frequencies worldwide, many of its deliberations can be highly 'political' because there are important political prizes to be won in the international process of allocating and securing frequencies. These, however, are properly within the ITU mandate. The main political discussion of recent years which considerably disrupted the work of the ITU directing body, the Plenipotentiary Conference, in 1982, was an attempt to have Israel excluded from the Plenipotentiary Conference and all future ITU Conferences. At the Nairobi Conference meeting of that year, the debate on this issue consumed four of the six weeks available for the general debate. The Resolution was opposed by the United States and others on the ground that the ITU

Covenant did not provide for the exclusion of a member state and that the principle of universality of membership of the UN System would be jeopardized. The United States also argued that the Plenipotentiary Conference lacked the competence to take such action and threatened to suspend immediately all financial support for the Organisation if the Resolution was carried. A number of Western delegations then introduced an amendment to the original Resolution which in effect retained the condemnation of Israel for its activities in Lebanon but removed the exclusion provision. This amendment and, in the final vote, the amended Resolution were carried. Following the adoption of the Resolution, the challenge to Israel's credentials disappeared.

*ILO.* In some ways the most outstanding development on the political front in recent times started with the International Labour Conference in June 1983. It constituted something of a high point in the history of the discussion of human rights in a UN Agency which has an established constitutional *locus standi* on such issues, in particular those aspects associated with freedom of association.

The Committee on the Application of Conventions and Recommendations (the Committee of Experts), the body responsible for reporting on the observance of International Labour Conventions by states which have ratified them, produced what the West regarded as 'a strongly balanced report' which was adopted by the Conference by an impressive majority, (including most developing countries) despite strong Soviet and Eastern bloc opposition. The Soviets called for an overhaul of the ILO supervisory machinery to eliminate the procedures which had drawn attention to Soviet violations. This move was defeated in a vote in which a significant number of Third World delegates must have supported the Western position. The result owed much to the introduction of secret ballots into the ILO's procedures, one of the most important gains from the withdrawal of the United States from the ILO in 1977. Secret ballots were introduced in 1979 and the United States returned in 1980.

In an examination of freedom of association, the Committee had looked into more than 100 complaints from about 70 countries, and its report contained a number of adverse verdicts on cases from Chile, Turkey, Nicaragua, the Soviet Union and Czechoslovakia and other Soviet allies. Over all this hung the shadow of the Solidarity issue, but the Polish case was not discussed at that Session because the ILO governing body had decided to establish a Commission of Enquiry which precluded discussion until the Commission's work was concluded.

The Polish Government's reaction to the Commission's report

(1984) was to give notice of withdrawal from the ILO. In the following year this was supported by a 'Declaration of the Socialist Countries on the situation in the International Labour Organisation'[4] in which, *inter alia,* the ILO was accused of permitting 'attempts to use the Organisation for unseemly political ends against socialist and other progressive countries in order to interfere in their internal affairs', resulting, it was alleged, 'in subverting the ILO's universality'. There is no doubt that up till the United States' withdrawal, there had been a certain reluctance in the ILO to face up to Soviet and Eastern European transgressions in the human rights field. This partiality was one of the principal complaints of the United States against the ILO, and the redress of the balance owes much to the shock of the US withdrawal.

Apart from this major issue, there are other political issues raised at recent ILO Annual Conferences which have become almost traditional. There was, for example, the usual Arab Resolution attacking 'Israel's policy of settlement, expansion and discrimination and its actions with regard to the situation of Arab workers in Palestine and other occupied Arab territories', and 'Israel's racism'. This Resolution was defeated by a majority of 11 votes (again after a secret ballot). References to disarmament in a Resolution on Youth were also defeated. However, the Conference Committee on Apartheid produced conclusions which condemned a number of Western governments by name and called for member countries to stop dealing with banks operating in South Africa and went on to request details concerning the legal relations and activities of investors in South Africa. It also recommended ILO assistance to liberation movements, and trade union boycotts against selected major foreign investors in South Africa.

*The IAEA.* The main political issues raised in this organisation in recent years derived from the 1981 Israeli attack on the International Atomic Energy Agency-safeguarded Research reactor near Baghdad. This attack led to Iraqi attempts in 1982 to suspend Israel from the Agency – attempts strongly resisted by the United States, which in 1982 temporarily suspended its own participation in the Agency. However, a 1983 Resolution introduced by Iraq was more modest, and was approved. It called on Israel to withdraw its threat to destroy nuclear facilities in Iraq and other countries, and called on the IAEA to suspend research contracts in Israel and forbid the purchase of Israeli equipment or the convening of meetings in Israel. The Resolution was carried by 49 votes to 24 with 17 abstentions, but

4 Document GB/230/19/4, June 1985.

nevertheless the United States (which had by then resumed its participation) declared that 'its passing indicates a continuing tendency to
consider issues which, strictly speaking, are not within its competence.' In view of the status of the reactor as 'IAEA-safeguarded',
this was, at first sight, a difficult position to sustain; presumably the
United States considered that the condemnation of Israel in the UN
General Assembly Resolution of 1981 should suffice (this said that
Iraq was entitled to redress for the destruction of these facilities – redress which it never obtained).

## Politicisation in the Bretton Woods institutions

Politicisation in the World Bank and the IMF is the reverse image of
politicisation in most of the other UN Specialized Agencies, in that
the alleged political abuse of the Bretton Woods institutions is said
to emanate mostly from developed countries and in particular from
the United States. In this regard, US policy-making circles are said to
have drawn up a 'hit list' of countries for whom access to multilateral lending is to be denied where possible.[5] Among the countries
to face stern US opposition in the Bretton Woods institutions during
recent years are Vietnam, Cuba, Grenada (under the New Jewel
Movement) and Nicaragua. The basis of US opposition to loans for
these countries is political, rooted in its antipathy for radical socialist
regimes perceived to be falling into the Soviet orbit and manifesting
hostility to the United States. However, the arguments the United
States has used to oppose such loans, credits and other facilities are
technical. In 1981, the United States was influential in shaving a
proposed IMF credit to Grenada from $9m. over three years to $3m.
over one year, by arguing, contrary to IMF Staff who proposed the
loan, that the construction of the international airport in Grenada
would hurt the balance of payments of Grenada. This argument
almost certainly cloaked the real US preoccupation with the military
utility of the airport, but it did place apparent objections firmly
within the domain of the IMF.

Third World countries are accused of using 'artificial' majorities
to force extraneous political issues onto the agenda of other Specialized Agencies. The charge against the United States in the Bretton
Woods institutions is that of opposing the flow of financial
resources to countries which have expressed hostility to American
policies. In one instance, the US Congress withheld approval of new
funds for the World Bank until the President of the Bank, Robert

5 Cabel Rossiter, 'The Financial Hit List', *International Policy Report*,
Washington, DC: Center for International Policy, Feb. 1984.

McNamara, provided a House sub-committee with a note saying that no further loans would go to Vietnam in the near future.[6] A survey by the US Treasury appeared to confirm the importance of financial leverage to securing US interests when it discovered that in 85% of the cases where the United States sought to 'pursue a specific objective by seeking to change multilateral development bank policy, practice or procedure', it had been either successful or partially successful, by using financial leverage.[7]

Both the legislative and executive branches in the United States acknowledge that operations of the Bretton Woods institutions promote general US interests in liberalizing the world economy and opening markets to US goods and capital.[8] For this reason the United States is generally cautious about politicising the proceedings in these institutions, and the instances where this has occurred are rare and selective. Although the State Department appears to be the main agency responsible for introducing bilateral political concerns into the institutions, the problem is further complicated because of the ability of the US Congress to 'domesticate' the deliberations of multilateral institutions, by linking particular preoccupations in US domestic policies to US activities in international agencies.

Two observations arise from this consideration of 'politicisation' in the Bretton Woods institutions. First, the more that the decisions of these institutions are perceived by the Third World to be subject to the interests of the United States or of other Western governments, the less legitimacy they will have as impartial Agencies. Sporadic attempts by some governments to subordinate multilateral institutions to the exigencies of their national policies weaken the standing of these institutions and their influence in promoting the more liberal economic policies which most governments profess to be desirable. Secondly, politicisation in the Bretton Woods institutions serves to undermine arguments for weighted voting on budgetary issues in other Agencies. Rather than enhance efficiency, it may be counter-argued, weighted voting only serves to permit the decisions

---

6  Ibid.

7  R. Girling, *Multinational Institutions and the Third World*, New York: Praeger, 1985.

8  As Senator Charles Mathias candidly phrased it, 'There is a major element of self-interest in this because for every foreign aid dollar that we contribute to these multilateral institutions there is money spent in this country.' Hearings before the US Senate Subcommittee on International Economic Policy on IDA VII Replenishment, 29 Feb. 1984. This line of argument is not confined to the United States. Multilateral lending is frequently justified to the British Parliament by the commercial advantages which it has brought to the United Kingdom.

of international Agencies to be politicised in the interests of a different group of member states.

What lessons are to be learnt from this examination of 'politicisation' in the Specialized Agencies? The main one appears to be that the problem has arisen principally when groups of states have sought redress of their grievances in the proper fora and failed to secure any satisfaction. Often this has happened when (as in the case of Israeli settlements or Apartheid) the support for them in the proper fora has been overwhelming, but this has produced no changes of policy. The aggrieved states then cast around for any forum in which they can express their views and arguments, even if the only effect is to score a propaganda point. Their efforts are supported and exploited by other countries either for political purposes of their own or because they genuinely share the sense of grievance and want to show solidarity.

The first remedy for this situation, therefore, would appear to be to improve the efforts to deal with these problems by the proper UN machinery. Certainly the intrusion of such issues into the Specialized Agencies' discussions is a symptom of the inability of other organs of the United Nations, notably the Security Council and the General Assembly, to handle them effectively. This inability is due much more to political factors raised by these issues and to the sharpness of the political divisions in the United Nations, than to any weakness in the *machinery* for negotiating solutions. However, one aspect of the machinery, which has been carried over from the General Assembly into the Specialized Agencies, has in fact damaged the chances of serious negotiations rather than improved it. This is the procedure for dealing with these issues in a general debate in a large Assembly, followed by long resolutions painfully drafted and amended in the processes of public voting. Such procedures, though they can have an effect upon the atmosphere in which serious negotiations take place, are not conducive to extracting the concessions necessary for serious negotiations (cf. Chapter VI on Voting). The devotion to this form of procedure, however, is so well entrenched throughout the different organs of the United Nations that there is little prospect of changing it. To enable the Specialized Agencies to discharge their technical functions more effectively, therefore, the question becomes one of how to ensure damage limitation if it is accepted that some political issues will continue to be raised in ways of only marginal relevance to the functional purposes of these organisations.

One way to limit the damage is for those governments who feel strongly that discussion of some extraneous political issues is seriously interfering with the Agencies's work to bring pressure to bear on the Executive Heads, as well as to make representations to the offending governments, to persuade them to exercise some restraints in the interests of transacting some useful public business of a technical nature of benefit to all. As explained in Chapter III, much of the response will depend on the standing, prestige and general tactics of the individual Executive Heads; but the effect of Dr Mahler's appeal to the WHO Assembly of 1983 shows that the influence of the Executive Head can be great, particularly where his prestige is high and where member governments set great store by the proper discharge of the functional responsibilities of the Agency (as is the case with the WHO). Governments should also recognise – especially those governments which in the past have been the subjects of 'political' attacks in Specialized Agencies – that, whatever they may believe about the misuses of procedures, the mere fact and persistence of the attack is an indication of the sense of grievance which inspired it.

The prominence accorded to various 'political' issues varies over time. The major one in the mid-1980s has undoubtedly been the economic problems of the poorer countries; this will be discussed in Chapter XII. We may accept that the demands of, say, the International Development Strategy as it stands are not likely to be endorsed by the governments of developed countries. Nevertheless, there are fora within the UN System where they can be discussed and even on which general negotiations about them can take place properly, constitutionally and within the mandate (e.g. the GATT, the IMF, the IBRD and some parts of UNCTAD, as well as in regional banks and Specialized Agencies such as the FAO dealing with particular aspects of these economic problems). If governments, particularly of Western countries, decline to negotiate on these issues in any forum, or conclude that it is not to their advantage to make any concession necessary to ensure some progress on them in the proper forum, then they must expect trouble to continue in Agencies to whose concerns the issues are less directly relevant. Developing countries will use any platform to make their voices heard, and the only remedy is to make some progress in negotiations on the issues of substance in the proper places. The same is true of the Arab-Israeli issues and Apartheid, though these may be of less direct concern to many countries than the economic issues. Another way to limit damage is by some procedural change within each organisation, such as that in the ILO whereby contentious resolutions are discussed first in a procedural committee which limits the number coming forward to the main conference. Such procedures would have to be devised organisation by organisation, but the ILO forms a useful model.

A third method of bringing pressure to bear is by a member state's withdrawal. As has been previously pointed out, this method was used by the United States in relation to the ILO in 1977 with some beneficial results, and it was tried again in 1984 and 1985 by the United States and the United Kingdom in relation to UNESCO, with results that have yet to be seen. The major lesson to be drawn from the ILO incident, however, is that it is not the withdrawal of a country which matters, however important that country might be and however serious the ensuing break with the principle of 'universality'; what matters is the loss of the country's financial contribution. In the case of the United States with its 25% contribution, this is a serious loss indeed, but even that was not lethal to the ILO.[9] On the other hand, British withdrawal, with a loss of contribution of some 5%, would be more easily sustained. Finance apart, withdrawal does bring a loss of other inputs – intellectual, cultural and political – which could well impoverish the work of the organisation, at least over time.

No Specialized Agency, however, is likely to be much worried by this prospect. Each has up till now been confident that it is now such an established feature of the international scene that it will still be there after President Reagan and Mrs Thatcher have both departed, and whether or not reforms have been made; sooner or later their successors will come creeping back. This view is reinforced by much past history. Even Secretary Shultz's letter of withdrawal from UNESCO of 20 December 1984 envisaged not only that the United States would continue 'such participation in the activities of the Organisation as may be appropriate under the procedures and practices of the Organisation'. It went further and expressly stated that 'sufficient reform in the future could lead us, once again, to join in the important work that ought to be, and once was, UNESCO's pride.[10] Moreover, this is the pattern of most previous withdrawals from UN bodies, starting with those of Poland, Hungary and

---

9 The recent Kassebaum Amendment is causing such concern partly because it threatens a 5% cut *across the board* and would be that much more difficult to make up (see Chapter VIII).

10 The British statement sounded less forthcoming (*Hansard*, cols. 448–57, 5 December 1985). When asked a direct question on this point on 13 December 1985, the responsible minister, Mr Raison, replied: 'Before considering rejoining UNESCO we would need to be convinced that the organisation had adopted thoroughgoing and comprehensive reforms and that all member states and the secretariat were once again fully committed to working towards its constitutional aims and objectives' (*Hansard*, cols. 785–6, 13 December 1985).

Czechoslovakia from UNESCO in 1953 (because, as the Polish representative put it then, UNESCO had 'become a docile instrument of the Cold War'), through that of Indonesia from the United Nations itself and most of the Specialized Agencies in 1965, or the withdrawal of Portugal from UNESCO in 1971.[11]

Looked at across the UN Agencies as a whole, and with the ILO and UNESCO as prominent exceptions, the discussion of political issues outside their mandate has disrupted the transaction of their normal business only in limited ways and only from time to time. In so far as it had any widespread effect in the 1980s, this was only in relation to the issues embodied in the establishment of a New International Economic Order. This needs to be resolved in some way if the Specialized Agencies are to concentrate better on their functional responsibilities; whether the gains that are to be made by the Specialized Agencies functioning more effectively are worth the costs to some governments that would be involved in resolving the major North/South issues is a much larger question which individual governments, especially those of the West, have to decide for themselves.

11  UNESCO Executive Board paper 4X/EX/2, 28 Jan. 1985, offers an interesting exposé of this whole subject – not only in relation to UNESCO.

ANNEX

## SOUTH AFRICAN PARTICIPATION IN SPECIALIZED AGENCIES AS AT JANUARY 1986

South Africa retains membership of the UN, WHO, IMF, IBRD, ITU and GATT. The pressures placed on South African participation are outlined below by organisation:

UNESCO. South Africa withdrew in 1955. This was its only 'voluntary' withdrawal, i.e. not under threat of expulsion or suspension of voting privileges.

ILO. In June 1963 the Governing Body excluded South Africa from ILO meetings. In March 1966, South Africa withdrew.

WHO. Voting privileges were suspended by WHO in 1964.

FAO. The Conference of FAO excluded South Africa from its work in 1963. South Africa served notice of withdrawal almost immediately; this became effective in December 1968.

WMO. South African membership was suspended in April 1975, until such a time as the South African government renounced racial discrimination.

IAEA. Failed to redesignate South Africa (accept credentials) as a member in June 1977.

UPU. South Africa was expelled in 1979.

*Sources*: Richard Bissell, *Apartheid and International Organizations*, Boulder, Colo.: Westview Press, 1977; Deon Geldenhuys, *The Diplomacy of Isolation*, Johannesburg: Macmillan/South Africa (for South Africa Institute of International Affairs), 1984.

# CHAPTER VI

# VOTING AND DECISION-MAKING: HISTORY OF THE 'ONE STATE ONE VOTE' METHOD

The present crisis in the United Nations stems in part from its voting procedures. The problem was well summed up by Richard Gardiner writing in the *State Department Bulletin* (52:701–11) in 1965: 'The manifest disproportion between voting power and real power is now a central preoccupation of persons concerned with the future of the world organisation . . . If United Nations procedures can not be adapted to take account of power realities, the large and middle powers will increasingly pursue their national interests outside the UN System.'[1]

The basis of the difficulties which have arisen is the notion of each state having one vote as a normal attribute of sovereignty, regardless of its population, resources or military or economic power. This notion has long troubled international lawyers and writers on international affairs. As long ago as 1916, Leonard Woolf referred to 'the problem of the inequality of equal independent states' as one which would create difficulty for anyone trying to create an international authority, and concluded that 'if the world is ever to organise itself for the peaceful regulation of international affairs, that organisation must provide for the essential inequality of States.'[2] The legal arguments critical of the notion that 'equality' means that all states have the same rights and duties are based upon the proposition's manifest absurdity, since all states have not the same capacity to discharge them. Instead, some lawyers argue, the proposition should be interpreted as meaning that 'all states have the same capacity of being charged with duties or acquiring rights' or that equality before the law (meaning that the law will be applied to all states equally, irrespective of their size) does not necessarily require that all states 'participate equally in establishing the law, through equal voting, and share the benefits and burdens of that law, even though they are unequal in size and wealth.'[3]

---

1 This has in fact happened. Major issues – especially political issues – are handled either bilaterally or by the regional or specialist organisations which have sprung up outside the UN System.

2 L. Woolf, *International Government*, London: Fabian Society, 1916, pp. 118–120.

3 Zamora in *American Journal of International Law*, 74 (1980), pp. 566–608.

However that may be, the Constitutions of the Specialized Agencies set up after the United Nations Charter was drafted in 1945 applied the provision set out in Article 2.1 of the Charter: that 'the Organisation is based on the principle of the sovereign equality of all its members'. (This provision was approved by the United States, the United Kingdom, the Soviet Union and China (under Chiang Kai-shek) at the Dumbarton Oaks Meeting where the Charter proposals were prepared.) In addition, Article 18.1 of the Charter states that 'each member of the General Assembly [i.e. each member of the United Nations] shall have one vote'. However, although all the organs and committees of the United Nations follow this one vote per member procedure, there is a form of weighted voting in both the Security Council (in the veto given to the five permanent members, Article 27.3) and the Trusteeship Council (in the balance laid down between 'administering' and non-administering members of the Council, Article 86.1(*c*)).

The provisions of the constitution of UNESCO are fairly typical of the provisions in Specialized Agency constitutions relating to voting. Article IV 8(*a*) provides: 'Each Member State shall have one vote in the General Conference. Decisions shall be made by a simple majority except in cases in which a two-thirds majority is required by the provisions of this constitution, or the rules of Procedure of the General Conference. A majority shall be a majority of the Members present and voting.' (The cases requiring a two-thirds majority are principally the admission of new or associate members; the adoption of international conventions submitted for the adoption of member states; and the adoption of regulations governing the rules for the amendment of the constitution.) Even budgets in Specialized Agencies (unlike that of the United Nations itself) are normally passed by simple majority.

Article IV(4) of UNESCO's constitution is also important in this context. It provides: 'The General Council shall, in adopting proposals for submission to the Member States, distinguish between recommendations and international conventions for their approval. In the former case a majority vote shall suffice; in the latter case a two thirds majority shall be required. Each Member State shall submit recommendations or conventions to its competent authorities within a period of one year from the close of the session of the General Conference at which they were adopted.'

## The earlier alternatives

Before 1945 the simple principle of 'one state one vote' had not always been adopted as the basis of international organisations. In earlier organisations, various forms of weighted voting had been employed. For example, in the UPU the voting power of states seems to have depended on the volume of postal business in the 'metropole and its colonies' (France having four votes and Britain eight). In the functional organisations established between the Wars under the aegis of the League, many different systems of weighted voting were devised. (For example, the International Office of Public Health had six different classes of members, while the International Institute of Agriculture had five, with varying scales of voting power and financial contributions, which did not always correspond with each other.) Indeed a former Secretary of the ACC has written:[4] 'In many technical spheres, primitive forms of weighted voting had come to be accepted as a natural feature of intergovernmental co-operation within international organisations during the decades before the outbreak of World War I.' Moreover, despite the fact that the Covenant of the League of Nations had adopted as its normal rule the principle of one state one vote, it had been accompanied by another rule not present in the United Nations or its Specialized Agencies – the unanimity rule (see League Covenant Art 5.1).

## More recent developments

Thus by 1945, when the Charter and the Specialized Agency constitutions came to be drafted, the international community already had experience of two different systems of voting – namely weighted voting as practised in various technical institutions and one state one vote as practised in the League. Moreover, on the very eve of the negotiations leading up to the Charter, two international agencies, later to become Specialized Agencies of great importance on the international scene, had been established with weighted voting, and have remained operating effectively on that basis from that day to this. These are the IMF and the IBRD. They have systems of voting and decision taking which are weighted to their participants' resources or financial contribution and through which they take decisions binding on the participants.[5] Neither of these features is present in most of the decision-making procedures of the rest of the UN System. Nevertheless a number of international organisations have adopted weighted voting and have been successful in

4 Frederick K. Lister in *Decision-Making Strategies for International Organisations: The IMF Model*, a most valuable analysis of this whole question, published in 1984 by the University of Denver, on which parts of this Chapter draw heavily.
5 It should, however, be noted that, owing to the absence of most of the Socialist countries, their membership is not as 'universal' as that of most Specialized Agencies.

organising and (what is more important) financing programmes of development in developing countries. Notable among them are the Regional Development Banks and the International Fund for Agricultural Development which have voting arrangements reflecting the contributions of those who provided the funds.

In the case of IFAD there was a large Arab participation in financing it; indeed, weighted voting was a condition of the funds being provided. Moreover, in the 1980s, although there has been no attempt to amend the 'one state one vote' provisions in any of the existing constitutional instruments operating within the UN System, the number of attempts to introduce the principle of weighted voting into subordinate organisations or organisations outside the System has been increasing, especially where it is a matter of managing funds provided by members or of disposing of real resources. For example, the International Maritime Satellite Organisation,[6] established in 1979, which makes provision for allocating 'space segments' for use by shipping and rescue services etc., thereby improving maritime communication, employs a system of weighted voting in its Council based upon each member's involvement through investment shares.[7] Similarly, the new UNIDO arrangements, which came into force when UNIDO became a proper Specialized Agency in January 1986, provide for a powerful Programme and Budget Committee divided into various groups so that the market economy and the 'Socialist' countries if they vote together have a veto (an arrangement likely to be vitiated in practice – ironically – only by the market economy countries not maintaining their solidarity). Even more complicated voting arrangements will apply to the International Sea-Bed Authority which – if the Law of the Sea Convention ever takes effect – will organise the control and disposal of minerals lying on the bed of the sea. Here the main body on which all participating states will be represented, the Assembly, will take its decision by a two-thirds majority while the Council takes some decisions by a two-thirds majority, some by three quarters and some by consensus.[8]

## Voting procedures and decision-making

One of the things that is needed now if the United Nations and the

6 See INMARSAT Convention of 3 Sept. 1976, Articles 3 and 11–15.
7 It has in fact two organs – the Assembly which operates on one state-one vote procedures and the Council which operates on weighted voting plus a constituency principle to take care of the interests of developing countries.
8 See UN Document A/Conf. 62/122 of 7 Oct. 1982, especially Articles 157 and 159–162 of the Law of the Sea Convention of 1982.

Agencies are to become more effective and more action-oriented is a re-examination of the various schemes of weighted voting and of the circumstances in which they – or variants of them – can usefully be applied. The procedures for taking decisions in international organisations fall into four broad types. The first are those in organisations where decisions are legally binding only on those who have expressly concurred in them (these processes normally involve a formal ratification of the agreement concerned at a later stage, often by the legislatures of individual states). The second involves procedures for taking decisions legally binding on all but also requiring the concurrence of all (the unanimity rule). The third involves procedures for taking decisions legally binding on all members of the organisation without requiring their concurrence; this form of decision-taking is usually done in organisations which have simple majorities for some types of decisions and special majorities for others. Fourthly, there are the procedures for taking decisions which are only recommendations with no binding force; these are usually adopted on the basis of simple majorities (with special majorities only for special purposes).

## *Relating voting rights to actions and provision of resources*

The problem with decision-taking in the Specialized Agencies and similar organisations in the 1980s can be simply stated. It is that the developing countries (if they vote together) have a permanent majority; they can therefore always carry a vote on a recommendation. Something more than this, however, is needed if the recommendation is to lead to effective action. If Agencies with a functional purpose are to justify their existence they must become more action-oriented; they need to have a role beyond that of being mere clubs to spread international goodwill by bringing together those with a common interest. Where their resolutions require concerted action, what is needed is that those who have to provide the resources to make the action possible should be willing to do so; this means that the voting procedures should be designed to reflect the extent of this willingness.

Under all weighted systems, voting power must in the first instance depend directly upon the nature of the subject which the organisation is dealing with. The second criterion must be the extent of the interest of the individual participants. The third must be the extent to which individual participants are prepared to surrender control of resources to another authority, or indeed the extent to which the nature of the subject requires this. Each set of circumstances will be different, but in the voting systems which have resulted from the application of these criteria, certain patterns can be observed. First, there are some systems which use a single criterion to determine voting power, such as the export level or import level of a particular commodity in a country's trade. Secondly, there are those which use a number of criteria each accorded its appropriate weight (this is the basis of the voting arrangements in both the IMF and the IBRD). Thirdly, there are methods which involve voting by categories such as contribution levels or population size. Fourthly, there are methods which involve prescribing how a majority shall be made up (e.g. so many from each group). The fifth method is apparently becoming more popular in the UN System, namely that of setting up special subordinate bodies with limited membership to deal with some particular aspect of the organisation's business with voting powers different from those of the main body. There are of course various combinations of these systems.

Those who seek reforms along the lines of more varied voting procedures must accept that it would be very difficult to change present systems in existing organisations. There are too many vested interests determined to maintain the present arrangements even where these are proving ineffective and have resulted in public disillusionment and frustration. Any reforms will probably have to be piecemeal and partial and apply as new institutions are set up or new programmes started, generally as a price for raising new funds. Meanwhile, public opinion needs to be better educated on the significance within the UN System of resolutions, consensus, abstentions, reservations and the rest of the jargon, so that public attitudes towards them can become more realistic.

There is a continuing search throughout international organisations for systems of voting and decision-taking which avoid the defects of the 'one state one vote' method. Looking at international organisations as a whole, we seem to be moving towards a situation in which if it is a question of an organisation making recommendations which are not binding on member states, then the method of 'one state one vote' still applies; but where it is a question of decisions involving action, particularly decisions binding even on those who did not vote for them, then arrangements involving weighted voting operate. This, however, like so many other observations on the UN System, is something of an oversimplification, not least because it omits a major feature of the UN scene which has emerged since 1960 and of which the Charter gives no inkling: the notion of Consensus.

## Consensus

As often used in the United Nations, Consensus is not really a voting procedure at all but a gentleman's agreement to avoid voting on a particular issue or resolution. This is an alternative to a method written into the constitution of UNCTAD when this was being negotiated in the early 1960s. The UNCTAD device was that of a 'conciliation procedure' whereby voting on proposals 'substantially affecting the economic and financial interests of particular countries' could be postponed for six months while special committees worked to reach a compromise. The device has never been used, for the simple reason that developed countries have up till now regarded the demands made upon them by UNCTAD as so severe that they usually have no desire to reach even a compromise solution.

In the United Nations, since the 1960s, the term 'Consensus' has acquired a very particular meaning. It describes a practice designed first to elaborate the text of a resolution and then in some sense to get it adopted without taking a vote.[9] Sometimes the term is used (as it often is in ordinary parlance) when a vote is hardly necessary because there is such widespread agreement on the text. In the United Nations, however, it is often used when to take a vote would reveal such deep divisions between members that the practical uselessness of carrying the motion would be apparent to all. Johan Kaufman has described this second form as 'pseudo consensus'.[10] He cites as the perfect example of the genre the Resolution adopting the Programme of Action for the Establishment of a New International Economic Order adopted at the Sixth Special Session of the General Assembly. On this, the United States and the EEC entered such reservations that, although the Resolution was carried by Consensus, in some of its most important provisions it was a dead letter as soon as it was 'adopted'.

The first use of Consensus in the special United Nations meaning of the term was during a major political clash between the United States and the Soviet Union in 1964 over the financing of peace-keeping operations in the Congo and Suez. The Americans had proposed to make these operations a charge on the general United Nations budget, and therefore a matter for mandatory contributions under Article 19 of the Charter. Other nations, including France as well as the Soviet Union, strongly contested the obligatory nature of

9 An interesting study of consensus in relation to the Security Council is contained in a UNITAR pamphlet by F.Y. Chai entitled *Consultation and Consensus in the Security Council* (1971). But not all that it says can be applied *mutatis mutandis* to the Specialized Agencies.

10 Johan Kaufman, *Conference Diplomacy*, Dobbs Ferry, NY: Oceana, 1968.

this expenditure. The Soviet Union which under this procedure would have been obliged to contribute, threatened to withdraw from the United Nations. Following consultations, U Thant announced that an 'understanding' had been reached whereby issues other than those which could be disposed of 'without objection' would not be raised. This procedure was successfully followed until a compromise agreement had been reached on the financing of the two peace-keeping operations. Having once been successfully used on a contentious political question between the Great Powers in the General Assembly, the procedure spread to debates on contentious economic issues and to the Specialized Agencies and other bodies such as UNCTAD, particularly where the majority of states wanted to pass resolutions which would have imposed obligations on a minority of richer states which the latter were not prepared to accept. A ritual was invented to achieve a solution which is mysterious to those who have not participated in it, involving countries negotiating in groups (usually the Group of 77 representing the developing countries, the group of market economy countries, and the group of 'Socialist' countries). A refinement of the ritual is the 'contact group' in which representatives of each of the main groups meet, usually with the Secretary-General or his representative present, to invent forms of words in resolutions which all can somehow agree upon or at least agree not to vote against. This in turn leads to the strange spectacle after a resolution has been adopted by Consensus of delegates rising to say that if it had gone to a vote they would have had to abstain or even vote against certain clauses.

The device of Consensus has spread outside the United Nations. It was employed at the Helsinki Conference on Security and Co-operation in Europe (CSCE) in 1973, where the participants are reported to have defined it as meaning 'the absence of any objection put forward by a representative as constituting an obstacle to the adoption of the decision in question'.

The Consensus device has been useful in buying temporary peace in organisations in which contentious issues were being raised (it has been much favoured in UNESCO). It may even be useful in preventing a breakdown in discussions while the possibilities of further negotiation are being explored. Nevertheless its limitations are serious. The misunderstandings which have flowed from it have damaged international co-operation in the longer term. They have led the public to believe that there was a larger measure of agreement on certain controversial issues than in fact existed. They have also led public opinion to expect too much from some resolutions which prescribe general policies in controversial areas, and to believe that the United Nations and some of its Specialized Agencies are supranational bodies capable of legislating by majority vote for the whole world. This they are not. The powers of all international organisations (unless their constitutions, as freely accepted by their members, provide otherwise) are limited to making recommendations.

There is no legal obligation on any state to carry out any resolution, in whole or in part, which has not obtained its agreement, and it is a disservice to international co-operation to pretend otherwise. Consensus has enabled the United Nations and some of the Specialized Agencies to save face in cases where their pretensions have exceeded their powers. It obviates the need for serious negotiation of the kind which might lead to concerted action. As this fact has become more generally perceived it has added greatly to public disillusionment with the United Nations and all its works and to the frustration of those (especially in developing countries) who expected great consequences to flow from UN resolutions adopted by Consensus. There is a place in the UN System – and it ought to be an important one – for 'consensus' in the proper *Oxford English Dictionary* sense of the word, namely 'general concord of different organs in achieving a common purpose', especially where what is involved is the provision of real resources for the achievement of clearly specified objectives. There should be no place for 'pseudo consensus', except perhaps as a means of terminating debates on contentious issues which are not ripe for negotiation.

## The Kassebaum Amendment

The question of voting powers and rights is of course intimately bound up with the question of contributions and finance which will be discussed in the next Chapter. In August 1985, however, there was an important development in the United States which affects both issues and indeed also the staffing issues dealt with in Chapter XI. This was the passing of the Kassebaum Amendment, about which more will be said in Chapter VIII.

CHAPTER VII

# FINANCES OF THE SPECIALIZED AGENCIES

As explained earlier, the Specialized Agencies are financed mainly from three sources: the assessed contributions of their members (which they have to pay by virtue of being members of the organisation concerned and which are assessed on a UN formula designed to reflect their national capacity to pay); the subventions the Agencies obtain from the UNDP, which is itself financed by the voluntary contributions it receives from the members of the United Nations; and finally by various 'Funds in Trust' or special funds which the Agencies negotiate from various donors, both multilateral (such as the IBRD) and bilateral, or which (like the UNFPA) have been established to finance special programmes or activities and to which member governments of the United Nations contribute voluntarily. Financially, therefore, the System is complicated. It has grown up in a manner that is less than rational partly for reasons of internal politics and partly because this piecemeal approach has in one way or another served member governments' interests.

Many attempts to rationalise the finances of the System have been made over the years, the best of which have been only moderately successful. These attempts at rationalisation have had two broad objectives. The first was mainly the concern of the developed countries (both capitalist and Communist) to get the assessed budgets under control so that in response to the votes of the majority they did not expand excessively; in the first half of the 1980s this attempt, as will be shown later in this Chapter, had largely succeeded. The second was to channel most of the voluntary funds through the UNDP, not least so that they could be better administered and above all so that the UNDP could become the major channel for technical assistance funds going through the System and could use them as an instrument for co-ordination at both inter-Agency and country level. This attempt, it seems, has not succeeded – at least up to the time of writing – partly because of Agency resistance and partly because it is an ideal to which the donors have all too often paid no more than lip service. A measure of its failure is that whereas in 1968 (the year before the publication of the Jackson Report) the UNDP's share of the technical assistance funds passing through the UN System was 65%, by 1980 this had sunk to 38%. The growth has been in technical assistance financed through the Specialized

Agencies' regular budgets and through the growth of special funds of one sort or another as sources of money. By 1984, the situation was that, of UN technical co-operation expenditure of US$1.368 billion, UNDP central resources accounted for 38.5%, UNDP administered funds 5.92%, UNFPA 8.76%, Agencies extra-budgetary sources 30.69% and regular budgets 16.08% (of which the WHO had the largest share).[1] Some aspects of this question will be examined in more detail in Chapter XV on the UNDP and it will be referred to again in Part Three.

## Definitions

The definition of the various sources of the money flowing into the system is most simply given in the new constitution of UNIDO. Not all Agency constitutions define the position so clearly, but the practices of most are now broadly similar. Article 13.2 of the UNIDO constitution states:

2. The expenditure of the Organisation shall be divided into the following categories:
(a) expenditures to be met from the assessed contributions (referred to as the 'regular budget'); and
(b) Expenditures to be met from voluntary contributions to the Organisation and such other income as may be provided for in the financial regulations (referred to as the 'operational budget').
3. The regular budget shall provide for expenditure for administration, research, other regular expenses of the Organisation and for other activities, as provided for in Annex II.[2]
4. The operational budget shall provide for expenditures for technical assistance and other related activities.

The second article in UNIDO's constitution of importance to the question of finance is Article 15 which provides:

1. Regular budget expenditures shall be borne by the Members, as apportioned in accordance with a scale of assessment established by the Conference by a two-thirds majority of the Members present and voting, upon

1  Source Table 1 of DP1985/65 of 1985.
2  Annex II of the articles provides that 'Administration, research and other regular expenses of the Organisation shall be deemed to include:
(a)  interregional and regional advisers;
(b)  short term advisory services provided by the staff of the Organisation;
(c)  meetings, including technical meetings, provided for in the programme of work financed from the regular budget . . .;
(d)  programme support costs arising from the technical assistance projects. . . .'

the recommendation of the Board adopted by a two-thirds majority of the members present and voting on the basis of a draft prepared by the Programme and Budget Committee.

The scale of assessments shall be based to the extent possible on the scale most recently employed by the United Nations. No member shall be assessed more than twenty-five percent of the regular budget of the Organisation.

Such limitations of the maximum contribution are not universal as a constitutional provision in all Agencies but 25% has up till now generally been regarded as the upper limit on the major contributor, i.e. the United States, even though strict application of other principles, such as GDP *per capita* would indicate that she ought to pay a higher percentage, (in fact over 50%).

Finally, there are two articles which provide for 'voluntary contributions to the Organisation' (Article 16) and for the setting up of an 'Industrial Development Fund' (Article 17). Article 16 authorises the Director-General to 'accept voluntary contributions to the Organisation, including gifts, bequests or subventions, made to the Organisation by governments, intergovernmental or non-governmental Organisations or other non-governmental sources . . .' Article 17 states that 'in order to increase the resources of the Organisation and to enhance its ability to meet promptly and flexibly the needs of developing countries, the Organisation shall have an Industrial Development Fund which will be financed by the voluntary contributions to the Organisation provided for in Article 16 . . .'

In looking more closely at the three different categories of finance – assessed contributions, voluntary funds outside the Agency's control, and voluntary funds directly under its control – it is important to bear in mind their inter-relationship, which is two-fold. First, the voluntary funds make an important contribution to the ordinary administrative overheads of Agencies (e.g. 13% of the cost of each UNDP project goes to the executing Agency). Secondly, voluntary funds have in fact expanded over the years, partly as a means of resisting developing country pressure for increases in regular budgets; they have also enabled donors to retain greater control of the selection and execution of projects. Developed countries (both market economy and Socialist) naturally tend to resist pressure for the expansion of all sorts of expenditure. The chosen instrument of the market economy countries for doing this in the case of the assessed budgets is the Geneva Group.

### The assessed budgets and the Geneva Group

The Geneva Group was formed in 1964 by the major market

economy contributors to the Agencies' assessed budgets in an attempt to bring these budgets under control. Before discussing how it has operated and with what success, it is necessary to get the problem into perspective. Appendix A shows how the total budgets of the ten Specialized Agencies dealt with by the Geneva Group emerged from the budgetary exercises of 1984/5. In total their expenditure is less than $2 billion. This is only a small fraction of the total national budgets of the eleven states who make up the Geneva Group, even assuming that they had to bear the whole amount (which they do not). In financial terms, therefore, it is a comparatively minor problem for the states who are members of it. Politically, however, it is of much greater importance because it is a form of international taxation which can be imposed upon them in the last resort without their consent as long as they remain members of the Organisations; this has long caused resentment in some of their legislatures, notably in the US Congress. It has, therefore, a political importance which far exceeds its financial importance.

The date of the Geneva Group's foundation – 1964 – is significant. It was the year UNCTAD was founded and the developed countries were beginning to show concern at what they regarded as a developing country attempt to 'gang up' on them in various institutions within the UN System. They therefore decided to form a group of those countries in Group B (the 'market economy' countries in UNCTAD terms) who contributed more than 1% on average to the budgets of the 'Big Four' Specialised Agencies – the FAO, the ILO, UNESCO and the WHO. In mid-1986 the Group consisted of Australia, Canada, France, the Federal Republic of Germany, Italy, Japan, Netherlands, Spain, Sweden (with observer status only – from its own choice), and the United Kingdom and the United States, which act as joint chairmen of the Group. The Group are civil servants not ministers (thereby virtually guaranteeing that the Group will not be innovatory), and they meet early each year, usually in Geneva.[3] The Group's terms of reference are directed mainly to budgetary control and management improvement with the object, it is claimed, of producing more effective and efficient UN Agencies for the benefit of the entire membership. The central Geneva Group is supplemented by a number of separate Agency 'Geneva Groups' set up not only in the four main Agencies but also in a number of bodies, such as UNCTAD, which are not, strictly speaking, Specialized Agencies.

The Geneva Group and its subsidiaries have no constitutional

3  The idea of extending Geneva Group institutions to New York and the organisations based there has been generally resisted by Missions in New York.

position. They are at best an inter-governmental pressure group. They make their influence felt first by establishing (if they can) a common position on budgetary questions and administrative matters, and then by making representations to the Secretariats of the Organisations (sometimes also to the Agency Heads themselves) about what rates of budgetary and programme growth might be reasonable.

Throughout the life of the Group their position has suffered from two weaknesses. First, all they can do is to try to persuade; at the end of the day they are constitutionally bound to pay up or get out – or at least so it was generally understood (despite the continued participation of many governments who are in arrears) until the Kassebaum amendment arrived on the scene. Secondly, for a variety of reasons, they have not always been able to agree among themselves. Not only are there many genuine differences among them about aid policy – for example some of them are as a matter of principle more in favour of multilateral than of bilateral aid – but also various extraneous factors come into play (for example, an Agency's location – the Italians are unlikely to be difficult about the budget of the FAO as long as its headquarters remain in Rome).

Nevertheless, over time the Geneva Group, assisted by a number of other factors, has been successful in introducing a measure of budgetary restraint. For example, when the Group was set up in 1964 the budgets of the four major Specialized Agencies were increasing at about 15% a year. By the biennium 1982–3 this had been reduced to 2.2% for the WHO, 8% for the FAO, 6.3% for UNESCO and 8.8% for the ILO (all figures in real terms). As can be seen in Appendix A, the figures for the following year were even lower, in some instances being below zero real growth (which is understood to be the Geneva Group target for all Agencies). There are, however, marked differences between the Agencies, with UNESCO and the FAO always being the most awkward as far as the Geneva Group is concerned.

How successful the Geneva Group has been in its second aim – that of improving administrative efficiency – is harder to determine. It has given support to the JIU and to such procedures as M. Bertrand's programme budgetting techniques, but the results of all these special procedures and institutions still leave much to be desired. Again the Geneva Group governments are not all as united in underlining the importance of administrative performance as some members of the Group would like them to be. Some Geneva Group governments, even in their national administrations, take a more relaxed view of these matters than do others.

To a third point of their declared aims, however, the Geneva

Group seems, on the evidence available, to have given inadequate attention. According to a Canadian source, in addition to budgetary control and administration, the Group was also supposed to concern itself with 'programme development'. Except in the sense that it made efforts to limit programme expansion on the grounds that it would lead to increased expenditure, the Group does not seem to have seriously considered programme content and its relevance to the work of the Specialized Agencies, not even to their work as providers of technical assistance and feasibility studies. This is an omission about which more will be said later.

## Expenditure of the UN Agencies from non-assessed voluntary sources

Assessed budgetary expenditure of the Specialized Agencies apart, it is now very much easier to obtain accurate and comprehensive information about the resources being spent on technical co-operation by the Agencies than it was before 1980. This is largely thanks to two sets of annual reports about which more should be said as an introduction to this aspect of the subject and which everybody interested in it should consult further.

The first is the UN Secretary-General's Report on the Operational Activities of the United Nations System which has been appearing since September 1981.[4] The 1986 Report is especially important since it is the Secretary-General's triennial review to ECOSOC (the first since 1983). Three general points are worth noting about this series of reports. The first is that they are not confined simply to finance; they deal also with System-wide questions of co-ordination and evaluation; these are considered in later Chapters. Secondly, although they give a wealth of statistical material which is clearly set out and analysed, it is sometimes not easy to reconcile this with statistics available from other sources, notably those from the Agencies themselves. The reasons for this (apart from differences of format) are alleged to be that in the past the Agencies were deliberately obfuscatory, but it is also claimed that the situation is improving. Thirdly, although the analysis in these documents is generally clear, the language occasionally becomes opaque for diplomatic reasons and lapses into UN prose. For example, para. 32 of A/46/698, when writing about 'round-table meetings', says 'Significant shortcomings in this co-ordination mechanism became evident in the early 1980s. . . . The principal criticism of beneficiary

4  A/36/478 of 30 Sept. 1981; A/37/445 of 28 Sept. 1982; A/38/258 of 8 June 1983 and A/38/258 Add 1 of 19 Sept. 1983; A/39/417 of 18 Sept. 1984; A/40/698 of 22 Oct. 1985; A/41/350 of May 1986.

countries was the disappointing level of resources mobilised; for aid partners there was an expectation for better quality macro-economic preparations and a more substantive policy dialogue.' This simply means that the poorer countries were disappointed that the 'round table' did not seem to produce more aid; while donor countries were disappointed that it did not give them more chance to comment on how poorer countries were running their economies. Once such language difficulties are overcome, however, the reports are illuminating.

The second series of valuable reports for anyone studying the finance of the UN System has been published since 1973 but has been much improved in recent years. This consists of the Reports of the Administrator of UNDP on 'Information on UN System Regular and Extra-Budgetary Technical Co-operation Expenditures'. These are reports to the UNDP Governing Council. The Agencies co-operate with the UNDP in producing them and they give, Agency by Agency and sector by sector, the technical co-operation expenditures of each Agency, how much was financed from regular budgets and how much from extra-budgetary sources (including the UNDP).[5]

Progress has also been made in another direction. As a result mainly of the work of M. Bertrand and of the JIU, the United Nations and the Agencies (except the Bretton Woods Institutions) have – with varying degrees of willingness – adopted a common budgeting and programming cycle, and a common system of pro-gramme budgeting. It is at last somewhat easier for governments to compare the budgets and programmes of each organisation, and to gain a fairly coherent picture of the work of the System. Much remains to be done in this direction to achieve full 'transparency' and full comparability, but progress has at least been made – however slowly. Far less progress has, regrettably, been made with plans that were drawn up in the 1960s and early 1970s for computerising the whole of the operational work of the System in one accessible form. There is still no one official source from which a government, a newspaper or a financial or non-governmental institution can obtain System-wide information on operational activities.

## The scale of Technical Co-operation funds passing through the UN System

Over the years 1981 to 1984, the level of technical co-operation funds

5   The references for the last five years are: DP/545 of 2 July 1981; DP/1982/63 of 21 Oct. 1982; DP/1983/57 of 20 June 1983; DP/1984/66 of 8 June 1984; DP/1985/65 of June 1985.

passing through the UN System amounted to about US$1.4 billion a
year. The table below, drawn from the UNDP Administrator's
reports, gives a breakdown for each of these years. To put these sums
into proportion, however, it has to be said that during the same four
years total world aid from all sources, capital and technical assistance, amounted to about US$34.3 billion a year,[7] of which multi-
lateral funds came on average to about US$6.2 billion a year. There-
fore, funds passing through the United Nations System were
averaging about 4.8% of total world aid funds and only about 23%
of total multilateral funds. It is also useful to see in what sectors the
UN technical assistance funds were spent. During 1984, some 9.7%
of the funds were spent on natural resource development, some
18.7% on agriculture and forestry, 7.7% each on industry and transport, 20.7% on health and 3.7% each on education and
employment.

### UN TECHNICAL CO-OPERATION EXPENDITURE, 1981–4[6]

| Type of Expenditure | ( × US$1,000) 1981 | 1982 | 1983 | 1984 | Total | % |
|---|---|---|---|---|---|---|
| Regular Budget | 213,265 | 198,594 | 257,405 | 220,071 | 889,335 | 15.2 |
| Extra-budgetary other than UNDP UNFPA and UNDP-administered funds | 501,117 | 410,240 | 396,908 | 420,025 | 1,728,290 | 30.64 |
| UNDP-administered | 572,900 | 61,428 | 63,953 | 81,046 | 206,427 | 3.68 |
| UNDP central resource | | 660,600 | 560,100 | 527,495 | 2,421,095 | 42.95 |
| UNFPA | 39,109 | 113,727 | 122,523 | 119,892 | 395,251 | 7.1 |
| *Total* | 1,426,391 | 1,444,589 | 1,400,889 | 1,368,529 | 5,640,398 | |

One other point needs to be borne in mind in considering these
figures; about 75% of them are provided by ten countries who also
provide the major part of the assessed contributions and who are
represented on the Geneva Group (i.e. the United States, Japan, the
Federal Republic of Germany, Canada, the United Kingdom, the
Netherlands, Sweden, France, Italy and Australia). The same ten
countries also provide the bulk of the world Official Development
Assistance, both bilateral and multilateral.

However, the major feature to note is that fifteen years after
Jackson some 46% of all UN resources were outside the control of
the UNDP and its ancillaries.

6 These are actual expenditure figures, not commitment figures.
7 See Chart on p. 94 of OECD Report *Twenty Five Years of Development Co-
operation*, Paris, 1985.

## The financial complexities of the System – UNESCO

This, in broad outline, is the way in which the technical co-operation activities of the UN System and the operations of the Specialized Agencies are financed. To get the full flavour of the complexities of the finances it may be useful to examine the budget of one Ageny for one year in greater detail. We will take for this purpose the non-asessed part of the UNESCO budget for 1985/6, not because it is especially typical either of UNESCO or of the Agencies as a class, but because UNESCO has many outside-financed activities and because for this financial year it has provided a great deal of detailed information.

As a breakdown of funds by sources for its operations UNESCO provides the estimates shown in the table below.

|  | 1986–7 *projection* | 1984–5 *estimates* |
|---|---|---|
|  | $ | $ |
| UNDP | 80,000,000 | 83,000,000 |
| UNFPA | 14,000,000 | 11,300,000 |
| UNEP | 4,390,000 | 5,300,000 |
| UNFSSTD | 1,000,000 | 1,850,000 |
| Other UN sources | 10,692,000 | 9,500,500 |
| World Bank technical assistance | 8,150,000 | 8,290,000 |
| Regional development banks and funds | 10,100,000 | 10,195,000 |
| Funds-in-Trust | 60,935,000 | 63,272,000 |
| Associate Expert Scheme | 7,200,000 | 7,102,000 |
| Special accounts, voluntary contributions and other funds | 20,520,800 | 20,450,800 |
| *Total* | 216,987,800 | 220,260,300 |

On these figures UNESCO comments on its budget proposals:

Under the 'United Nations Development Programme' a biennial delivery of $80 million is projected for 1986–1987, which is $3 million lower than the estimates for 1984–1985 ($83 million). The present trends of project approvals and expenditures indicate that the 1984–1985 target of $83 million may not be achieved. The conservative approach adopted by UNDP in programme planning and the resulting low level of approvals, and the appreciation in the value of the US dollar, which permitted programme delivery at a lower cost in dollar terms, are some of the factors worth mentioning.

UNDP continues to be the dominant source of extra-budgetary project-financing. However, while UNDP expects that the programme will gain momentum in the coming years and that resources will increase on the one hand, the changes in priorities for resources allocation and the gradual expansion of new execution modalities might affect UNESCO's share of projects on the other. In view of the tripartite character of project formulation and execution, and the key role played by Member States in the

allocation of IPF (Indicative Planning Figure) to different sectors of activity, which governs the choice of the executing agency, *the volume of
resources made available to the Organisation by UNDP could be influenced
favourably by Member States* [emphasis added].

This last sentence, of course, is a clear example of Agency salesmanship via member states. The UNESCO document continues:

The United Nations Fund for Population Activities finances projects in the
fields of population, education and communication. These projects aim at
the integration of population content in the training and teaching programmes in national systems of education, research and communication.
Special attention is devoted to rural areas, and to women and youth groups.
Given the positive trend in UNFPA allocations for projects to be executed
by UNESCO, it is expected that $14 million would be available during
1986–1987, representing an increase of $2.7 million over the 1984–1985 esti-
mates ($11.3 million).

UNESCO will continue its co-operation with the United Nations Environment Programme for the execution of projects related to ecology, renewable
energies, microbiology, biotechnology, geology, seismology, environmental effect of water projects, marine pollution, land management, urban
systems, biosphere reserves, and environmental education and information.
Funds available from UNEP for UNESCO executed projects show a
declining tendency, and accordingly an amount of $4.4 million dollars has
been retained for 1986–1987, compared to 5.3 million in the previous budget
period.

The Interim Fund for Science and Technology set up by the Vienna Conference on Science and Technology for Development was subsequently
replaced by the United Nations Financing System for Science and Technology for Development.[8] Donor support to this Fund has been only a small
fraction of that originally expected. Nevertheless, UNESCO has executed a
certain number of projects in science and technology research development
and information. Given the current financial constraints of the Fund, a
reduced sum of $1 million has been estimated for 1986–1987, as against $1.9
million foreseen in 22 C/5.[9]

'Other United Nations Sources' include the Co-operative Programmes
with the World Bank, UNICEF, and the World Food Programme; the
United Nations Fund for Drug Abuse Control and United Nations Trust
Funds for the United Nations Decade for Women and Sudano-Sahelian
Activities.

The reference to assistance projects financed by the World Bank
and Regional Development Banks is also interesting. The agreements under which these programmes are financed go back to 1964

8  See Chapter XIII.
9  A reference to a UNESCO paper.

and many activities concerned with the educational development of developing countries have been financed under them. During the period 1973–84 the World Bank alone, according to UNESCO, approved '200 loans or credits to 82 countries for a total value of $US4770 million', and UNESCO has been involved in 143 of these. However, these figures, though true, are clearly deceptive and symptomatic of UNESCO's attempts to inflate its own importance by implying that the scale of this financing is somehow due to the efforts of UNESCO rather than to the policies of the IBRD. UNESCO has also acted as executing agency since 1971 for the technical assistance of 67 World Bank projects to the value of $50 million. Thereafter, however, UNESCO's share in such projects by the World Bank seems to have been declining and was down to about $12 million for the period 1979–83. UNESCO has also developed contacts with the African and Asian Development Banks, the Arab Bank, the Islamic Development Bank and the Caribbean Development Bank. (Such arrangements with the Banks, however, are by no means universal throughout the Agencies. For example, the World Bank has similar arrangements only with UNIDO, the WHO, the FAO and IFAD.)

The major share of UNESCO's funds, after the UNDP, comes from 'Funds in Trust', described as being 'contributions from Member States for the purpose of carrying out specific activities which are consistent with the aims and policies of the organisation, either for the benefit of another Member State or Organisation or for the benefit of the funding source itself. The projects are executed by UNESCO in accordance with specific agreements concluded for each project with the funding sources and the beneficiary state.' These 'Funds in Trust' have grown to cover some 27% of UNESCO's expenditure compared with UNDP's contribution of 37%. If the sums in other 'special accounts' are added to the 'Funds in Trust' the operations financed from non-UNDP sources are almost identical with those financed by the UNDP.

The problems of finance in the UN System are as much those of complexity as of adequacy, or at least they were before Kassebaum and Gramm-Rudman, as described in the next Chapter. As regards the operational funds, the UNDP has not acquired the paramount role envisaged for it in Jackson. Its role, however, is still of key importance and Chapter XV is devoted to discussing its policies and problems. What has sabotaged the Jackson approach has been the growth of voluntary funds other than the UNDP and of 'Funds in Trust'.

These have grown because it suited the convenience of most of the parties to the operation of the UN System to see them grow. It suited the Agencies because they feared the discipline of having a single or dominant paymaster. It suited the developing countries because they believed that the more 'Funds' were established, the more resources might be expected to flow in their direction. It suited the developed countries for a variety of reasons. First, many of them favoured the rise of 'voluntary' funds as an alternative to being subjected to the pressures (which constitutionally they were powerless to resist) for an increase in assessed budgets, to which they would each be bound to contribute their alloted share. Secondly, they favoured them because they could not solve some of the problems of multilateral funding among themselves – especially that of 'burden-sharing', as well as that of contributing to expenditure from which they could not get an assured return through the process of aid-tying. The result, unhappily, is a muddle and an indiscipline which many have a vested interest in preserving.

The relationship between finance and 'coherence' or 'co-ordination' in the UN System is one of the unresolved issues of the 1970s and 1980s. Many argued at the time of the Jackson report that it was wrong to try to link the two to the extent that Jackson proposed. They considered it would impose too rigid a straitjacket on donors and Agencies alike, and that the UNDP world lack the administrative and intellectual capacity to exercise so tight a degree of centralisation over the Agencies operationally even if it were their main paymaster. The assessed budgets, on the other hand, appeared by 1985 to be coming under reasonable control in a way which would produce results in improved efficiency if not greater coherence.

In 1985 came the Kassebaum Amendment, of which the most important immediate effect, as explained in the next Chapter, is to cut the budgets of the United Nations and all Agencies by 5%, unless other countries can make up the difference. It will, however, do more than that. It will demonstrate much more forcibly than the withdrawals from the ILO and UNESCO the lack of confidence of the US Congress in the way the United Nations and its System have been operating and in the principles of world solidarity on which they were based.

# KASSEBAUM AND GRAMM-RUDMAN

In 1985 two important developments occurred in the United States that affect the issues of voting rights and powers, finance, and staffing that are surveyed in earlier Chapters of this study. The first blow came in August with the Amendment by Senator Nancy Kassebaum (Republican, Kansas) to the Foreign Relations Authorization Act of 1985. The Kassebaum Amendment stipulates that the United States should pay no more than 20% of the assessed annual budget of the United Nations or any of the Specialized Agencies that do not adopt weighted voting procedures on 'matters of budgetary consequence'. With its passage in August 1985, the Kassebaum Amendment became the spearhead of a drive in the United States to regulate United Nations operations (see Annex to this chapter for full text).

By 1986, however, Kassebaum was not the only threat to United Nations and Specialized Agency finance emanating from the US Congress. There was also the Gramm-Rudman Act enacted in December 1985.[2] This provided for a programme of reduced Federal deficits over the following five years leading to a balanced budget in 1991. It also provided (starting in the current fiscal year), that if deficits were expected to be higher than those specified, then funds would automatically be cut ('sequestered' is the word used) across the board to produce the necessary savings. This produced an immediate shortfall in the United States payments to the Specialized Agencies and to funds and programmes. The effect of Gramm-Rudman is such that, because payments to some Specialized Agencies had been made before it became law, a heavier burden was bound to fall on the others to meet the terms of the Act.

There is a third element in this financial crisis which should be mentioned.[3] To quote the Secretary-General's Report; 'As at June

---

1 This chapter was contributed by Mr Arthur Kilgore, a researcher and lecturer in International Relations at the London School of Economics and Richmond College, London.
2 The full title is *The Balanced Budget and Emergency Deficit Act of 1985*, PL 99-177.
3 The Sundquist Amendment is a possible fourth element. It stipulates that the United States should withhold contributions equivalent to the amount that East European employees of the United Nations are required to remit to their governments (known in the United States as Eastern bloc 'kick-backs'). Although such a figure is difficult to determine, it is thought that it could result in the United States withholding up to $20 million.

1985 only 33 member states or less than 21 percent of the total membership had paid their full assessed contributions to the regular budget in full and 26 member states, or an additional 16 percent of the total, had made a partial payment toward their assessment for 1985.'[4] Some states are in arrears not only for 1985 but also for previous years. This shortfall of course does not relate directly to the Specialized Agencies (no figures are available for them as a group), but it will affect those institutions mentioned in this book, such as UNCTAD, which are financed from the United Nations budget. However, the situation for the Agencies must be similar. For example, the ILO figures of Receipts and Expenditure for the period 1 January–30 April 1986 show that on a total budget for 1986 where contributions were due to total $126.5 million, $9.9 million was owed by sixteen member states who were more than two years in arrears. Sixty-two states (including the United States and the Soviet Union) had arrears of less than two years' standing amounting to $11.7 million.

The consequences of the Kassebaum Amendment and other developments for the future of the UN System are now being investigated both at the United Nations and in Congressional Committees in Washington. The seriousness of the crisis is perhaps best indicated by the fact that in the spring of 1986 the situation was the subject of emergency meetings of the United Nations in New York. From a UN perspective, the United States ship of state is rudderless and on course to run it down. It is difficult to predict the precise damage that the current US government actions will have on the United Nations, but if the current momentum of the anti-UN legislation is maintained, it could ultimately be severe.

The case that we argue here is that the United Nations suffers from two problems in the United States – too much notoriety, and too little importance in the cut and thrust of domestic politics. These problems have finally conspired to help create one of the greatest crises faced by the United Nations since its founding. The notoriety of the United Nations was amply demonstrated in the debate on the Kassebaum Amendment in Congress. One of the main reasons given for the introduction of the Amendment was the UN decision to 'build a $73 million conference centre in Ethiopia' in the midst of famine and despite the opposition of the US, British, Dutch and Luxembourg governments. As Senator Kassebaum put it, 'the cost of the first phase of this building will be $73.5 million, of which the United States' share will be 25 percent and it will cost us $18.5 million to pay for that conference center in Ethiopia so that they can

4 A/C.5/40/16 of October 1985.

stand on the twenty-ninth floor and watch the rest of the country starve to death.' This statement, whether true or false, reflects the strength of feeling in Congress on the complex of questions involved in voting rights, budgeting and staffing throughout the UN System.[5] The United Nations' lack of importance in United States domestic politics, on the other hand, means that US contributions to the United Nations and its Specialized Agencies are more vulnerable to cutting under the provisions of the Gramm-Rudman Act than other domestically cherished programmes.

Given that the actions of the United States, coupled with the continuing failure of other member states to pay their contributions, will have a decided effect on UN operations, it will be useful to consider the scope of possible UN response to the crisis. A number of factors make such an exercise difficult. Prime among these is that the total amount of funds to be lost through US cutbacks is as yet indeterminate, since some of the cuts are still subject to US Congressional approval or the discretion of the State Department. This may tempt the United Nations and affected Specialized Agencies to bide their time with *ad hoc* responses in the hope that over time they will be able to regain the lost US contributions. But for a number of reasons which we will discuss below, this scenario appears unlikely. It is much more likely that the United Nations will respond in an *ad hoc* piecemeal manner because certain internal groups and member states will resist any long-term reorganization that might affect their interests. It has already been reported that the committee on Palestine, when asked what they would do if its budget was cut by 10%, refused to discuss the idea, while another would not even contemplate giving up first-class air travel by its members.[6] A third category of response could be labelled 'constructive' – that is, taking the opportunity provided by the crisis to initiate meaningful long-term reforms to make the United Nations more effective and to enable it to regain the respect of major donor countries. This is by far the most difficult response to initiate, but the Secretary-General convened a Group of High-Level Experts in February 1986 to investigate the long-term response to the crisis, while the publication of the Bertrand Report (discussed elsewhere in this study) gives further impetus to thoughts about reform of the UN System at this crucial moment.

## The adoption of the Kassebaum Amendment

When considering the importance of the Kassebaum Amendment, it

5 *Congressional Record*, 7 June 1985, S7793.
6 *Sunday Times*, 16 March 1986.

is necessary to distinguish between the political forces that enabled it to be passed, the intentions of the sponsors, and the other governmental actions and processes that have engulfed Kassebaum since it was approved.

The Amendment was readily passed through the Senate by an overwhelming vote of 71 for, 13 against, and 16 not voting. To get it approved, the sponsors capitalized on a coalition of groups within Congress. Its supporters can be divided into three groups, representing a continuum of opinion about the United Nations. First are the isolationists who are suspicious of most international organisations and who advocate US withdrawal from the United Nations and removal of its headquarters from US soil. This is a vociferous, but not particularly powerful group. Secondly, there are those who see the United Nations as useful only inasmuch as it is an instrument of US foreign policy. This perhaps is the fastest-growing and most influential of all the groups. Its thinking reflects that of the Heritage Foundation (a US libertarian pressure group), and overall it is concerned to reassert US authority over UN activities. Thirdly, there is a core of sincere reformists who, on the whole, support the UN System, though not in all its aspects, and whose intent in supporting the Amendment was to promote genuine reform within the organisation in order to improve its credibility in the United States. The Amendment's author, Senator Nancy Kassebaum, could be counted among this group.

It is important to note that 'reformists' were the initial sponsors of the Amendment, and although they relied on a coalition that included people more hostile to the UN System than themselves, the ambitions they had regarding the impact of the Amendment are distinct from those of other more destructively minded members of the coalition. Their intentions are revealed in a passage from the conference report: 'It is the intention of the managers that this substitute [i.e. revised amendment] promote meaningful reform in budget procedures at the United Nations and its specialized agencies and not to be used simply as a way to reduce the US assessed contribution to the United Nations or its specialized agencies.' To this end the 'managers' of the Amendment stipulated that the amount of funds required to enable the United States to fulfil 'its full obligations to the United Nations in calendar years 1986 and 1987' should be included in the Department of State authorization legislation; that the minimum amount the United States would pay would be 20% of the assessed contribution; and that 'the authorization for funds in excess of 20 percent will remain available to permit payment of a further assessed contribution should the intended reforms be

achieved in the UN fiscal year for which the funds are provided.'[7]
The US administration indicated that it shared the concerns of
Congress about budget reform. It would therefore seem that the two
branches of the US government were allied in recognizing and
working towards the intent of the Amendment.

Once passed, the Kassebaum Amendment became law, with no
expiration date and subject to no process of renewal, and unless it is
either repealed or amended, the United Nations is encumbered with
it as one of the 'eternal' facts of life. The implication of this is that it
will take a conscious act of political will now to reconsider the Kassebaum Amendment and generate sufficient numbers either to amend
or repeal the law.

The stipulation that each UN Agency must resort to weighted
voting in its budgetary procedure (granting votes proportionate to
the contribution of each member state), was clearly an insurmountable hurdle in most of the UN System. Where the United Nations is
concerned, the budget-making process is governed by Articles 17
and 18 of the UN Charter, which states that the General Assembly
'shall consider and approve the budget of the Organisation' by a
two-thirds majority, with each member of the Assembly having one
vote. To alter this process or remove ultimate authority from the
General Assembly would require reform of the Charter, through a
process that is set out in Chapter XVIII, Articles 108 and 109. These
provisions require that any amendment or alteration of the Charter
be adopted by a vote of two-thirds of the member states, and ratified
by at least two-thirds of the member states, including all five of the
permanent members of the Security Council, before such changes
can come into force. The difficulties presented by this process are
multifarious. The developing countries would sacrifice their
decision-making power over the budget only with the greatest reluctance, making it unlikely that the necessary two-thirds majority
could be mustered in the first place. Beyond that there is the question
of Soviet sensitivity about their position as co-equal with the United
States. A weighted voting system on budgetary questions would
disrupt the equality of the superpowers in the United Nations, and
would therefore be unlikely to receive a Soviet ratification even with
a two-thirds vote in favour of necessary Charter reform. In addition
there are other question marks, such as the People's Republic of
China's reluctance to allow the big powers to run the show in the
United Nations (witness the PRC's willingness to veto non-Third

---

7 It is noteworthy that this effectively rules out retroactive payments beyond the
fiscal year.

World nominees for the Secretary-Generalship) or the many difficulties of Charter reform. Certainly, numerous obstacles to the introduction of weighted voting on budgetary issues lurk just below the surface in the United Nations, and there appears to be no channel through for the required reform.

As in the United Nations, the institution of weighted voting procedures in most Specialized Agencies would require an amendment to the constitution of each individual Agency concerned; and, as in the United Nations, the possibility of obtaining such an amendment is extremely limited, although for certain Agencies such as the World Bank and the IMF the issue is moot since they already have weighted voting in place. The process of amendment varies widely throughout the Agencies in the UN System,[8] but generally speaking most proposed amendments would go through two stages before becoming effective. The first stage is approval, usually by a two-thirds majority, in the competent body of the organisation. The second stage would entail ratification of the amendment by, usually (once again), two-thirds of the member states. Procedures for amending constitutions vary. There are those that allow the ratification stage to be dispensed with for certain types of amendment (usually ones that do not involve new obligations for members or do not alter the basic aims of an organisation), as in UNESCO or the FAO. And there are those that only require ratification – but, importantly, ratification by particular categories of member states, as in the ILO where any amendment must be ratified by at least five of the ten members of the Governing Body that are designated as states of chief industrial importance. But in almost all instances the initial hurdle is as high in the Agencies as it is in the United Nations, because amendments must be approved by a two-thirds majority of the conference or assembly of an organisation. What this would require, in effect, is that substantial numbers of small or poor states vote away one of the few levers of power they may manipulate in international politics in order to satisfy the requirements of the Kassebaum Amendment. History has generally shown that power is non-negotiable, and hence weighted voting is unlikely to receive a more positive response in the Specialized Agencies than it receives in the United Nations proper. The sponsors of the legislation were not unaware of this aspect, and in the autumn of 1985 began devising a strategy that would permit the freeing of (Congressionally) 'seques-

8  For a discussion of amendment procedures see D.W. Bowett, *The Law of International Institutions*, London: Stevens, 1963; see also Egon Schwelb, 'The Amending Procedures of Constitutions of International Conciliation', *British Yearbook of International Law*, 31 (1954), pp. 49–95.

tered' US contributions to the United Nations without the adoption of weighted voting on budgetary matters.

The House Delegation to the US mission to the United Nations was instrumental in getting the US representative to put forward a package of reforms that, if adopted by the UN, would justify the amending of Kassebaum so as to allow the United States to meet its full assessed contribution where meaningful reforms had been instituted. Among the reforms sought by the United States were a freeze on UN salaries, and the introduction of certain budgetary review procedures in the UN System. Some of the US demands – such as the freeze on salaries – were met by the United Nations during the autumn session of the General Assembly in 1985, but in the eyes of the US delegation and Congress, these were not nearly enough to justify reconsideration of Kassebaum.[9]

As initially conceived, the Kassebaum Amendment was a crude carrot-and-stick device. The carrot of the full US contribution was held out for those organisations willing to undertake the requisite reforms. One must query why, in the first instance, the carrot was placed so far out of reach, since weighted voting on budgetary matters was extremely unlikely to be adopted in the UN and Specialized Agencies. If it was a strategy to probe the limits of reform to which UN Agencies might be tempted, such a strategy certainly bore attendant dangers that the authors would not be able to muster the votes necessary to amend Kassebaum when the time came to reward Agencies that had made sincere efforts to reform. If the authors truly intended to reward Agencies, they may well have stepped over the brink beyond which they could not deliver the *quid pro quo*, i.e. an amended or repealed law as a reward for sincere reform. An alternative conclusion is that the managers were somewhat disingenous in their desire to reward reform.

A second cause for concern lies in the hidden agenda behind the Kassebaum Amendment. There was no clear indication of what, other than weighted voting in budgetary matters and reduction in the salaries and pensions of employees, the United Nations and its Specialized Agencies could do. Moreover, the specifics of Kassebaum focussed on reforms that would control expenditure in the UN System. It did not put any emphasis on meaningful reform to make the institutions more effective. It is hardly surprising that a certain scepticism exists among UN functionaries about the intentions behind Kassebaum.

9 According to one Congressional source, about 'one-fifth' of what might have been adequate to alter the mood in Congress, had been adopted by the United Nations.

## Gramm-Rudman and beyond

Whatever the uncertainties surrounding the Kassebaum Amendment, any reformist intentions underlying it were soon displaced by other Congressional and Administrative processes. In particular, the Gramm-Rudman Balanced Budget Act was passed through Congress in December 1985. The intent of this Act is to curb deficit spending by the US government and to balance the US budget by 1991. The practical effect is to impose progressive cuts in government spending over the five years up till 1991. The US Administration and the Congress are responsible for meeting certain specified targets for reducing the budget each year.

The Administration responded to the requirements of the Gramm-Rudman Act by withholding $34 million of its current contribution to the United Nations and by eliminating altogether from the 1987 budget the 5% of UN budgets that were being withheld in accordance with the Kassebaum Amendment. In other words, the Administration had eaten the carrot that was intended to reward reforming Agencies. When other cuts imposed as a result of Gramm-Rudman are taken into account, it is estimated that the United States will contribute well below 20% – in the most extreme scenario the figure is 7% – of UN System budgets for 1987. With the European Community already having warned the United States that it will not make up budgetary shortfalls in the United Nations, a major financial crisis going well beyond the intent of the Kassebaum Amendment has been precipitated.

## Short-term prospects

In this collision with US governmental processes, what damage limitation can the United Nations undertake? It would appear that for the time being the ability to win back all or some of the US contribution cuts is out of UN hands. Even if UN Agencies were to take that most revolutionary – and therefore unlikely – step of employing weighted voting procedures on budgetary questions, the funds are no longer there to be restored. But given that no amount of reform in the United Nations was likely to prove persuasive or decisive in a debate focussed primarily on US deficits and balanced budgets, a sort of divine intervention was required.

One source of possible delivery is the US Supreme Court, which in July 1986 struck down a key clause of the Gramm-Rudman Act as unconstitutional. This clause would have obliged the US Comptroller General automatically to institute across-the-board cuts in the budget if the Administration or Congress failed to meet targets specified in the Act. The loss of this section overrides the automaticity of the Gramm-Rudman Act. But one must be careful about envisioning the Supreme Court action rescuing the United Nations from its troubles. First, Gramm-Rudman remains intact *sans* Comptroller, which means that budget-cutting procedures remain for the Congress and Administration to balance against appeals for the restoration or maintenance of certain welfare, defence, etc. programmes. The likelihood of convincing the Administration and Congress to overlook their obligation under Gramm-Rudman will depend on the size and/or political importance of the constituency that benefits from any programme. In terms of these criteria, the constituency for the United Nations has insufficient numbers or power to carry the day. Indeed, the weakness of the UN lobby in the United States makes the United Nations potentially vulnerable to deeper cuts. Conceivably, Congress or the Administration could be tempted to retain certain politically sensitive programmes while adhering as closely as possible to the terms of the Gramm-Rudman law by countering any increased spending in other areas with cuts in contributions to multilateral programmes.

As we write this in the autumn of 1986, even the near future is shrouded in a thick fog of uncertainty. But we have a duty, as we go to press, to weigh up the possibilities as best we can. One possible salvation may come in the form of a tax increase in the United States. Such a move would make spending cuts less imperative, and at the very least ease the pressure to cut contributions to the United Nations as an exercise in deficit reduction. There may even be slight cause for optimism on this score since there is strong support for a tax increase, both within Congress and in other sectors of society. Some analysts even suggest that it is only a matter of time before the Reagan Administration itself, entering on its final two years, sees the light and realises that the political, social and economic costs of maintaining high levels of defence spending, coupled with cuts in other areas of public spending and tough monetary policies, are too high to sustain. But the Administration appears to have put its faith in tax reform to generate revenue in the long term while sticking to its convictions in tax-cutting as an electoral boon in the short term.

The short-term outlook for the United Nations recouping lost monies from the United States is bleak. But it would be a serious mistake for the United Nations and its Agencies simply to await the outcome of further developments in the United States – such as a Democratic Administration following that of Reagan, or a change of circumstances in the US economy – in the hope that the *status quo ante* could then be restored. To do so would be to misinterpret the extent of disillusionment with the UN System in the United States[10] and elsewhere.

Indeed the UN Secretary-General has taken steps in an attempt to mitigate the immediate effects of the financial crisis;[11] however, these are acknowledged as being insufficient to withstand the blow falling on the United Nations from the autumn of 1986. Despite the unlikelihood of short-term relief from the financial crisis, the United Nations and its member states should nonetheless initiate a sincere consideration of feasible solutions to make the UN System relevant to the diplomatic needs of major donor countries as well as other countries. Otherwise the label of 'forums for subsidized agitation' will stick, and the chance to regain credibility will pass by. Some of the feasible, if modest, steps towards regaining credibility are suggested in Chapter XXI. Should the Agencies of the UN System fail to do the re-thinking that is necessary, then it will become much more likely that the current financial crisis becomes a chronic one. Already the Soviet Union (in this it is not alone) has demonstrated unwillingness to finance fora irrelevant to its needs by maintaining a 'permanent' arrears.[12] If the number of those with a standing distrust of UN Agencies is enlarged to incorporate major Western donors, especially the United States, this will only increase the gap between the UN's purported role in the international system and its ability to fulfil that role.

10 For the 'liberal' case against the United Nations, see Thomas Franck, *Nation against Nation: What Happened to the UN Dream and What the US can do about it*, Oxford University Press, 1985.
11 See Secretary-General's report A/40/1102, May 1986.
12 It is notable in this respect that at the height of what some have labelled the 'second cold war' in the early 1980s, the United States, the Soviet Union and the United Kingdom found common cause in delivering a warning to the UN Secretary-General about the consequences of excess spending and inefficient practices.

ANNEX

## THE KASSEBAUM AMENDMENT[13]

*United Nations Organisations: Reform in Budget Procedures*

(*a*) *Findings* – The Congress finds that the United Nations and its specialized agencies which are financed through assessed contributions of member states have not paid sufficient attention in the development of their budgets to the views of member governments who are major financial contributors to these budgets.

(*b*) *Voting Rights* – In order to foster greater financial responsibility in preparation of the budgets of the United Nations and its specialized agencies which are financed through assessed contributions, the Secretary of State shall seek the adoption by the United Nations and its specialized agencies of procedures which grant voting rights to each member state on matters of budgetary consequence. Such voting rights shall be proportionate to the contribution of each such member state to the budget of the United Nations and its specialized agencies.

(*c*) *Limitation on Assessed Contributions* – No payment may be made for an assessed contribution to the United Nations or its specialized agencies in excess of 20 percent of the total annual budget of the United Nations or its specialized agencies (respectively) for the United States fiscal year 1987 and following years unless the United Nations and its specialized agencies have adopted the voting rights referred to in subsection (*b*).

13 Section 143 of the Foreign Relations Authorization Act, Fiscal Years 1986 and 1987, p. 21.

# CHAPTER IX

# THE CENTRAL REGULATION OF THE U.N. SYSTEM AND OPERATIONAL CO-ORDINATION

The question of finance has always been closely related to the problem of the central regulation and co-ordination of the UN System. Co-ordination of the Agencies' activities was identified at a very early stage of the UN's history as one which was causing difficulty; an examination of the many reports and discussions of it shows that while the essential features of the malady were diagnosed early – indeed the problem was foreseen in the UN Charter itself, as is shown below, – the remedies have tended to be complicated and the improvements not commensurate with the efforts made to introduce them.

As has already been explained, the League of Nations, in the last stages of its life, had appeared to be moving towards a centralised system for organizing those Agencies which were performing a functional role. The solution adopted after 1945 was different. The system was to be decentralised and the Specialized Agencies were to be made autonomous. However, article 57 of the Charter provided that 'The various specialized agencies, established by intergovernmental agreement and having wide international responsibilites, as defined in their basic instruments, in economic, social, cultural, educational, health, and related fields, shall be brought into relationship with the United Nations in accordance with the provisions of Article 63.' Article 63 then provided that 'The Economic and Social Council may enter into agreements with any of the agencies referred to in Article 57.' Article 63.2, in the most important provision of all for the history of this problem, then went on to provide that the Economic and Social Council 'may co-ordinate the activities of the specialized agencies through consultation with and recommendations to such agencies and through recommendations to the General Assembly and to the Members of the United Nations.' The salient features of Article 63.2 as a definition of the role of ECOSOC are immediately apparent. It is only permissive ('may co-ordinate'); and it is only consultative and advisory ('through consultation and recommendations'). Right from the outset, there was no central direction – ECOSOC had no power, and the failure to provide it was an express omission from the Charter.

The results became apparent very early in the history of the United

Nations. The problems have grown in scale and complexity as the years have passed; the UN's activities in the economic and social sphere have expanded, while the various attempts at reform have enjoyed only limited success. As early as 1960 a report prepared by a committee of past Presidents of the ECOSOC and Chairmen of its Co-ordination Committee identified the difficulties of achieving common policies through the budgetary and policy-making bodies of separate and autonomous agencies. Apart from their budgetary independence and their constitutional autonomy, this early report identified as contributory factors 'the lack of co-ordination between national ministries, which leads to governments speaking with different voices in different agencies' and to delegates 'innocent of any instructions' who 'express no views but their own'. These issues will be dealt with in more detail in the next chapter.

It has been argued that 'this functional decentralisation, with wide freedom of action for individual Agencies in their respective technical tasks, has been a source of great strength and vitality to the UN System.'[1] From the outset, however, it also gave rise to great problems of co-ordination at the functional, administrative, staffing and financial level. To some extent this was inherent in the constitutions of the Specialized Agencies themselves, many of which, despite their highly sectoral approaches to the world's economic and social problems, overlapped. (UNESCO, with its constitution which gave it interests in so many fields, was the most obvious example; but the ILO overlapped with the FAO in the field of agricultural employment, with the WHO in the field of industrial health, and with UNIDO in industrial development; many others besides could be cited). Quite apart from the constitutional provisions, the very nature of the activities in which the UN System was involved, embracing almost all aspects of economic and social development around the world, was such that there had to be co-ordination if they were to be undertaken with even moderate success. The need for co-ordination was increased in 1960 with the introduction of the First UN Development Decade – which, in effect, was a plan undertaken at the UN General Assembly's instigation to promote development worldwide in accordance with a set of targets laid down by the United Nations. It also increased as the sectoral approach of the Specialized Agencies provoked sharp competition between them for the limited resources for development made available in the UN System.

1  Martin Hill on 'The Administrative Committee on Co-ordination', in Evan Luard (ed.) *The Evolution of International Organisations*, London: Thames and Hudson, 1966, p. 104.

Various institutions were created in the United Nations to deal with different aspects of co-ordination, such as the Advisory Committee on Administrative and Budgetary Question (ACABQ), responsible to the General Assembly, and the Co-ordination Committee of the ECOSOC. However, the main responsibility for functional co-ordination (the subject of this chapter) falls to a body of which no mention is made in the Charter, but which was set up as long ago as 1947 – the Administrative Committee on Co-ordination, better known as the ACC.

## The ACC

The composition of the ACC possibly provides an explanation for both the strengths and the weaknesses of the UN System. Its Chairman is the Secretary-General of the United Nations, and there is evidence to show that the quality of its performance over the years has depended partly upon the extent to which individual UN Secretaries-Generals have had the time or the inclination to devote themselves to its affairs. Its members are the Executive Heads of the Specialized Agencies themselves (ILO, FAO, UNESCO, ICAO, WHO, IBRD, IMF, UPU, ITU, UNFPA, WHO, IMO, UNIDO, and IFAD), together with the Executive Director of the GATT, the UN Under-Secretary for Economic and Social Affairs, the Secretary-General of UNCTAD, the Adminstrator of the UNDP, the Executive Director of UNICEF, the High Commissioner for Refugees, the Comissioner General of the UN Relief and Works Agency, the Executive Director of the World Food Programme, the Executive Director of the UN Institute for Training and Research and the Chairman of the ACC's Preparatory Committee (which manages the ACC's business between its thrice-yearly meetings). Most of the members of the ACC therefore have a direct interest in co-ordination by virtue of their substantive offices; but for the same reason they also have a vested interest in the preservation of their empires and the interests of their organisations. The ACC's subordinate machinery was considerably reorganised following General Assembly Resolution 32/197[2] of 1977, and it now consists of an organisational committee, the Consultative Committee on Substantive Questions, and sub-committees on nutrition, statistics and information, and information systems.

The broad terms of reference of the ACC were set out in ECOSOC Resolution 13 (III) of 1946. The main one was that 'of taking all

2  See especially para. 55–56 of the Annex to General Assembly Resolution 32/197 of 20 Dec. 1977.

appropriate steps, under the leadership of the Secretary-General, to ensure the fullest and most effective implementation of the agreements entered into between the United Nations and the specialized agencies'. References have already been made to these agreements in earlier Chapters. In form they mostly follow those entered into in 1946 with the ILO, UNESCO and the FAO, under Article IV of which the Agencies undertook to co-operate in 'measures necessary to make co-ordination of the activities of the specialized agencies and those of the United Nations fully effective' and in particular 'to participate in and to co-operate with any body or bodies which the Council may establish for the purpose of facilitating such co-ordination'. The ACC reports to ECOSOC but its meetings take place strictly in private, a fact which in the past has disconcerted ECOSOC.[3]

Early in the life of the ACC, the tradition was established that the representatives of the Agencies at its meetings should be the Executive Heads in person (although in practice this tradition has not always been observed, e.g. by Mr McNamara when he was Head of the IBRD). This meant in consequence, first, that, the ACC could meet only two or three times a year and, secondly, that it had to confine itself to broad issues of policy. As an instrument for close co-ordination across the whole UN System, even in pursuit of major lines of policy, the ACC could not be expected to be a very effective instrument. Its main defect however, has been that its members are primarily responsible to their own governing bodies and not to ECOSOC at whose behest the ACC was established – or at least so they can argue and so they have behaved; the fact that the same governments, partly at least, are represented on ECOSOC as are represented on the governing bodies of the Specialized Agencies in practice makes no difference. Moreover the Executive Heads of the Agencies, corporately assembled as the ACC, have over the years steadily and successfully resisted all attempts by ECOSOC to acquire greater control over their activities. Therefore the view in ECOSOC came to be that the ACC 'has tended to be used by the agencies as an instrument to safeguard entrenched interests and limit interference by the Council'.[4] It was indeed already recognised by 1960 that the ACC's role was not only to assist ECOSOC by preparing the ground for an important range of ECOSOC's decisions, but also to try 'to ensure that the Council's decisions were such as could be accepted

---

3 There is an echo of this malaise in para. 56 of the Annex to Resolution 32/197 which says that 'Arrangements should be made to improve communications between the ACC and the intergovernmental bodies concerned.'
4 Martin Hill, op. cit. p. 124.

and implemented by the governing organs of the agencies'. If these 'governing organs of the Agencies' had been genuinely and effectively under the control of the member governments (as they were according to their constitutions), this would have been a sensible provision. In practice, as has been pointed out in earlier chapters, they are much more under the control of those very same Executive Heads who constitute the ACC. There can be small surprise therefore if the ACC has tended to represent the views of the Agencies rather than those of either the United Nations or its member governments.

## The attempts at reform

The resulting frictions have led to various attempts at reform or at least to the introduction of measures and devices which might improve the situation in certain respects. It is impossible to describe them all in detail. They fall into four broad categories which will be described below. Before doing so, however, there is one point which should be made about the achievement of the ACC. Stimulated by ECOSOC and the General Assembly, it has certainly taken steps to make the Agencies aware of what each of them is doing. Most of them even have departments devoted exclusively to 'co-ordination' – in this sense – with other Agencies, with other parts of the United Nations, and with regional organisations. These departments have sometimes even been described as 'professional co-ordinators'. However, the fact that most Agencies are aware of what other Agencies are doing in areas of interest to them does not mean that they try to co-operate in the discharge of particular tasks or to produce a division of labour which would ensure the most economic use of resources in dealing with any problem. What often happens is that, as new situations arise, Agencies compete either to be first in the field or to take the lead role or to obtain a larger share of any resources which may be provided than their circumstances would justify.

Two recent examples illustrate the point. The first is the disaster in 1984 at the Union Carbide plant in Bhopal, India, where the escape of a toxic gas killed some 2,500 people and incapacitated many more. This was an event which could be of legitimate concern to a number of Agencies or organisations by reason of their constitutional responsibilities – the ILO, the WHO, UNIDO, UNEP to name but four. Within a few weeks, however, seminars were being organised not only by the ILO but also by the Committee of UNCTAD responsible for policy on transnational corporations, and others were trying to take separate initiatives. There was nobody

with the authority to allot lead responsibility within the UN System
to one Agency (the job properly belonged to the UN Commission on
Transnationals), which might organise international co-operation – including co-operation from other Agencies – on all aspects
of the question; governments interested in the problem were faced
with difficult choices as to which meetings to attend and which
organisation deserved the major share of their attention.

The second example is both wider, more important and,
unhappily, more typical. It concerns the food crisis in Africa as it
developed in 1984 and 1985. Quite apart from all the public and
private emergency relief aid that was being provided bilaterally, four
multilateral funds existed or were created, all of which took a hand
in dealing with the problem. One for dealing with irrigation schemes
was set up by the FAO; one for food aid was set up by the World
Food Programme (whose relations with the FAO have long been
'delicate'); one for long-term agricultural development was run by
the World Bank; and one for financing peasant farmers was run by
the International Fund for Agricultural Development. The United
Nations then established a new (and temporary) office in New York,
with a staff of thirty-five, to co-ordinate all these activities – The
Office of Emergency Operations in Africa (OEOA). This did not
prevent Mr Saouma, the Director-General of the FAO, formally
complaining to the Director of the OEOA when the latter accepted a
sum of money from the Netherlands government to buy rice seed for
Chad, on the grounds that seed-buying was the FAO's job. Mr
Saouma has also continued a long-standing argument with the WFP
about the authorisation of food aid shipments to Africa. Finally,
when the OEOA called a special meeting of donors to co-ordinate
their programmes of help to Africa, Mr Saouma did not attend, and
the FAO held its own meeting of donors two weeks later. There was
neither any organization nor any individual within the UN System
with the authority to make a single organisation the leader in co-
ordinating all these activities, even in the face of a major international disaster of chronic character and unprecedented proportions.
The waste of effort and of scarce resources was considerable.

The methods which have been tried over the years to deal with this
situation fall into three broad classes. The first might be described as
directional – the attempt by resolution, often of the General
Assembly, to lay down some broad plan for economic and social
development which the United Nations and its Specialized Agencies,
their subordinate bodies, their regional organisations and their
member governments are exhorted to follow. The most widely
known and the most ambitious of such resolutions have been those
by the General Assembly dealing with the three Development

Decades and with the New International Economic Order. These have on occasions been accompanied by the creation of special machinery, such as the UN Committee on Development Planning, to prepare for them and to supervise their execution. Their effect, critics have alleged, has been to suggest to the Specialized Agencies new territories which they might conquer, rather than areas over which they might co-operate. Raúl Prebisch is supposed once to have said: 'Resolutions are the poetry of UNCTAD – they express the aspirations of the members not their intentions.' Certainly the effect of resolutions such as those on the Development Decades has been to inflate the aspirations of the Specialized Agencies rather than inspire their co-operation. Another effect has been to raise expectations in developing countries which have not been fulfilled.

The second set of remedies, as might be expected in an organisation as bureaucratic as the United Nations, is institutional – the creation of new pieces of machinery to deal with special aspects of the problem and to introduce piecemeal reform. Indeed, over the years, machinery to improve the processes of co-ordination throughout the UN System has proliferated. We need give only a few examples. The General Assembly set up the Advisory Committee on Administrative and Budgetary Questions (ACABQ), the 'Ad Hoc Committee of Experts to Examine the Finances of the UN and its Specialized Agencies', the Enlarged Committee for Programme Coordination (ECPC) (although this ceased to exist in 1969), and the Joint Inspection Unit. Meantime ECOSOC established the Committee for Programme and Co-ordination (CPC), the Committee on Development Planning (CDP), the Governing Council of the UNDP and the Advisory Committee on the Application of Science and Technology (ACAST). Already in 1968 the UN Secretary-Geneeral drew the attention of member states to this trend to proliferate co-ordination machinery,[5] while in 1969 the General Assembly itself passed a resolution (GA Resolution 2537) stressing the need 'to avoid duplication of effort and waste of resources in the activities of control and investigative bodies and organs concerned with administrative questions'.

One important point should be noted at this stage which we refer to again later. It was partly the problems of co-ordination between existing Agencies which led in the 1960s to the creation within the UN System of new institutions which had both a responsibility for co-ordination of the operations of existing institutions and (without being themselves Specialized Agencies) an operational responsibility in their own right. The most famous of these is UNCTAD,

5 Document A/7201 of September 1968.

established as an 'organ of the United Nations' by virtue of General Assembly Resolution 1995 of 1964. Article 2 of this resolution expressly states as one of UNCTAD's functions. 'Generally to review and *facilitate the co-ordination* of activities of other institutions within the United Nations System in the field of international trade and related problems of economic development, and in this regard to co-operate with the General Assembly and the Economic and Social Council with respect to the performance of their responsibilities for co-ordination under the Charter of the United Nations' (emphasis added). Similar considerations led to the creation of UNIDO, where Article 27 of General Assembly Resolution 2152 of 1966 declares that UNIDO is 'to be responsible for reviewing and *promoting the co-ordination* of all activities of the United Nations System in the field of industrial development' (emphasis added). Later still, the same purposes underlay in part the creation of the UNDP with the Interagency Consultative Board as its executive arm.

These institutional changes seem, on the whole, to have complicated the situation rather than clarified it. In one way they even seem to have made the problem somewhat worse by effectively weakening still further the co-ordinating role which Article 63 of the Charter gave to ECOSOC (as described above). ECOSOC has always been the weakest of the institutions created by the Charter.[6] As to why this should be so, opinions differ, but constitutionally its role *vis-à-vis* the other institutions of the UN System is not strong. Originally this was attributed to the small size of its membership – only eighteen states – which, in an organisation of 159 states, would clearly have weakened its impact. But its subsequent increase to 54 members does not seem to have produced a corresponding increase in prestige and influence. Furthermore, its Secretariat has a poor reputation. Even if the road to progress lay through better centralized control, it is probably too late to look for much help in ECOSOC to secure better direction of the System as a whole, without radical changes in the Charter which would give ECOSOC more authority.

The third method by which attempts have been made to impose some discipline upon the system has been through finance. Some aspects of this have been dealt with in Chapter VII. To recapitulate, the principal financial instrument which in theory the United Nations has tried to use for this purpose has been the UNDP and the

6 Everybody interested in the performance of ECOSOC in the 1980s should read a short report entitled 'Reporting to the Economic and Social Council' prepared by M. Bertrand for the JIU and circulated by the Secretary-General under cover of A/39/281 of 31 May 1984.

resources channelled through it for development of developing countries. The General Assembly established the UNDP in a resolution passed in 1965 by combining two existing programmes of the United Nations – the Expanded Programme of Technical Assistance and the Special Fund – under a new governing council, an intergovernmental body known as the Governing Council of the UNDP. In the 1960s the Director General of the UNDP established a 'Capacity Study' under Sir Robert Jackson, who in his report published in 1969, stated, *inter alia*: 'The fact that the UNDP now controls the greatest proportion of these development co-operation funds is one of the main reasons for advocating its evolution as the central co-ordinating organisation.'[7]

The UNDP has not acquired this role; the Agencies – and the member governments that have abetted them – have seen to that. Their argument is best set out in the UNESCO Executive Board resolution of May 1970 on the Jackson Capacity Study. In it the Board

'*Affirms* its conviction that the regular programme of UNESCO constitutes the indispensable basis to support the Organisation's operational activities whether financed by UNDP or by extra-budgetary resources; *Insists*, particularly from the point of view of UNESCO that programming would not be separated from execution, and that intellectual and educational concerns should not be separated from operational activities, lest programming become so abstract as to lose its effectiveness and lest operational activities be in danger of sacrificing human factors to purely quantitative results.'

This is clearly another way of saying to the UNDP: 'You will give us the money. We alone are competent to decide on how it is to be spent in the areas of education and science.' But before one criticises the attitude of UNESCO too fiercely, it is important to recognise the element of truth in its resolution. It is a fact that the Agencies and not the UNDP have the technical knowledge necessary for the design and implementation of projects in their special fields. Very often this technical knowledge is considerable; if it were not readily available to governments from within the UN System, standards of administration world wide would probably fall. This, however, does not automatically make the Agencies good judges of the relevance of their specialized knowledge to the development of particular countries, or of the priority these activities ought to be accorded over other inputs. On the other hand, there is little evidence that the UNDP has the staff resources to make it a better judge on these issues.

7 *Study of the Capacity of the United Nations Development System,* Geneva: UN, 1969.

The attitudes expressed in the UNESCO resolution quoted above, and in similar resolutions, rapidly communicated themselves to the field and affected the result of another of the major Jackson recommendations – namely that more effective systems of co-ordination should be established on the ground in developing countries by setting up development teams of Specialized Agencies' representatives under the leadership of the local UNDP Resident Representative (later, in countries where his responsibilities were extended, he was called the Resident Co-ordinator). Reports indicate that, partly for reasons which will be amplified in the next Chapter, this has had only limited success – Agency salesmanship is as bad as ever[8] – but since 1980 the idea has been making some progress, at least in the poorest countries.

Apart from the doctrinaire reasons set out in the UNESCO resolution, there is another reason why the Jackson formula has not worked as well as its supporters hoped, namely that UNDP funds as a proportion of the total funds available to Specialized Agencies for spending on their programmes have been declining. The reasons for this have already been examined and will be discussed further in Chapter XV. Sir Robert Jackson's dictum quoted above had been based upon the assumption that they would increase.

In 1977, one comprehensive General Assembly resolution on the Restructuring of the Economic and Social Sectors of the UN System[9] embodied all these different methods of reform. It is symptomatic of the inherent difficulties of the subject that it took a Committee of the General Assembly, under the patient chairmanship of Ambassador Dadzie, two years to draft this resolution. It falls into all three of the classes just described. It is in itself 'directional', in that it attempts to issue guidance to a whole range of UN institutions from the General Assembly, through ECOSOC to the ACC and its sub-committees. It is institutional in that it both proposes the abolition of some of the committees which had sprung up to deal with aspects of this matter and the establishment of an office for Development and International Economic Co-operation under the UN Secretary-General and other changes in machinery. It is also financial, notably in that it proposes new arrangements for financing Specialized Agency programmes, through 'a single annual UN pledging conference for all UN operational activities for development' (a proposal which has been adopted, although in practice it has not produced more resources or better budgeting).

8 See, for example, *UNDP in Action: A Study on UNDP Field Offices in Selected Countries in Africa or Asia*, Stockholm: Swedish Ministry of Foreign Affairs, 1985.
9 Resolution A/RES/32/197.

As was pointed out in Chapter IV, the passing of this resolution, in spite of producing some changes for the better, has in fact not fundamentally altered the situation. It lays down a number of principles which are wholly admirable. For example, it calls on the General Assembly to 'concentrate on the overall strategies, policies and priorities for the system as a whole'. It prescribes a balanced distribution of work between the Second and Third Committees of the General Assembly. It tries to promote ECOSOC as 'the central forum for the discussion of international economic and social issues of a global or interdisciplinary nature' for consideration by the General Assembly and member states. It calls on 'all UN organs and programmes, the specialized agencies, the GATT, the IAEA and *ad hoc* world conferences' to be guided by the overall policy framework established by the General Assembly and ECOSOC. It stresses the importance of proper co-operation with regional organisations. On operational activities of the UN System, it specifies as a desirable aim 'the achievement of optimum efficiency and the reduction of administrative costs with a consequent increase in the proportion of resources available to meet the assistance requirements of recipient countries'.

However, all these recommendations, admirable as far as they go, suffer from three weaknesses. First, the resolution and its Annex exhorts only: it does not order – because over much of the area with which it deals it does not have the power to do so. Secondly, despite that drawback, it attempts to secure better co-ordination from the top downwards. It requires the General Assembly 'to promote solutions as to international economic, social and related problems and, to that end, to function as the principal forum for policy-making and for the harmonisation of international action in respect of these problems'. This is altogether beyond the powers of a body like the General Assembly or indeed of any other organisation in the present international system. Finally, in order to ensure 'the provision of effective leadership to the various components of the UN system in the field of development and international economic co-operation', it proposes the appointment of a Director-General for Development and International Economic Co-operation with a small staff responsible to the Secretary-General – a task which is almost certainly too big for anyone who holds the office.

A fair degree of success has attended the work of the two Directors-General who have held office up to the time of writing in relation to the second of these tasks, namely the supervision and control of the economic and social work of the United Nations itself, as distinct from the Agencies. But the provision of leadership to, and any substantial co-ordination with, the rest of the System have proved elusive. The Director-General's efforts have been unnecessarily hampered by the difference in status between himself, an appointee of the Secretary-General, and the Agency heads, appointed by member governments in conclave. This has put the Director-General at a disadvantage; it would help him if his standing could be raised nearer to equality with that of the Agency heads. This could be done in various ways. It might be possible for him to be appointed - or elected - by the members of ACC; or, perhaps more effectively, he might be appointed by the General Assembly. The first possibility is open to the criticism that a Director-General appointed by the ACC would be even more patently the ACC's subordinate; this might be got round by having his appointmet endorsed by the General Assembly. The second possibility is open to the criticism that it might embarrass the Secretary-General if the Director-General were appointed by a majority larger than had appointed the Secretary-General himself; this could be circumvented by having the Director-General appointed by the General Assembly on the Secretary-General's recommendation.

There is a fourth method which might bring about some improvement in the situation. This is that member governments – who, after all, are represented on all the governing bodies of the Agencies – could work together to take more energetic action and to insist upon some change. This remedy has never been seriously tried although individual governments, notably that of the United States, have on occasion used their muscle to produce some order in particular instances of concern to them. More will be said on this aspect later.

The autonomy which the drafters of the Charter in 1945 accorded to the Specialized Agencies was almost certainly deliberate. It was designed to encourage them to show initiative and enterprise in their functional fields. The intention appears to have been that any central direction that was required should either be engineered by ECOSOC (which was after all an intergovernmental body) or be imposed on the Specialized Agencies individually by their own governing bodies, which also in theory represented the views of member governments. The system has failed to produce the necessary degree of co-ordination because the member governments, from developed and developing countries alike, could not identify a common purpose and therefore could not produce a common policy in relation to Specialized Agencies on the basis of which they could impose some co-ordination on them.

Almost the only common purpose which the Western governments could recognise was that of restraining the Agencies' budgetary growth. With this as its primary aim, they set up the Geneva Group which, as described in Chapter IX, has had some limited success towards this end. This in itself, however, alienated the developing countries, which were persuaded that an increase in each Specialized Agency budget, to which they contributed so little, gave them access to extra funds. But because of the way many developed countries manage their budgets, it very probably did not do this; moreover, few Western governments were sufficiently critical of how the Agencies' funds were spent or of the technical competence of those responsible for spending them.

There were other reasons why developing countries condoned the Specialized Agencies' empire building. The first was that the Agencies were part of the UN System, and developing countries increasingly identified the United Nations and its offshoots as the major protector and promoter of their interests. Another reason was that the Specialized Agencies looking after particular functions affecting domestic policies in developing countries (such as agriculture, health and education) could do something to promote the domestic importance in these countries of the Ministries looking after these particular subjects. Equally, it was often the functional Ministries which represented their countries on the Specialized Agencies' governing councils, and they often put their departmental interest above their national interest. (The FAO, for example, was once described as 'an international ploughboys' club'.) The result has been to create a situation in which it was easy for the Specialised Agencies to divide and rule, and sometimes misrule.

From what has been said above it is clear that within the system as a whole the Agencies have a strong body in the form of the ACC to 'co-ordinate' their efforts without sacrificing their autonomy, even where such sacrifice would be in the interest of providing a better service in the economic and social spheres to the international community as a whole and particularly to the developing countries. The governments, owing to the weakness of ECOSOC, lack any corresponding body. Any effort to create one would be unlikely to succeed, judging by the experience of their effort to achieve institutional reform, unless all governments could see some interest common to developed and developing countries alike in improving the functional performance of the Agencies. There are some signs, which will be discussed later, that this may be happening.

# CHAPTER X

# THE ROLE OF MEMBER STATES

It was argued in the preceding Chapter that part of the answer to the problem of securing better co-ordination between the Agencies of the UN System must lie with member states, in particular with their organising themselves better both domestically and externally to cope with UN business. However, member states face many obstacles. The first is the sheer volume of business transacted by the United Nations and its Agencies as well as the methods of working followed in the UN System. The number of meetings held by the United Nations and the Specialized Agencies, the Funds and Programmes, and their conferences, committees, sub-committees, symposiums and boards run to several hundred a year (834 in 1984).[1] Their duration varies from a few days to several weeks. Even if they are held at the main headquarters of the organisations concerned, these are scattered around the world: admittedly there are concentrations of them in Geneva, New York and Vienna, but others – and by no means the least important – are in Washington, Paris, Rome, Nairobi and elsewhere. In addition, a number of conferences (sometimes very important ones) are held every year under the auspices of the United Nations or its Agencies in places as far apart as Torquay and Tokyo. It is a physical impossibility for most governments to be represented at all of these meetings, and it is very difficult for many of them, even if they can send a representative, to send someone with appropriate knowledge, or who is adequately briefed on the subject matter (itself often very specialised), even though it may have an important bearing on his country's interests. The volume of paper generated by these bodies and their meetings is enormous as is the task of digesting and commenting on it and

1 In 1984 the United Nations itself, in addition to the General Assembly, had six committees plus thirteen subsidiary bodies. ECOSOC had twelve Commissions responsible to it and fifteen 'organs and programmes' related to it (ranging all the way from UNCTAD to the ACC). In addition there were eight special bodies, ranging from the UN Institute for Training and Research to the UN Habitat and Human Settlements Foundation. Finally there were the eighteen Specialized Agencies proper, many of them with their own structure of subordinate bodies. This is all in the addition to a number of regional organisations dealing on a regional basis with subjects which the UN and its offshoots are dealing with on a world basis, and therefore involving the same people to do the work. Indeed regional organisations have proliferated (there are now 280 of them), partly to meet the shortcomings of the UN and to make up for its failure to take account of local variations in its global decisions.

framing policies on the matters it raises. It strains the capacities of many small states to deal with it at all, and it strains the capacity of many larger states to deal with it coherently and competently and in ways that demonstrate a consistent line of policy – particulary when the same issue is being discusseu in different organisations in any one of the widely scattered cities already mentioned.

The result is that it is not too difficult for the Secretariats of the Specialized Agencies, faced with weak and poorly informed representatives of member governments who are ill prepared to discuss the issues confronting them, to get their plans approved and the expenditure voted, and then to execute these plans with minimum supervision. Paradoxically, the problem is further complicated by the fact that a number of these meetings are held at the regular conference centres of Geneva, New York, Vienna and Washington where many governments, even of some of the smaller countries, maintain permanent representatives. They or members of their staffs would normally be expected to attend the meetings of the organisations with headquarters in the place where they are located. Frequently, however, the machinery of government in their national capitals is not well enough organised to provide them with adequate briefing to represent their government's views on the issue under discussion. Indeed, the governments concerned have often been unable to formulàte views. In such circumstances, therefore, the representatives in effect write their own briefs which are as likely to follow the views of a member of the secretariat of the organisation concerned as the views or even the interests of the country from which the representative comes. This is particularly the case in a place like Geneva, where a small staff, without any adequate support from the government at home, may have to represent their country on organisations as disparate as the ILO, the WHO, the GATT, UNCTAD, the UNHCR, the WIPO, the Organisation for the Protection of New Varieties of Plants etc., or at *ad hoc* conferences on a wide range of issues.

A variant of this phenomenon deserves notice too. Sometimes the support from capitals takes the form of the same delegate who reappears year after year at the meetings of a particular body within which he becomes a one-man institution. Frequently he identifies himself far more with his cronies on the body concerned than he does with the policies or even the interests of his own government. He becomes a predictable force in favour of the *status quo* and of Agency power.

A particular aspect of the problem of inadequate briefing is that because some member governments have not the resources to study the substance of the issues arising at these meetings, they will brief their representatives simply to vote on certain issues in the same way as the delegate of some other named power. This is a valuable and time-saving device for ensuring group solidarity but not for considering the merits of issues and still less for negotiating solutions. (There is a variation of this practice not infrequently seen among some developed countries who over time have. acquired a 'liberal' reputation for themselves by not voting *against* certain measures because they were safe in the knowledge that predictable opposition from other powers, notably the United States and the United Kingdom, would ensure that these measures were never implemented.)

The problem of securing adequate representation at these many meetings, and ensuring that it is properly briefed to express well thought-out consistent policies at all meetings, is more difficult for the developing than for the developed countries.[2] Most developed countries have some internal machinery or interdepartmental arrangements elaborated over the years which ensures both the production of briefing material and some measure of consistency in the analysis of problems and in the subsequent expressions of policy worldwide and over time. This machinery differs from country to country, and generally the details are not revealed although the results are obvious. (For example on any discussion of commodity problems, whatever the forum, the French can be guaranteed to advocate *'l'organisation des marchés'* and have been doing so for the past forty years.) Secondly, developed countries have better group arrangements for considering collectively many (but by no means all) of the issues which will be raised in international fora. Notable among these are the OECD, with its highly competent secretariat analysing issues of economic importance (helped by an elaborate committee system which includes the Development Assistance Committee), and the Geneva Group described in Chapter III which is concerned overwhelmingly with budgetary questions among some of the Specialized Agencies (viz. ILO, UNESCO, WHO, FAO, ICAO, UPU, WIPO, WMO, IAEA and ITU). Some of the developed and developing countries also have machinery for regional groupings of one kind or another which play an important

2 In 1957 this whole question of Co-ordination at the National Level was the subject of an ECOSOC Report E/3107, based on a survey of developed and developing countries ranging from Afghanistan to Yugoslavia (through Canada, Sweden, the Soviet Union, the United States and Britain). In detail it is by now probably out of date, but it is still worth reading for the way in which it analyses the problem and illustrates possible solutions. It discusses *inter alia* Devices for General Co-ordination, Devices for Co-ordination in respect of Particular Aspects of Economic and Social Activities, and Arrangements for Representation at Conferences and Meetings.

role in briefing, even though the main purpose of such groupings may be wider than the working out of common positions for meetings within the UN System. For example, the EC countries now express a joint view on issues raised in international fora which are within the Community competence, and they also form caucuses on other issues, though sometimes without reaching a common position. The existence of these institutions and arrangements (especially the OECD) ensures a better analysis of many of the issues and a more consistent expression of view on them than would otherwise be the case.

On the question of the internal arrangements for framing policy, there is an inherent difficulty. Issues coming before the Specialized Agencies usually have three aspects. The first is diplomatic: they affect the relations between governments in the context of an international organisation. As such, these issues would normally be the responsibility of ministries of foreign affairs. The second is financial: they cost money to implement, and thus they arouse the interest of ministries of finance (which, if the sums or resources involved are large, can be predominant). The third aspect is functional. They therefore become the domain of whichever ministry has the primary responsibility for the subject under discussion – be it agriculture, health, education, transport, labour, trade, finance or aid to developing countries. Measures of internal co-ordination within countries are required before policies can be framed, positions established and briefs prepared. Different countries have devised different solutions to this problem. The British method is believed to be through a Committee system run by the Foreign and Commonwealth Office combined with a system of 'lead departments' responsible for dealing with the affairs of different organisations. The major responsibility for preparing briefs lies with the lead department, which then circulates them in draft for comment to all the other departments involved in the Committee system (whether or not they have any ostensible interest in the subject). If necessary, a meeting is held to resolve differences. Some countries give the responsibility for co-ordination to special departments within their ministry of foreign affairs. Others devise different systems of consultation for different subjects.

The results, either way, are much the same. On the issues being raised at the UN or the Specialized Agencies, individual developed countries speak on the whole (and with some exceptions) with a much more consistent voice over time, and in no matter what forum, than do the developing countries. This is most clearly illustrated by examining how economic issues (say the NIEO) are discussed in the General Assembly, in the meetings of the Bank and Fund, or in those of UNCTAD; furthermore, differences *between* the developed countries remain much more consistent, for example, the more 'liberal' attitudes taken by the Scandinavian countries, compared with those of the United States and the United Kingdom, are repeated in many organisations, as are the idiosyncratic positions often adopted by the French. Consistency in developed countries is generally their strong point; what is lacking is elasticity or flexibility. The machinery is perfectly geared to preserving a prepared position or even a vested interest: it is less well adapted to negotiating change, even a change of policy within a particular government machine. Often, for a country to change its traditional position would be either disturbing to its allies – in which case the ministry of foreign affairs would object; or it would cost money – in which case the ministry of finance would protest; or it can run contrary to some domestic interest, which it is the responsibility of the functional department to protect. In a rapidly changing world, the system of briefing in many countries, especially developed countries, tends to ensure no change and to weaken the usefulness of the Specialized Agencies as fora where new solutions can be examined or negotiated. This in turn increases the frustration of those who – mostly in developing countries – are seeking change through the medium of such Agencies. It also frequently means that those attending meetings become lazy and merely reiterate old positions, so that the intellectual quality of the input to the debates in such organisations tends to decline over the years. This has been true not merely at the political level but also at the technical and functional level, where over time the contribution of the developed countries has tended to weaken in some Agencies, partly from familiarity with the way some subjects are debated, partly from disappointment at the allegedly deteriorating performance of the Specialized Agencies in their specialized tasks, and partly because the developed countries have not been prepared to think out new policies and positions even on functional issues. (It should be borne in mind that to devise new solutions for the technical problems of developing countries, especially in such matters as health and agriculture, demands expenditure on real resources for research and development of appropriate techniques. If a ministry is not responsible for the subject, it will have small interest in promoting and financing the research.)

Indeed, the internal arrangements in developed countries for briefing for meetings of the Specialized Agencies can have a considerable influence on both the content and the quality of the briefing in ways that are not always apparent to an outsider. For example, in the United Kingdom the lead department for briefing on issues coming before Specialized Agencies whose principal area of activity is the developing countries is the Overseas Development Administration (ODA), even if (as with agriculture and education) the functional subject-matter lies with a domestic ministry such as the ministry of agriculture or the ministry of education. Moreover, the cost of financing the developed countries' share of such activities falls primarily upon the vote of the lead department (in the British case, the ODA). These arrangements can have the effect that the domestic departments concerned pay inadequate attention to the possible international effects of their policies or devote insufficient resources to the study of them. To some extent these adverse effects can be limited by advisory groups and committees; but the tendency for any ministry to concentrate on matters of purely domestic concern can be reinforced by briefing arrangements which give it no *responsibility* for matters of international concern. Other difficulties arise in the case of countries with federal constitutions such as the Federal Republic of Germany, where responsibility for dealing with some of the subject-matter of Specialized Agency activities can fall to both the federal and state governments. The practical tendency of both these factors is the same: to make it difficult to change accepted lines of policy even in response to changing circumstances. This tendency can be reinforced if, as is now generally the case, countries are represented at meetings of the Specialized Agencies and their subordinate bodies more often by officials than by ministers.

For the developing countries the problem presents itself differently. First, many of them lack the administrative resources to handle the volume of business generated by the United Nations and all its Specialized Agencies. Secondly, many of them lack the technical resources and skills to make any contribution or judgement on the technical merits of many of the proposals coming before the Specialized Agencies even though they are matters of great importance to developing countries. Their representatives at meetings therefore seem to prefer to discuss matters which involve expenditure or politics rather than issues involving judgements of functional performance. Developing countries, like all countries, tend, when in doubt, to vote in a way that maintains group solidarity rather than to judge issues on their merits. This suits officials of Specialized Agencies very well if they are more concerned with maintaining their Agencies' importance than with the efficient discharge of their functional responsibilities.

Another aspect of administration in many developing countries plays into the hands of those Specialized Agencies which do not want member governments or the United Nations itself to exercise effective control over them. This is that there is often no clear government policy or machinery for implementing it which covers all aspects of government activity – foreign, domestic and economic – especially in the field of economic development, and which ensures a fairly clear government line on everything from finance to agriculture, health, education, transport and trade.[3] Instead policy is often decided by the ranking of individual ministers in the government pecking order in which the dominant places are taken usually by the Prime Minister and the Ministers of Finance and Defence. The 'functional' departments, especially those dealing with such domestic subjects as agriculture, health, or education, often do not rank high or have much influence. When, therefore, such a department is approached by a Specialized Agency with ambitious plans for activity within the area of its sectoral responsibility and money to back them, the proposal tends to be examined not in the light of what contribution it might make to the country's development but of how it might enhance departmental prestige. The situation is often made worse when there are representatives of the Specialized Agencies on the spot and the phenomenon of 'Agency Salesmanship' castigated by Jackson appears in full vigour. The earlier attempts to deal with this by combining Agency representatives into development teams under the aegis of UNDP resident representatives failed, partly because of inter-Agency jealousy and partly because the governments regarded attempts to impose some external discipline on the Agencies as one which should be left exclusively to them. This is probably true in theory. In practice, however, their departments of development planning have not proved strong enough to exercise this control. On the other hand, Agency intervention can sometimes be positively beneficial where a particular subject has not been receiving proper attention in a country's development plans (as has frequently happened in the past with agriculture, for example). It remains to be seen whether the more recent experiments with 'Round Tables' and Resident Co-ordinators, referred to later, will enjoy a greater success.

There are other factors within the administrations of developing countries which make proper co-ordination of effort in the development field hard to attain. One factor is the difference of approach to some major economic problems manifested by the different Specialized Agencies. This can be exacerbated in some developing countries by the fact that some of their ablest officials dealing with these issues have themselves been trained by some of the Specialized Agencies

---

3 As the 1957 ECOSOC Report E/3107 put it: 'The conduct of foreign affairs on a multilateral basis, through the instrumentality of intergovernment agencies, must be considered as an inseparable part of the larger problem of organisation for the conduct of national affairs as a whole.'

who are most at odds with one another. Those who have been trained by the IMF, the IBRD or institutions under the influence of UNCTAD tend to go on talking with the voices of their mentors long afterwards, and in the absence of a strong ministerial line this can seriously weaken government attempts at co-ordination. Another element is the fact that proper systems of co-ordination of multilateral assistance in all its forms require the co-ordination of bilateral assistance as well. Many efforts have been made to deal with this problem – from the 'Round Tables' led by UNDP for the least developed countries to the consortia and Consultative Groups led by the IBRD for the wealthier countries. But success has in the past been limited. In particular, bilateral donors tended to become more reluctant to take a constructive part in such co-ordination procedures as more and more of their 'aid' became tied to the promotion of their exports. This also has worked in favour of those who wished to 'divide and rule' on behalf of the Agencies.

By the 1980s, however, there were signs that matters might be improving.[4] Donors themselves have shown renewed interest in the question. The United Nations, using the resources of UNDP in particular, has made a fresh effort to stimulate local co-ordination, and in the poorest countries has established 'Round Tables' of bilateral and multilateral donors to work together with local governments and the local UNDP Resident Representative (renamed Resident Co-ordinator) in deciding inputs of both capital and technical assistance. (In March 1986, there were twenty-seven such groups either in existence or planned under UNDP auspices. The previously established consortia and consultative groups for the larger countries continue their work, largely under the auspices of the IBRD.)

The need for co-ordination on the ground – regardless of what happens in the higher echelons of the UN System – is now generally accepted among donors and recipients alike. Consciousness of the need has grown especially in those countries in the drought regions which have been subject to emergencies. There are signs that in some places the new procedures are bringing Agency salesmanship under control. Nevertheless some undesirable features of the past persist. Donors compete for attractive projects, and recipients are disappointed with the results of these co-ordinating processes which involve them in a great deal of work. However, it is encouraging, that attempts to improve the System from the bottom up show more signs of success than attempts to reform it from the top down. We shall return to this theme.

4  Those interested in a short up-to-date account of the institutional arrangements for international aid co-ordination will find one in the *OECD Review of Twenty-Five Years of Development Co-operation*, Paris, 1985 (pp. 200–10).

# THE ROLE OF PERSONNEL POLICY

Some 80% of the budgets of the United Nations and of most of the Specialized Agencies are devoted to staff costs. This seemingly high proportion is sometimes cited as evidence that the organisations are nothing but bloated bureaucracies; in fact, their functions dictate that staff should account for the greater part of the expenditures, since it is mainly through staff that the organisations implement their programmes. With the exceptions of the World Bank, the International Monetary Fund and the International Fund for Agricultural Development, which do not apply the UN Common System of Salaries and Allowances to their staff, the Specialized Agencies are not financing or loan-granting institutions. Apart from relatively small amounts spent on publications and the holding of conferences and meetings, it is through staff that they do their work – staff to collect and publish data, to prepare studies, to organise meetings, to design and administer programmes, to plan and provide technical assistance. The main resources of the organisations are without doubt their human resources and it is therefore appropriate to inquire what share of responsibility the staff may bear in the current disaffection of governments and public for the UN System as a whole and the Specialized Agencies in particular.

In this Chapter we will examine the changes that have occurred in the staffing of the Specialized Agencies since the happy era of the 1950s and 1960s when the UN System enjoyed the general support of governments and peoples, and we will try to estimate what part these changes may have played in the change of attitude. A discussion will follow of what should be the policy on staffing matters of those governments, groups and individuals who believe that the Specialized Agencies are worth saving, and what actions could be taken at different levels.

---

1 This Chapter is based mainly on material provided by Mr Roger Barnes who was a staff member of UNESCO from 1947 to 1975, *inter alia*, a Secretary of the Executive Board, Director of Conference Services and Director of the Bureau of Personnel. From 1975 to 1980 he served as the first Executive Secretary of the newly-established International Civil Service Commission. From 1980 till his retirement in 1982, he was Secretary of the Consultative Committee for Administrative Questions. Dr K. H. Reich of the University of Fribourg and formerly with CERN also offered valuable comments.

## The principles underlying the staffing of international organisations

From the time when the establishment of the League of Nations was under discussion, it has always been recognised that the question of staffing presented particular difficulty. The organisations are representative of nation states, and their staffs are drawn from those states. Once appointed, should primary staff loyalty be with the state from which they come or the organisation which they serve? Article 100.1 of the UN Charter appears to settle the issue beyond doubt as far as the United Nations and its Agencies are concerned. They are to be purely international and not merely 'intergovernmental' and staff should manifest loyalties to the organisation rather than to the nation states from which they come. The attitude which member governments should adopt towards their nationals serving with the United Nations is equally clearly stated: 'Each Member of the United Nations undertakes to respect the exclusively international character of the responsibilities of the Secretary-General and the staff and not to seek to influence them in the discharge of their responsibilities' (Article 100.2).

Almost from the beginning of the United Nations, however, this approach has been under attack. It was dealt a severe blow in 1952 and 1953 in the United States by Senator McCarthy and his associates, who claimed that as 'a matter of hard, cold fact quite a few American communists have infiltrated the United Nations and ought to be tossed out.' The US Senate National Security State Committee succeeded in forcing the then Secretary-General, Trygve Lie, to permit certain US members of his staff to be subjected to Committee interrogation, thereby in effect subjecting them to improper political pressure.

Even more important, it has been openly repudiated by the Soviet Union and the bloc of Socialist countries. Communist representatives in the Fifth Committee of the United Nations (which deals with budgetary and staff questions) have argued that the very concept of an impartial civil service is undesirable; members of the UN Secretariat should openly further their own governments' policies rather than acting like rootless cosmopolitans. In 1961 Walter Lippmann quoted Khrushchev as stating: 'While there are neutral countries, there are no neutral men.'[2]

Dr T. H. Franck[3] has summed up Soviet objectives (particularly

---

2 *New York Herald Tribune*, 17 April 1961, cited by Dag Hammarskjöld in his Oxford lecture, *The International Civil Service in Law and Fact*, 30 May 1961, published by the Clarendon Press, Oxford.
3 T. H. Franck, *Nation aganist Nation*, Oxford University Press, 1985, p. 105.

in the post-Stalin period) in staffing UN Agencies as follows:

1. to ensure that the Soviet Union and other Socialist states occupy approximately one-third of the professional positions in the Secretariat.
2. to ensure that these positions are filled by persons proposed by Government, rather than through direct, or competitive, recruitment by the United Nations.
3. to prevent the creation of a career international civil service and to ensure that Soviet citizens be limited to serving a five- (exceptionally eight-) year contract, after which they are to be recycled back home, with some possibility of serving a second term later.
4. to ensure that Soviet citizens serving in the Secretariat act as representatives, directly serving Soviet interest in the UN and, to some extent, representing UN interests in Soviet circles.
5. to secure specific important, and even semi-important, posts as the hereditary right of Soviet citizens, to be passed along from one incumbent to the next.'

Dr Franck's observations are corroborated by a Soviet source. Mr Arkady Shevchenko, a former Soviet Under-Secretary-General of the United Nations who defected while serving in New York, reported that before taking up his post he was briefed by the Soviet Foreign Minister, Andrei Gromyko, as follows: 'Never forget, Shevchenko, that you are a Soviet ambassador first, not an international bureaucrat.' On arriving in New York he received further briefing in the Soviet Mission to the United Nations by the 'KGB Resident' who reportedly said: 'I don't have to tell you, Arkady Nikolaevich, that the United Nations is our best watchtower in the West. Our people there collect valuable information about the United States and other countries. You'll have a special opportunity to get to know Americans and other Westerners in your job. And you can help promote our officers in the Secretariat and protect them in case the CIA or FBI tries to make trouble for them.'[4]

Over the years, ever greater tension has developed between the two 'models'. There is no doubt which one best serves the cause of efficient international action. There is, equally, no doubt that temporarily at least some accommodation between the two is needed if international collaboration is to continue.

## Changes, 1945–1985

*Increased numbers.* The most evident change in the staffing of the

---

4 Arkady N. Shevchenko, *Breaking with Moscow*, London: Cape, 1985, pp. 218 and 237–8.

Specialized Agencies in the four decades since most of them were established is in the size of the staffs, corresponding to the increase in budgets, in programmes and in numbers of member states. This carries with it, to a greater or less degree, the inevitable consequences of the mutation from small, compact and fairly coherent groups to large, decentralized, heterogeneous bureaucracies. (The advantages of smallness and homogeneity are preserved in secretariats like those of the WIPO and the WMO, and the benefit of homogeneity in spite of size in a professionally uniform organization like the WHO. At the other extreme is UNESCO which, small or big, has always suffered from the diversity of the professional backgrounds of its staff.)

*Wider geographical distribution.*[5] The expansion in membership of the organisations and in the size of their staffs has been accompanied by a very marked change in the national and cultural make-up of the personnel. In the early years, when there were some forty or fifty member states, the staff were drawn mainly from a few Western European countries and India. Efforts are now made to recruit staff from the hundred or more states which have come into existence and joined the organisations since then and, in some organisations and at some levels (particularly the highest), this has resulted in 'over-compensation'. For example, the proportion of posts above the D2 level occupied by nationals of African member states in the major Specialized Agencies greatly exceeds the proportion which even the most generous quota system in use in any of the organisations would give to these countries.[6] It is commonly said that the priority given to 'improved geographical distribution' has been responsible for a lowering of the quality of the staff. As for the competence and commitment of individual staff members, there is no reason why this should be so; there are individuals to be found in the Third World countries quite as competent as those in the original group of member states. However, the organisations have not succeeded on the whole in finding and attracting these people. This is due partly to shortcomings in their recruitment methods, partly to pressures exerted by governments (of developed and developing countries alike) to secure the appointment of candidates who are not always the best qualified they could offer, and perhaps most of all to the fact that other more rewarding careers are open to outstanding citizens of developing countries, whose governments are understandably

5  Statistics about geographical distribution, in 1985, are given in Appendix B.
6  On the other hand, below the D2 level more than 50% of the posts are still held by people from the United States, Western Europe and Japan.

reluctant to release them for long periods of service in the United Nations and its Specialized Agencies.

On the other hand, what can be said with certainty is that the vastly greater cultural and linguistic diversity of the staff members of the organisations, whatever benefits it may have provided in terms of broadened understanding and sympathies, has not always led to greater efficiency. It is clearly important that the staff of an international organisation should so far as possible reflect the geographical composition of the membership if it is to retain the latter's confidence and support. It is indeed a Charter requirement that 'due regard shall be paid to the importance of recruiting the staff on as wide a geographical basis as possible.' However, the same Article also lays down that: 'The paramount consideration in the employment of the staff and in the determination of the conditions of service shall be the necessity of securing the highest standards of efficiency, competence and integrity' (UN Charter, Article 101.3). There may in consequence be a conflict between 'the highest standards of efficiency' and the need to show the widest possible cultural diversity befitting an international organisation. Many governments genuinely attach more importance to cultural diversity than to administrative efficiency.

*The change of function and the change of terms of service.* A further major change in the staffing of the Specialized Agencies concerns the professional characteristics of staff. This follow from the evolution in the nature of their functions, from largely head-quarters-type activities of international regulation (standards) and exchanges of information (clearing-house activities, meetings and symposia of experts, publications) to greater emphasis on direct development assistance activities. Even those organisations whose essential functions continue to be regulatory, such as ICAO, WIPO, the IMO and the ITU, have significant development programmes. Consequently, fewer openings exist which can be filled by general-ists, there is an increased need for specialists with practical experience in their speciality for assignments in the field, and for staff with field experience for assignments at headquarters and in regional offices. Many such staff members are employed by the organisations for limited durations – say, of up to five years – either because they themselves see international service as only one phase in their profes-sional careers, or because the organisation cannot predict its require-ments in staff for development co-operation work sufficiently far ahead to offer longer-term employment. Because of this trend, and under pressure from some member states (ostensibly in the interest of improving geographical distribution), most Specialized Agencies have considerably reduced the number of staff to whom they guarantee permanent employment. Whereas, in earlier years, life-time security of tenure of the kind found in a national civil service was the norm, and the majority of staff held indefinite career appointments, now a high proportion of the staff in most organisations are employed on fixed-term (contract) appointments. These may be renewed repeatedly so that, seen in retrospect, the staff members may have 'enjoyed a career' of twenty or more years – but without ever having the assurance of continuity which is a character-istic of civil service employment. The *reductio ad absurdum* in this trend was reached in UNESCO in 1985 when the contracts of senior staff with many years' service were grudgingly renewed by dribs and drabs of two or three months at a time.

The 'career' nature of service in the Specialized Agencies has been further eroded since, for many posts, staff are needed with several years of experience in the practice of their speciality, which can only be acquired outside the international organisations; thus the average age of first appointment is high (over 40). Coupled with a mandatory age of retirement (in most organisations, 60 years of age)[7] which is low by many national standards, the 'career' for most of those staff who seek long-term service is limited to a span of twenty years and two or at most three promotions.

*Some consequences of these changes.* These changes in the compo-sition and characteristics of the professional staff of the Specialized Agencies have inevitably had an effect on the attitude of staff members towards the UN System and their own organisations. In particular, they have resulted in a diminished degree of commitment to the organisation – although not necessarily to the cause of inter-national co-operation. The independence from improper outside pressures and influences which in earlier days was generally seen as an essential condition of a true international civil service has been diluted. Inevitably, staff members with no guarantee of continued employment with the organisation beyond the end of their current three or five-year fixed-term contract may depend on the goodwill of their national administration in finding further employment,

7 A change of the mandatory retirement age to 62 is now being considered, for reasons connected with the financial soundness of the Pension Fund; this change is opposed by those who want to keep maximum flexibility to allow for the 'improve-ment of geographical distribution' – even when statistically there is little further need for such 'improvement' and when, if certain countries are still 'under-represented', the problem is not lack of vacant posts to be filled by their nationals but lack of qualified candidates permitted by their government to apply and the government's deliberate policy of recalling its nationals after four or five years.

(whether or not they are actually national civil servants on second-ment). It is understandable that they should pay at least equal attention to the interests of their past and prospective future employer as they do to the interests of an organisation which cannot or will not offer them the security they need to be able to maintain the same impartiality in relation to their own country as to all others.

As for staff members who are nationals of Socialist countries or of authoritarian regimes, such independence and impartiality has, of course, been out of the question for the reasons already stated. Many of them have declared open opposition to the very mention of it. To Communist governments it is inconceivable and unacceptable that one of their citizens should place his loyalty to an international organisation above his loyalty to his own country, and they have always sought to prevent such a deviation occurring by only permitting their nationals to serve in UN organisations for limited periods and by the very tight control they exercise over them through their permanent missions and embassies. They have not always succeeded. There are shining examples of staff members from Communist countries with fixed-term appointments whose loyalty to the organisation and whose impartiality matches up to the highest standards set for the career international civil servant, just as there are cases of staff members from other countries with permanent appointments whose conduct does not meet these standards. However, this exception to the proclaimed standards of conduct for international civil servants, which has always existed and which has regrettably been condoned, has had unfortunate consequences. There can be little doubt that other countries, seeing that different standards were tolerated for staff members from Communist countries, have progressively adopted those same methods vis-à-vis their own nationals. This apart, the changes which have occured in the staffing of the Specialized Agencies – some of them for valid functional reasons, others because governments have put their short-term national interests before those of international co-operation – have led them rather far from the traditional concept of an independent and impartial international civil service. This may be a necessary price to pay for any sort of Soviet bloc co-operation with international agencies, but the degree of damage it does to their standing is serious.[8]

8 Similar difficulties arose in the League of Nations, notably with the citizens of Italy and Germany after the countries became dictatorships. In particular, Mussolini's *chef de cabinet*, Marchese Paolucci, became an Under-Secretary-General of the League and is alleged to have organised fascist cells among the staff.

## The role and impact of the Executive Heads

We say much elsewhere about the part which – for better and for worse – Executive Heads have played in the evolution of the UN System. As regards the staffing problem, the experience of the last four decades has underlined the importance of the Executive Heads of the Agencies in their dual role – that of representing their Agency to the outside world and that of managing the staffing and the operations of their organisation. Not for nothing are most of them styled '*Directors*-General' rather than '*Secretaries*-General'. Article 101 of the Charter lays down the 'paramount consideration' in the appointment of staff as being 'the necessity of securing the highest standards of efficiency, competence and integrity'. The best Executive Heads have demonstrated more than this – namely extraordinary qualities of leadership which could both inspire their staff and persuade member governments of the wisdom of their policies. Others have harmed their organisations by their failures in one or both respects. This is partly the fault of those who selected them, who rarely give attention to these important qualities in making their selection. It reflects also the strength of the position of the Executive Head, consitutionally, as against that of member governments who have so little leverage in persuading recalcitrant Heads to accept advice even on professional and functional matters in which the Head's competence may be limited.

## Role of staff problems in loss of support for the UN Specialized Agencies

To what extent do the changes described above bear a responsibility for the current loss of support for the Specialized Agencies and confidence in them by governments and public?

First, it is likely that part of the widespread disillusionment with the organisations of the UN System is caused, or at least aggravated, by the observation that the organisations have not maintained the high standards which their constitutions proclaim with regard to their staff: the concept of an élite corps of men and women of total integrity, with international not national loyalties, of the highest level of professional competence, acting with perfect impartiality, 'having the interests of the Organisation only in view' and in complete independence of any improper instructions or influence. No doubt these standards were impossibly demanding in a naughty world; and one may doubt whether in practice they were always so admirably exemplified by the staff of the League of Nations and the pre-war ILO as proper respect for our elders leads us to believe.

The requirement of personal integrity is one which should not be impossible to satisfy within reasonable limits; and notwithstanding occasional sensational revelations in the press, the standard of the international secretariats in this respect is little below that to be found today in the best national civil services – and vastly better than that prevailing in the national civil services of the majority of the member states. But the charge that the international secretariats have lost their impartiality and individual staff members their independence in relation to improper outside influences is not surprising. As has already been noted, staff lacking security of tenure of their posts may well find it hard not to be attentive to the wishes of those on whom they may depend for their future employment.

It must also be remembered that the outside influence which some staff are accused of being subject to is often a genuine difference of approach, representing the perceived interests of a group of countries rather than the specific national interest of their own country. To the extent that this is true, they are in fact often reflecting the position of the majority of the member states. When the staff of UNESCO – and in particular its Director-General – are criticized for pressing policies which others may regard as contrary to the fundamental principles of the organisation, it must not be forgotten that they have been acting in conformity with the directives adopted by the majority of member states. The Head of an Agency may have a responsibility to try to moderate extreme positions taken by the majority if he perceives these to be misguided and if they seriously offend the minority, and to avoid exacerbating such conflicts by the way in which he implements the majority's decisions. But it is not the responsibility of other staff members to do so – their role is to follow the policy directives given by their Head who interprets the political decisions of the legislative organs. Individual staff members should not be blamed for upholding and promoting positions which have the sanction of the majority of the membership. However aberrant these positions may seem to some member states, this is not necessarily due to loss of impartiality or integrity – although the Western press and governments may find this difficult to accept.

The loss of professional competence and efficiency is more serious because, as perceived by national authorities (and to a lesser extent by public opinion), it is a cause of loss of confidence in the organisations. It must be observed that this criticism of the staff of the Specialized Agencies, like criticism of loss of impartiality and independence, applies particularly to the more 'political' organisations, most of all to the United Nations itself (which is outside our scope in this book) and to UNESCO which is polytechnical rather than specialized and deals in some politically-loaded subjects. To some extent it applies also to the ILO, the FAO and the WHO when aspects of their work have political implications, to a much less degree to organisations such as ICAO or the ITU, and hardly at all to purely technical organisations such as the UPU or the WMO. It is true also that these last organisations have not been subject to the same pressures regarding the composition of their staffs as the larger, more political ones, but it is not charged that their staffs are lacking in impartiality or are less efficient than they were in the 1950s. The problem is thus limited to a few organisations – which happen to be among the most conspicuous ones.

Whether the charge of diminished efficiency is justified or not in relation to organisations such as UNESCO is probably impossible to judge with certainty, given the absence of external, independent evaluation, and given that much of the work done today is different from, and in many respects more difficult than, that of earlier years. At the level of the individual, there have of course always been staff members who were less than fully qualified for the jobs to which they were appointed, or less industrious than might have been hoped (as indeed there are in all organisations). Perhaps what is different is that these were formerly seen as isolated instances of poor selection or of yielding to pressure in recruitment, whereas now there is an impression that, in certain areas, the appointment of unqualified persons is more or less systematic, even deliberate – either as part of a design to prevent the international organisations from becoming too effective and interfering in national affairs, or as a means to the self-perpetuation of privileged cliques. It is undoubtedly easy to attribute the failure of the organisations to achieve all their objectives to the inefficiency of their secretariats, but other causes should not be overlooked: inadequacies in the decision-making processes, lack of effective support at the national level, even the impossibility of dealing with some of the tasks undertaken (e.g. peace in the Middle East, suppression of trade barriers without loss to any group etc.).

That the staff are often blamed for shortcomings for which their responsibility is either limited or non-existent is no doubt a manifestation of the common tendency to blame the civil servant for everything which goes wrong, in the village, in the country, in the world – a tendency which is all the more easily indulged as the civil servant is prevented from defending himself and at the same time is sheltered by his cloak of anonymity. With the international civil servant there is also a strong streak of envy, which developed in the 1950s and 1960s when he or she was indeed well-paid and privileged, but is much less justified today because, thanks to the linkage of UN salaries to those in the US civil service,[9] the material conditions of UN civil servants have declined and are inferior to those of, for example, employees of multinational corporations.

## Possible corrective measures

Whatever part the alleged loss of impartiality of the staffs of the Specialized Agencies and their decreased efficiency may play in the loss of governmental and popular support for the organisations, it is certain that improvements must be made if the UN System is to regain that support or even to continue to exist. Those who view the System positively must take a position on the crucial question of how the international civil service is to evolve. We are now in the trough of disillusionment with the traditional concept and have a perhaps exaggerated perception that it has broken down irreparably. Should countries which support the Charter concept go on fighting to maintain the old standards – or would it be not only easier, but more effective to abandon it and to concentrate on making the best out of a new order?

It must be recognized that some of the departures from the traditional concept which have occurred are functionally valid and could not be reversed without damage to the organisations' ability to do their jobs – in particular, the move away from life-time career staff to a high proportion of staff on fixed-term appointments who must have technical qualifications which can only be acquired and kept up to date outside the international organisations. To meet this need while preserving a longer-term affiliation with the organisation, a kind of rotating career between international and national service has been suggested, but this seems unlikely to be realised in more than a few cases, mainly because of the reluctance of both categories of employer to tie themselves to a pattern of secondments and resumptions of service over a period of many years. In so far as life-time security of employment was seen as one of the foundations of the concept of an international civil service (e.g. in relation to impartiality and independence), it must be recognized that this will no longer be applicable to a high proportion, even a majority, of the staffs of the Specialized Agencies (the situation in the UN Secretariat, with a higher proportion of generalists, is different). To formalize the distinction between these two categories of staff – to say, for example, that only those whose professional characteristics enable them to be appointed on a permanent basis (i.e. essentially the generalists and the administrators) are true international civil

9 This is the so-called 'Noblemaître Principle'; see Appendix B.

servants, the others being some kind of contractual employees – would be damaging to the notion of an international civil service. It would also be difficult to apply in the light of the increasing (and wise) trend not take a decision about a candidate's suitability for permanent employment till after five or six years' service.

For the same reasons (need for specialist qualifications, hence late age of entry), the use of competitive examinations for initial selection (which is often cited as a characteristic of civil service employment) is unlikely to be expanded, despite the valiant efforts of those (in particular, Inspector Bertrand) who see it as a means of ensuring greater equity of qualifications between entrants coming from different countries. The number of junior, entrance-level posts for which such examinations could be made compulsory is too small to justify the enormous effort entailed in organising international competitions. (This is not to say, however, that within each organisation and for each specific vacancy, selection should not be made on a competitive basis; in some of the Specialized Agencies this is already the practice, e.g. in the ILO and WIPO; the Executive Head's prerogative to appoint the staff is not impaired, but a guarantee is provided against arbitrary exercise of that prerogative.)

So what remains of the traditional concept of the international civil service, i.e. that the secretariat as a body is at the service of the member states as a whole? The alternative is for the individual staff member to be recognized as an agent of his or her national government informing it of matters of official business of interest to it and promoting its interests over those of member states. Fortunately, this state of affairs has not yet become generalised; obviously, there could be no discipline at all in a secretariat most of whose members behaved in this way. Yet the trend seems to be towards this. As has been said, the very concept of loyalty to the organisation above all other loyalties is not readily accepted or understood by all cultures. It seems vain to hope that the Communist states could be persuaded to adhere to it; but then they have never done so and a *modus vivendi* has been reached which, if not morally satisfying, at least avoids too flagrant breaches of the professed standards of conduct. With other member countries guilty of such practices, there is perhaps hope of being able to persuade them that their national interests would be better served by a secretariat which included some of their nationals but which was at the service of the membership as a whole, rather than by their having in the secretariat a few of their nationals who would act as the government's agents but would inevitably be outnumbered by the much bigger contingents from larger countries.

The alternative being chaos and the end of the international organisations as they have existed – not too unsuccessfully – for the past forty years, it is still worth trying to win acceptance for the original concept. When the International Civil Service Commission was established in 1975,[10] it was hoped by some that it would reinforce the idea of the true international civil service; indirectly it did indeed achieve some results in this direction in its early years, but regrettably it is now so dominated by the political outlook of the General Assembly that there is little more to be hoped from it in present circumstances. However, there is still room for renewed efforts by those governments that are so minded and by non-governmental, professional, learned and other groups to obtain broader acceptance, both in governmental circles and in public opinion, for the concept of the international civil service as a system that has worked, can still work given a fair chance and can provide better service to the international community than any alternative.

As a corollary, governments should be urged to show restraint in respecting the independence of the Executive Heads and the secretariats. Nearly all governments have at one time or another yielded to the temptation to bring pressure to bear on Executive Heads. The path is extremely narrow and difficult to follow between interfering in the prerogative of the Executive Head to manage his staff (e.g. to get a promotion for a particular national) and, at the other extreme, holding oneself completely aloof from the way in which the secretariat is run. Many Western governments (France is a notable exception) have increasingly allowed themselves to be almost completely excluded from senior posts in the Agencies;[11] for example, in 1985 Britain had only one top-level post in the whole UN System and has been squeezed out entirely from the administrative area in the United Nations itself, where it had traditionally held senior posts and had made a notable contribution (although Britain probably still has a disproportionate number of posts elsewhere in the System and it is said that one of the reasons for its eliminations was that insufficient attention has been paid to providing candidates of the requisite calibre.)

A further point in connection with top-level posts in the secretariats is that governments should oppose the tendency to attribute certain posts to certain nationalities or regions more or less permanently (although here the fact that the President of the IBRD

10 On the ICSC an admirable pamphlet was published by UNITAR after this book was in an advanced stage: John P. Renninger, *Can the Common System be Maintained: The Role of the International Civil Servant*, New York: UN, 1986.
11 Table 5 of Appendix B shows, however, that they have retained the largest proportion of professional staff throughout the System.

is always an American and that of the IMF always a European sets a bad precedent). A reasonable rotation at the highest levels is beneficial. Those countries which have once provided an incumbent for one of these posts should not automatically hold on to it regardless of whether they can offer the best or even a reasonably qualified candidate for the succession; otherwise whole sectors of the secretariat can become heavily tinged with a particular national or regional flavour. This is not the best way to run an international organisation. It is a particular problem in UNESCO where the two major sectors, education and science, have been headed by officials of the same nationality for more than ten years; it has also been a problem in UNIDO. It is obviously easier for the Executive Head to perpetuate the *status quo* rather than to engineer delicate exchanges to maintain an appropriate balance at the top while avoiding the 'colonisation' of particular sectors; encouragement, support and understanding by the governments would help him to adopt the bolder course. Rotation among professionals is equally important, not least to bring the advantage of particular national experience and to widen the sources of information.

The importance of the personal actions of the Executive Head in all matters concerning staffing is very great. When the Executive Head demonstrates unambiguously his own attachment to the principles of the international civil service, and when he is known to be firm (without making a public display) in resisting improper pressures, member governments and staff members know where they stand; when the Executive Head is seen to be prone to abdicating his constitutional prerogatives and yielding to the political decision of the governing bodies matters which he is paid to deal with, serious doubt is cast on the independence of the international civil service. The selection of Executive Heads is entirely the business of governments – yet how much attention do governments pay to the managerial abilities and demonstrated strength of character of potential candidates? It would seem that almost every other qualification is given greater importance than these. Would it be too much to hope that the next time an Executive Head is to be chosen, some governments at least would stress these considerations, rather than looking for the candidate who is least likely to give offence to any group of member states? Even if the candidate is in the end defeated, at least a blow will have been struck for the recognition of the secretariats as functional units with a job to do demanding good management at the top in order to ensure effective performance at all levels.

The reasons why the secretariats can no longer be composed mainly of life-time career officials have already been described. Yet there is no reason why the stability and security which comes from an assurance of permanent employment (subject only to satisfactory conduct and performance) should be denied when there is no functional ground for witholding it. Since the mid-1970s it has become a matter of doctrine and of pride for organisations to show that they have reduced almost to zero the number of staff holding permanent appointments. The valid functional reason applying to a proportion of the posts has been distorted to make it appear a virtue that no staff enjoy permanency; this has been engineered by the small number of states that for ideological, almost philosophical, reasons cannot accept the notion of the permanent international bureaucrat, and has been enthusiastically espoused by those envious of the fact that the staff members granted permanent status in the first twenty years of the lives of the organisations were (not surprisingly) nationals of the member states which constituted the organizations in those years. As has already been argued, the contention that the granting of permanent status to suitable staff members would impede the further improvement of geographical distribution is unfounded; any further improvement should – and can – come from the increased availability of qualified candidates from the countries still deemed 'under-represented' and from a change in the policies of those governments which do not allow their own nationals to stay long enough in international service to become experienced and influential, thus forcing the organisations to expend efforts in recruitment campaigns merely to maintain the existing levels without any real hope of ever meeting whatever quotas have been set. The situation concerning the availability of persons of high qualifications worldwide is changing, so that if member governments and Executive Heads so wish, it should become easier to reconcile the standards of efficiency and competence with those of geographical distribution.

A further point we should not overlook is the impossibility of having an efficient and devoted staff if its members are not justly remunerated. The unnecessarily generous level of remuneration in the 1950s and 1960s (paradoxically, at a time when there were still plenty of young people who were ready to devote some years of their lives to international service without too much concern for the material rewards) have done a disservice to the United Nations; but since the mid-1970s the situation has been reversed. The mathematical linking of UN remuneration to that of the US Federal Civil Service came at an unfortunate moment, just when successive US Administrations, but above all that of President Reagan, were cutting civil service remuneration in relation to that of other sectors of employment in the country (the resulting shortfall of US civil service pay compared to that of other sectors of employment with which, according to the law, it should be comparable is more than 20% generally, and more than 30% at the top levels.) It is understandable that governments which are themselves obliged to enforce austerity in their own countries should be reluctant to approve pay increases for the international organisations; yet there are few, if any, national civil services which, like the UN organisations, have granted no pay increase in ten years. This is perceived as an injustice by the staff, with demoralizing effects at all levels (even among the Executive Heads, who are responsible for the management of their staffs but are unable even to get a hearing when they seek to present to the General Assembly the case for a review of the salary levels).

Issues of personnel policy have played a part in the tensions which have developed in the UN System. There is, nevertheless, nothing in them which has dealt – or is likely to deal – a mortal blow to the System as a whole. Although there is discontent over the freezing of salaries, existing working and social conditions seem to be broadly right. Some would argue that these conditions do not take proper account of 'extreme duty situations' – the enormous pressures of work or even physical danger – which sometimes arise, but this is true of most national civil services engaged in the conduct of 'international affairs'.

Since the end of the Second World War there has probably been a decline in the idealism which originally motivated many of the staff, but this could probably be restored if they could have more operational success by being given more resources and better policies for using them – and these depend mostly on attitudes of member governments. Some of these issues will be discussed further in Part Three.

To improve the situation, more governments need to accept that they will get a better service from secretariats which are competent and efficient, regardless of nationality. While geographical spread is important, nations acquire international prestige only if those they nominate for international organisations are persons of ability, *national* prestige is acquired only in appointing persons of ability to *international* organisations. More governments need to adopt a self-denying ordinance in bringing pressure to bear over appointments on Executive Heads and secretariats.

CHAPTER XII

# ECONOMIC POLICY ISSUES: EFFECTS OF THE 'RICH VERSUS POOR' DEBATE ON THE U.N. SYSTEM

As pointed out earlier, one of the causes of discontent with the UN System is the failure to make progress in dealing with many of the world's economic problems – especially in the discussions which have taken place on them in the UN debates between 'rich' and 'poor'. This has produced disappointment and frustration in many developing countries, and the repeated expression of these feelings in the United Nations and the Specialized Agencies has caused exasperation in developed countries and weakened their willingness to co-operate. We cannot attempt to analyse all aspects of the topic, still less suggest solutions to the world's economic problems. Rather, we are concerned here with the consequences of the present debate – and of the failure to make progress in it – for the work of the Specialized Agencies.

Several points should be stressed at the outset. The first is the obvious one that there are many more important reasons for finding solutions to the world's economic problems than that of reducing the difficulties of the Specialized Agencies. A much more useful approach is to see how the Specialized Agencies, working within their existing constitutions, can contribute to a solution of the world's economic problems and what are the conditions in which they can do so.

The second point is that some of the difficulty is caused not so much by the substance of the debate on economic issues as by the way it has been conducted since the 1960s within the UN System. Three of the main organs with constitutional responsibility for dealing with various aspects of the world economy – the IMF, the IBRD and the GATT – antedate the creation of the United Nations and have voting procedures which put them under the control of market economy countries which provide their resources. On the other hand, the organisation most responsible for articulating the demands of the developing countries – UNCTAD – was not created till 1964. The procedure adopted by UNCTAD, and later by the General Assembly, for formulating its demands is most clearly exemplified in General Assembly Resolution 3201 (S–VI) and 3202(S–VI) of 1 May 1974, in which the establishment of a New

143

International Economic Order was declared and its details set out.[1] The formula has been to bring in long resolutions recommending the introduction of a complex set of measures in the field of commodities, finance, trade, aid and related matters. Whatever might be the long-term effects of these proposed measures on the level of world prosperity (a point which is open to argument among the experts), the short-term result would be to impose the costs of introducing them largely on the developed countries. This makes many of the individual measures quite unacceptable to developed countries which, however, have been unwilling, for political reasons, to reject the package in the General Assembly by voting against it *in toto*. Instead, developed countries make reservations on particular points in these resolutions which they find unacceptable; to do otherwise would mean (in the words of the US Delegate to the General Assembly in 1974) that they had 'made commitments which they did not intend to fulfil'. Despite these reservations by the states which would have to provide the resources to implement these resolutions, they are pushed through by the majority votes of the remainder or declared carried by 'consensus'.

This procedure has had a number of unfortunate results. One is that, because of its obvious futility, it has led to these resolutions being taken less and less seriously by those responsible for taking economic policy decisions. Another is that because of the certainty that resolutions would be carried by built-in developing country majorities, the intellectual level of debate on these issues by the representatives of developed countries in UN fora has steadily declined. Some of the discussions have become not so much a dialogue of the deaf as a dialogue – on one side at least – of the indifferent.

However, it would be wrong to suggest that the main difficulties in dealing with these issues lie in the procedures. The real difference between the two sides lies in the substance and in a fairly deep ideological divide which has deepened during the 1980s. In the General Assembly of 1974 the British delegate, Mr Ivor Richard, in entering his country's reservations on the New International Economic Order Resolution, could say 'that the drawing up of a general declaration of principles caused little difficulty, but when we went on to the details of the Programme of Action we immediately ran into serious problems.' It is doubtful if a representative of the British government more than ten years later would be equally co-operative even on a general statement of principles. In any event, disguised behind

1 See also The Charter of Economic Rights and Duties of States in Resolution 3281 of Dec. 1974 and Resolution 3362 (S-VII) of Sept. 1975. Resolution 2626 of 1970 on the Second Development Decade is also relevant.

a few reservations on points in the Programme of Action, there was always a serious clash of ideologies and a difference of view between the two sides in their perceptions of their own self-interest. This difference dates from 1964 and the analyses by the first Secretary-General of UNCTAD, Dr Prebisch, of the main constraints on the development of the Third World countries. He identified these constraints as lying in the nature of the links between the developed and developing countries; he argued that these were such as to provide a serious tendency for the terms of trade of developing countries to deteriorate. Many economists in the industrialised countries opposed this thesis from the outset, but nevertheless it became the prevailing philosophy of the UN System outside the confines of the IBRD, the IMF and the GATT.

Following a wealth of analyses of the main 'linkage areas' provided by its Secretariat, UNCTAD went on to propose a number of structural changes in each of them. In the area of commodities, for example, it proposed not only a common fund to establish a measure of price stability but also an 'integrated approach' to many of the other facets of commodity markets, including proposals for the indexation of prices of commodity exports to prices of imports into the developing countries. On monetary issues, it proposed measures to supplement the financing of support for development programmes of developing countries threatened with disruption through unforeseen commodity price fluctuations. It has considered ways to alleviate the debt burden. It has also proposed, and in some cases successfully negotiated, arrangements in other 'linkage areas' such as shipping, insurance and the transfer of technology. But whereas the measures adopted by the IMF and the IBRD were broadly based on the principles of a market economy, the theories underlying UNCTAD (subsequently endorsed by the General Assembly) were interventionist, the theory being that since the poverty of developing countries was caused by the drain on their resources resulting from the operations of existing institutions, only government intervention to change the operations of these institutions could redress the balance. The underlying assumption was that 'the division of the benefits of economic interchange between the rich and the poor countries must be reviewed as a consequence of the relative bargaining strengths of the two groups' rather than be left to the working of 'normal market forces'. Indeed, the 'normal working of these market forces must be seen as a reflection of the powerful entrenched institutional position and bargaining power of developed countries'.[2]

2  Article by Maizels in the *IDS Bulletin*, vol. 15, no. 3, July 1984.

The developed countries have always maintained not only that these theories were intellectually invalid but also that they were contrary to their economic interests. This last point, in turn, has always been challenged by the UNCTAD Secretariat and its supporters, who claimed that the implementation of its measures was in the common interest of all – developed and developing countries alike – and would produce a general increase in world prosperity to the benefit of all. This thesis (which eventually found expression in the Brandt Report of 1980), although it raised some public support in developed countries, was never accepted by their governments, and in the mid-1980s is less acceptable to them than it has ever been. Another reason for the opposition of the developed countries, and one which has a bearing on the future of the Specialized Agencies, is that the UNCTAD proposals would involve international intervention planned and exercised on a huge scale by international institutions; such institutions, from experience to date, are judged by developed countries to be quite incapable of under-taking this intervention. The proposals would also deprive the governments of many market economies of control over their economic resources in ways which would be unacceptable to them politically and in which few of their political parties, trade unions or commercial groups would concur.

The attempt by UN resolution to dictate and supervise change on a world scale in economic, social, financial and scientific institutions has been a failure. Moreover, it is a failure which damages the credibility of the UN System. Its weaknesses are several. First, the resolutions themselves are frequently too generalised to be useful guides to policy. Their prescriptions are not specific enough to have significance (especially where developing countries are concerned), and the obligations they need to define if they are to be effective are too vague. Secondly, they lay far too much emphasis on institutional changes, as though it is institutions which always dictate the content of policies rather than the reverse. Thirdly, there is an implicit belief that many of the institutional changes they propose can be dictated by governments, whereas most governments would find the changes politically or administratively impractical. Fourthly, the resolutions are mainly concerned with the redistribution of existing resources rather than with the creation of new resources. Finally, they make policy recommendations, often on a world scale, without regard to their financial, administrative or technical implications.

For these reasons, the resolutions have repeatedly – and not only in the realm of economic relations – shown themselves to be ineffective as prescriptions for action. Nevertheless, as indications of where policy adjustments are called for, they can serve a useful purpose. For example, General Assembly Resolution 3201(S-VI) on the New International Economic Order and related documents are right to draw attention to the changes taking place in the world economy and the need for adjustments to meet them. They are right to draw attention to the need for more resources to promote development in developing countries, whether through increased trade, more aid or better systems for balance of payments support. They are right to draw attention to the special difficulties of countries which are large producers of raw materials. They are right to draw attention to the benefits which would flow from a degree of stabilisation of commodity prices; to the problems which flow from the introduction of synthetics; to the extent to which existing international monetary arrangements are unsuited to the circumstances of many developing countries; and to the need for international agreements which will promote food security. However, in the view of many Western (and other) governments, they are wrong to imply that the main reason that 'the gap between the developed and the developing countries continues to widen' is that 'the existing international economic order' was 'established at a time when most of the developing countries did not exist'. There are plenty of other factors which contribute to the problem and which need to be identified and removed if progress is to be made. They are probably wrong to assume that if 'every country has the right to adopt the economic and social system it deems the most appropriate for its economic development', this can necessarily be done without economic consequences for the country concerned, which may follow whether or not it is subjected to 'discrimination' from outside. It is unjustifiable to assume (as the documents appear to do) that it is easy to take measures for 'the recovery, exploitation, development, marketing and distribution' of raw materials produced in developing countries if this has to be done without regard to the way in which the country exercises its sovereignty over such raw materials. It is simplistic to assume that developed countries can, without much difficulty, 'make appropriate adjustments in their economies so as to facilitate the expansion and diversification of imports from developing countries', or that they can find 'measures to check inflation' which do not have an adverse effect on developing countries. Above all, experience has shown brutally that it is wrong to assume that because this resolution says that 'developed countries and others in a position to do so should contribute substantially to the various organisations, programmes and funds established within the UN System for the purpose of accelerating economic and social development in developing countries', any such countries will hasten to do so. They are more likely to judge the provision of finance on a fund-by-fund or programme-by-programme basis, on how effectively the money is likely to be used, and on how a contribution might serve their own national interest.

Experience is showing that to make progress on the range of issues now dividing the world in economic policy, three conditions are necessary. The first is to secure some agreement on aims and some consensus on methods. The second is to find machinery to work out the detail of the measures required to secure progress in the different problem areas and to identify the degree of international co-operation between governments and Agencies required to implement them. The third is to secure agreement about the finance to fund these measures and on an efficient way of administering it. Over the range of issues covered by the 'New International Economic Order' all three of these conditions, except perhaps for the second, may be harder to satisfy now than they were, say, in the mid-1970s. The second is now customarily described as 'problem assimilation' – meaning research and analysis. The creation and development of UNCTAD;[3] the expansion of the facilities in the World Bank, the IMF and the GATT for analysing different aspects of the problems of economic development and the relationship between different groups of countries within the world economy; and the accumulated experience of the OECD and bodies like the Commonwealth Secretariat – these have led to the possibilities for action being better *identified* than ever before. However, what is needed before fruitful negotiations can begin is some recognition among the developing countries that their interests are increasingly diverse, and that, despite the dangers which could come from a weakening of the solidarity established in the Group of 77, they must take full account of this fact in establishing their negotiating positions. Moreover, with the improved comparative position of some groups of developing countries in the world economy, the possibility of trade-offs rather than unrequited concessions in such negotiations should be considered more seriously. It is also desirable that groups of developing countries should establish better machinery for co-ordinating their positions before negotiations start. (The Group of 77 no longer corresponds to the heterogeneous character of the developing countries as they now exist.) Also, most developing countries need to recognise, more than they have done hitherto, the relationship between their domestic policies and their stances in

3 UNCTAD has rendered an important service not only through its Secretariat's contribution to the analysis of problems in the field of commodities, debt and 'invisibles related to trade', but also by providing technical assistance to developing countries working on these problems.

international negotiations. Developed countries, on the other hand, need to approach arguments about 'complementarity' with a more open mind and be willing to take a less short-term view of their own interests. In addition, governments need to make themselves more impervious to internal pressure groups safeguarding sectional interests and more open to arguments of 'international solidarity'. With these changes, there could be a fresh approach to negotiation.

Among the Specialized Agencies, such as the IBRD, the IMF, the GATT and UNCTAD, which have a constitutional responsibility for dealing with economic questions, the desirability of making such changes of approach is well recognised. Among those Agencies with a more marginal interest in economic questions, even among some (such as the FAO) dealing with activities which have a considerable economic impact, the same change of attitude is less apparent. There remains a willingness to proceed as before by rhetoric and confrontation, rather than by serious examination of the issues – a willingness possibly reinforced by the decline in the quality of their staffs in recent years and by the exigencies of inter-Agency rivalry.

On the question of aims and methods, the situation is more difficult. Because of the growth since 1945 in the economic importance of some developing countries such as Singapore and the Republic of Korea, the spectacular post-war economic development of Japan, the different role of Europe and the change of the United States to being a debtor country, the world has become a very different place in the 1980s from what it was when the Bretton Woods institutions were devised. Nevertheless the aims of those institutions as stated in their Charters remain valid. Above all, the desirability of international co-operation to secure either exchange rate stability or orderly adjustments in exchange rates, to provide international assistance in balance of payments adjustments, to promote increased employment, and to combat protectionism and increase international trade, is as great as ever. What is also apparent, however, is decreasing consensus on the best methods of achieving these aims.

There is also a decline in the willingness of the international community to provide the necessary resources for effective action. It is easy to ascribe this to 'a lack of political will' and to step up the rhetoric of the General Assembly about a new international economic order in the hope of remedying this deficiency. However, this approach is unlikely to be very fruitful. The demonstrable need for increased international co-operation is not enough in itself; the conditions for achieving this first need to be established. To this end more objective analysis of the successes and failures of existing institutions and policies would be a valuable first step. On institutions, there are tendencies – well exemplified in the debate in the mid-1980s on UNESCO – either to dismiss their defects simply because they are UN institutions, regardless of their performance, or to exaggerate them for the same reason. On Agency policies, there has frequently been a similar reluctance to examine which have been successful and which have failed. Secondly, there needs to be a greater willingness in both developed and developing countries to consider the international impact of their domestic policies and not to be over-sensitive when this is discussed in international fora. Thirdly, there is a need to try to establish and demonstrate in relation to any change of policy under negotiation the degree of common advantage it would serve – known in the trade as 'policy complementarity'.

Moreover, from the point of view of the System as a whole, a further organisational task needs to be undertaken – that of re-examining the role of the United Nations and all its offshoots in dealing with the world's economic problems. This should extend not merely to identifying the nature of the problems themselves and of possible solutions, but also to re-examining the machinery and the different organisational responsibilities for tackling them within the UN System; over the years, the different parts of the machine have stimulated sharp differences of approach to economic problems which in themselves have hindered negotiation rather than promoted it. These differences of approach, together with the weaknesses which have been revealed in the methods employed over the last twenty years, are well summed up in the following extract from an unpublished paper by Havelock R. Brewster, delivered at a Geneva Symposium in 1985, entitled 'Reflections on International Development Strategy'. Mr Brewster is a staff member of the UNCTAD Secretariat, but the views expressed in the following extract are his own and not those of UNCTAD or of its Secretariat: He writes as follows on 'Negotiation and Problem Assimilation':

In the economics field, setting aside the Bretton Woods institutions and the specialized agencies, the main intergovernmental bodies involved are UNCTAD and the Economic and Social Council (ECOSOC) of the General Assembly. The negotiation function nominally has fallen mainly to UNCTAD since its founding in 1964.

From the start it was a disputed function. Back in 1964 the British minister (Edward Heath) came directly to the point: 'The Conference will most speedily achieve its purpose if it guides and stimulates the work of existing bodies. These have the practical experience. They are used to translating broad ideas into workable plans.' By contrast, the Brazilian minister (João Augusto de Arcijo Castro) saw the Conference as a 'challenge to build a world commensurate with our responsibilities and our faith in justice and in the dignity of man'. And U Thant, the then United Nations Secretary-General, saw the Conference as 'designed for action'. These differing visions of the role of UNCTAD have persisted to the present day. What can be drawn out of experience of these twenty years of UNCTAD's existence? I venture to list them as follows:

'Language' which 'resolves' unresolved substantive differences, such as the mandate itself of UNCTAD, is ultimately worthless.

The scope for negotiation in UNCTAD *vis-à-vis* the responsibilities of other bodies, particularly the Bretton Woods institutions, has never been clarified but in practice has not amounted to much.

Negotiations in the true sense (setting aside certain issues in the commodities area) have not been taking place in UNCTAD. A lot of time and resources has been wasted on the symbolism of negotiations: groupings, spokesmen, 'decision', 'resolutions' etc. The charade reaches its apogee of absurdity in the four-yearly 'ministerial' Conference.

Negotiations and the problem-assimilation[4] function cannot be integrated within a single inter-governmental format. Their styles and requirements are very different and the 'mix' in UNCTAD has not served well the purposes of either. Governments have had trouble distinguishing, for purposes of an appropriate response, specific negotiating propositions from the exploration of ideas and the sifting of possibilities. And the secretariat has had trouble in interpreting the ambivalent requirements of governments.

Possibly reflecting the original differences in its conception, UNCTAD has not been equipped with the proper apparatus either for negotiations or for problem-assimilation. The style of business, the participation, the political status and intellectual quality of the participants, the appropriateness of the input, the purposes aimed at and expectations aroused are all wrong from the standpoint of both functions.

In other words, the UN machinery and the standard UN procedures are getting in the way of the successful negotiation of economic issues, especially as they affect the relations between developed and developing countries. If they cannot be changed, they need at least to be made to operate in a new way. Some suggestions will be made later.

4 I.e. research and analysis.

# CHAPTER XIII

# SCIENTIFIC RESEARCH: A CONTRAST IN STYLE AND METHOD OF INTERNATIONAL CO-OPERATION

In order to illustrate in greater detail some of the themes touched on in earlier Chapters, as well as points which will be made in Part Three, it is proposed in the next four Chapters to deal with certain topics and institutions in greater detail. One Chapter will deal with the Bertrand Report, which appeared when our study was in an advanced state of preparation and which is highly relevant to its conclusions. Others will deal with the World Bank and the UNDP, both of which play an important role in the United Nations operations to promote development. This Chapter, however, will deal with the two very different ways in which the United Nations and its Specialized Agencies have worked to promote scientific research on behalf of developing countries.

The United Nations became interested in scientific research as a means of promoting development in the poorer countries early in the 1950s. Several of these efforts were organized by Specialized Agencies. For example, UNESCO established an International Council of Scientific Unions to orchestrate basic scientific research worldwide for non-military purposes. The FAO had a global responsibility for making the world aware of the scope and content of agricultural research and stimulating its application to agricultural development. The WHO had a similar role in relation to health. Moreover, some of these early efforts had a degree of success, especially in alerting developing countries to areas of research that would be interesting and useful for them. The WHO's advertisement of malaria control by means of insect control is a good early example. By the 1970s it was apparent that these efforts were having limited impact, largely because there was no effective link between the scientists on the ground, who had the ideas, and the politicians at the centre, who alone could provide the money. Another reason for relative failure was that the politicians in the governing bodies of the Agencies tended to favour research into projects which would be politically attractive rather than into those which would be scientifically feasible.

The 1960s saw two very different international attempts at solving this problem, which are worth looking at in more detail for the lessons they offer for the future operations of the Specialized

Agencies. Both recognised that there were some problems of scientific research – and problems of organising it – which required international co-operation for their solution. However, the ways by which they each set about organising it were very different.

## The UN approach

In 1963 the United Nations organised a Conference in Geneva on Science and Technology which led in 1964 to ECOSOC establishing ACAST – the Advisory Committee on the Application of Science and Technology. The Committee consisted of twenty-four 'experts' (not government representatives), with four functions: to review progress made in applying science and technology to the problems of developing countries; to review the scientific and technological activities of the UN System to establish priorities and avoid duplication; to study and advise on any questions referred to it by the Secretary-General or the Heads of Specialized Agencies; and to study what organisational changes should be made to advance the application of science and technology in developing countries.

ACAST made a useful and sensible contribution to the UN's paperwork on science and technology – for example, it did useful work in preparing documents on the topic for the UN Second Development Decade – but it failed to produce any serious measure of co-ordination between the Specialized Agencies, despite the best efforts of the UN Secretariat to encourage them. On this matter, in the light of ACAST's work, the Secretariat produced a 'comprehensive report' to ECOSOC in 1969 on which ECOSOC's main conclusion after debate was that there was a 'need for further study'.[1] Moreover, although an ECOSOC resolution of 1969 claimed that ACAST had made 'an outstanding contribution to the general recognition of the role of science and technology in the development process', it is hard to discover that it led to the production of any research results anywhere of any use to developing countries.

In 1979 the United Nations embarked on a more ambitious attempt to stimulate and organise a scientific effort on behalf of developing countries: a conference of 142 countries in Vienna, which on 31 August 1979 'adopted by consensus a programme of action', later adopted by the General Assembly at its Thirty-Fourth Session. It is a lengthy document,[2] consisting of 118 paragraphs, written in typical UN prose. Its three sections deal respectively with

1 Document A/8003 of 1970.
2 Entitled *The Vienna Programme of Action on Science and Technology for Development*, United Nations, 1979.

'Strengthening the Scientific and Technology Capacities of the Developing Countries at national regional and international level', 'Restructuring the Existing Pattern of International Scientific and Technological Relations', and 'Strengthening the Role of the UN System in the Field of Science and Technology and the Provision of Increased Financial Resources'. For the third of these purposes the Conference established an Interim Fund with a target of $250 million.

It is impossible here to summarise all the proposals in such a document. It is enough to say that although they are worthy they are also vague, except where they recommend additions to the bureaucracy at national and international level. Thus they recommend *inter alia* that 'each developing country should establish one or more bodies for science and technology policy-making and implementation, supported at the highest level.' These bodies should 'embrace elements such as formulation of science and technology plans with a view to establishing targets for each science and technology sector, survey of the state-of-art in each science and technology sector and assessment of the availability of national resources and science and technology potential' – and much besides. Recommendations similar in tone are made for the regional level, where it is claimed that 'collective self-reliance among developing countries is a multi-dimensional process requiring the adoption of policies and measures that are both bilateral and multilateral in scope, with a view to a strengthening of the internal capacities of developing countries and improving their bargaining position.' The end conclusion is again bureaucratic, e.g. 'Developing countries should set up, as appropriate, a network of scientific and technological institutions or agencies which would carry out, in a co-operative manner, activities related to the whole gamut of scientific and technological activities' and so on. As a plan of action, it is so comprehensive as to be useless, not least because it fails to lay down any precise objectives which might have measurable results. The same emphasis prevails in the third section dealing with strengthening the role of the United Nations in this field where the main emphasis is on 'restructuring the organs, organisations and bodies within the UN system' and emphasis on 'the need for greater cohesiveness and co-ordination of the activities of the various organisations and agencies of the system'.

It is difficult to summarise the results of the Vienna Programme after five years of operations. On 9 April 1985 the Secretary-General himself published a Mid-Decade Review of it.[3] This shows, first, that

3  Document A/CN.11/63.

the Interim Fund is far from having raised the $250 million it was seeking. Governments contributed $40 million in the first instance, although another $50 million was forthcoming later in the form of Trust Funds. The reasons for this are not stated, but they are almost certainly that the principal donors considered the programme better designed to establish new bureaucracies than to create research institutions or programmes. Nevertheless, the report claims that in the period 1980-4, 100 projects had been funded and 1,020 fellowships provided, although no attempt was made to evaluate their usefulness. It admits, however, that 'in the area of mobilisation of resources for science and technology at national level, very little progress has been achieved so far.' One area where the Vienna Programme does seem to have made some progress is that of making all the UN organisations and the Specialized Agencies more aware of the importance of scientific research and technology to economic development; details were given of the contributions of eleven organisations and twelve Agencies to such scientific research and technology. However, the overall impression is that in the Vienna Programme the Agencies rather typically saw new possible worlds to conquer (e.g. more studies of the problem of undertaking research, conferences, data collection etc.) rather than new possibilities for real research to discover new facts that would help development in poor countries.

## *The Consultative Group approach: Two alternatives*[4]

Two other approaches to research which have involved the Specialized Agencies only partly ante-date the Vienna Programme and have produced real results of great value to developing countries. Both are very different from those first described, and both are in the areas of very specific applied scientific research. They involve several Specialized Agencies, together with governments and outside bodies.

The first is the Consultative Group of International Agricultural Research (CGIAR). Here the initiative came from the president of the Rockefeller Foundation, Dr J. George Harrar. In 1960 the Rockefeller and Ford Foundations combined their resources to establish the International Rice Research Institute (IRRI) in the Philippines to conduct research on the genetic improvement of the rice plant and on better agronomic practices transferable to farmers

4 The following section is mainly the work of Mr W.A.C. Mathieson, who from 1977 to the time of writing has been closely associated with the work of CGIAR. He was also Consultant to the UN Development Programme for 1976-81 and on the Executive Board of UNESCO for 1968-74.

156    *The Specialized Agencies and the United Nations*

which would make optimum use of its higher yield potential. The techniques they were using were developed from some used in Japan in the 1920s, the importance of which had gone unrecognised by the international community (including the FAO). The institution they founded was set up under Philippine legislation as an autonomous, non-profit, international entity governed by a self-perpetuating independent Board of Trustees of international composition. It was funded both as to capital and recurrent expenditure by the two Foundations, and land was granted by the host government. The scope of its concern was the rice growing areas of the developing world, and it was endowed by the government of the Philippines with privileges and immunities analagous to those available to a UN Agency. It recruited its international scientific staff and advanced their careers solely on the basis of merit.

The proved success of IRRI, scientifically, developmentally and institutionally, induced the two Foundations to develop a similar institution out of a Rockefeller Foundation co-operative programme with the government of Mexico for the advancement of wheat and maize, originally confined to Mexico but using internationally available germplasm. This programme had already produced spectacular results with semi-dwarf irrigated wheats. The International Maize and Wheat Improvement Centre (CIMMYT) was created in Mexico in 1966 on the same pattern as IRRI. Two other Centres followed, designed to bring research to bear on farming environments rather than on specific commodities: the International Centre for Tropical Agriculture (CIAT) in Colombia for the Latin American tropics (essentially beans and pastures) and the International Institute of Tropical Agriculture (IITA) in Nigeria (essentially pulses and root-crops). Both these Centres laid emphasis on the management of recalcitrant and fragile environments.

By this time the financial resources of the Foundations were becoming over-strained and suggestions were coming to them from various sources for the creation of similar institutions in other areas to tackle problems of tropical agriculture. A wider partnership had to be sought. A high-level meeting was organised by the President of the Rockefeller Foundation and the Rockefeller Conference Centre at Bellagio, Italy, in 1969, to examine the future of the international agricultural research institutes. The group assembled was remarkable for the power and authority exercised by those attending: McGeorge Bundy, President of the Ford Foundation; Robert McNamara, President of the World Bank; Paul Hoffman, Administrator of the UN Development Programme; Addeke Boerma, Director General of FAO; John Hannah, Administrator of USAID; Geoffrey Wilson, Permanent Secretary, British Ministry of

Overseas Development, and other luminaries. They came committed to agricultural development and with a strong conviction of the value of well-directed research. In summary, the group committed their respective institutions to support international organisations and foundations, with a mechanism for developing country representation, to be called the Consultative Group on International Agricultural Research (CGIAR). The World Bank would provide the Chairman and a small separate secretariat. A Technical Advisory Committee (TAC) of some fifteen eminent scientists would be created to advise the Group on global priorities, to be serviced by the FAO. The 'co-sponsors' of the Group, who would form a kind of steering committee, would be the FAO, the UNDP and the World Bank.

Since its first meeting in May 1971, with 23 members, four centres and aggregate expenditures of $20 million, the system had expanded by 1985 to 38 members supporting 13 centres with aggregate budgets approaching $200 million (current dollars). Pledges are made annually by the funding members directly to individual centres, with the Bank acting as a donor of last resort and operating a stabilisation fund. Individual donors (including several developing countries) know which activities their money is going to, and the TAC provides overall guidance on changing priorities and operates an evaluation service through quinquennial independent reviews of each centre's performance. The centres remain independent entities, each under its own international Board of Trustees as the ultimate determinant of its programme within the resources available. The result of all this effort is what is popularly called the 'Green Revolution', and it is noteworthy that it started as a private effort run by two American foundations. But its worldwide spread is due to an effort mounted and financially managed by the World Bank, mobilising resources within the Specialized Agencies and helped by governments, national and regional institutions and private resources.

The second comparable development came later, in 1977, with the establishment of the Special Programme of Research and Training on Tropical Diseases. The WHO acted as the executing Agency. Again, the World Bank and the UNDP joined with a Specialized Agency as co-sponsors of an activity outside the regular programme of that Agency. A joint Consultative Board (JCB) was set up, consisting of donor Agencies (Governments, international organisations, foundations and representatives of the WHO developing regions) and a Scientific and Technical Advisory Committee (STAC) of medical research scientists of world reputation to advise on priorities. No new institutions were established to conduct research. Scientific Working Groups (SWG) were created on each of the six endemic diseases selected for attack (malaria being the most important); sometimes several were created for various aspects of the control of each disease, which design and manage networks of co-operating scientists on a global basis. The SWGs assign resources to activities out of allocations made to them by the JCB on the advice of the STAC. There is also a Research Strengthening Group, which concerns itself with fortifying developing country resources in institutional capacity and trained manpower. The World Bank operates as fiscal agent for the programme, collecting contributions and accounting to donors.

Why have the CGIAR structures operated successfully in attracting resources and without much contention in doing their business? First, they have had clearly defined and limited objectives of incontestable importance, recognised as such by developed and developing countries alike. International staff of the operating units have been selected on merit without regard to geographic representation. Participants in the deliberative and advisory bodies are there only because they believe in the purpose and have no ancillary axes to grind. Representatives from governments are often from development assistance agencies who control the money available for the purpose in hand. They operate in the light of disinterested advice from the international scientific community. (By contrast, representation on the governing bodies of the FAO and the WHO is usually from Ministries of Agriculture and Health, who control no funds for development and may well be indifferent to any but domestic concerns.) In the CGIAR and the JCB no resolutions are tabled, no voting takes place, and national prestige is seldom at stake in any way. All decisions are by consensus and much depends on the skill and sensitivity of the Chairman. There are no assessed contributions, and donors can determine – or at least see – what happens to their money. Both enterprises have produced tangible results. It has been demonstrated that the rate of return on international agricultural research is the highest of any developmental expenditure. Health is more difficult for economists to handle and assess in their terms, but the alleviation of human debility can be observed. The presence of the World Bank gives donors confidence that financial management will be responsible and cost-effective. (Traditionally bankers are more trusted to handle money than a group of farmers or doctors.) What this demonstrates is that if a reputable objective can be fixed and a structure created within which committed people can pursue it, and small enough for all participants to know each other as individuals and persons not merely as 'representatives', there is a good chance of getting effective co-operation. You also need eminent and influential leadership to launch such an operation. This happened in both the examples quoted.

These operations have been successful in tapping the resources of information both inside and outside the Specialized Agencies and harnessing them to the financial resources available both inside and outside the UN System. And in the scientific advisory bodies and operational staffs, scientists from developing countries have been prominent and effective, freed from the constraints imposed by their national environments.

The aim of the Vienna Programme is somewhat different. Its principal purpose is probably to create what are called in the United Nations 'endogenous' research facilities – i.e. research facilities controlled and run by the developing countries themselves, more closely related – in theory, at least – to their own conditions and circumstances. The aim is laudable, but success in attaining it has been limited. This is partly because it has not set itself clear objectives, the attainment of which can be monitored and evaluated. Partly, too, it is because, rightly or wrongly, its methods have not so far inspired confidence among those who were called upon to provide the money.

# CHAPTER XIV

# THE I.M.F. AND THE I.B.R.D. AND ITS AFFILIATE INSTITUTIONS[1]

Most of the problems which have arisen in the UN System in general, and which have weakened the authority of and respect for multilateralism, have also been seen in the IMF and the World Bank. This is not surprising, of course, since these two institutions are Specialized Agencies within the System. Although their legal and financial arrangements and the management of their day-to-day operational responsibilities set them apart from other parts of the UN System, they exist nonetheless within the same international political environment. Thus, if the leading industrial powers become more inward-looking in their attitudes and policies, this has an impact on the IMF and the Bank, as it does on other institutions in the System. Similarly, if developing countries become disenchanted with multilateralism because it fails to address the global issues which they see as working against their interests, this attitude flows over into the two financial giants.

Yet despite this commonality of problems and concerns, the IMF and the World Bank are widely, if not generally, seen to be separate from the UN System. In fact most people would ask whether they are formally part of the System. Although the IMF and the Bank are specialized institutions under the Chapter and are both members of the ACC, and the answer to this question therefore has to be an unqualified 'yes', they have, both formally and in practice, only a tenuous relationship to the System as a whole. There is a formal reporting to ECOSOC each year, but the managements of the two institutions clearly believe that they are only answerable to their Boards of Governors, which meet once a year, and to the two full-time boards of executive directors which represent the Governors on the day-to-day approval of policies and operations. This attitude of their managements to the United Nations was most obviously seen in the 1960s when the Bank and the Fund noted the declarations of the General Assembly that lending to South Africa and to Portugal should cease, but refused to act on these declarations (although lending to both of them was phased out for other reasons).

---

1 This Chapter has been prepared by Mr Stanley Please, formerly Director of World Bank operational programmes in eastern Africa, senior advisor to the senior operational vice-president of the World Bank, and author of *The Hobbled Giant: Essays on the World Bank*, Boulder, Cdo: Westview Press, 1984.

## Weighted voting system

The most obvious and most important distinction between the Bretton Woods institutions and the UN System generally is the voting structure of the governors and the executive directors. An interesting point for speculation is what this voting structure might have looked like had the Bretton Woods meetings been held after the signing of the Charter rather than in 1944.

The weighted voting system of the Fund and the Bank gives overwhelming weight to the size of country quotas and shareholdings. The importance of this weighting has increased since 1944 due to the fact that quotas have increased, but the basic vote, which is identical for all countries, has remained unchanged and has therefore declined as a proportion of total votes. The pattern of weighting has varied considerably since the mid-1940s in order to reflect, in particular, the rise of west Germany and Japan to become industrial superpowers, and subsequently to reflect the financial strength to Saudi Arabia following the first oil-price increase in the 1970s. The periodic revisions of quotas have been central to the attempt to ensure that voting strength within the IMF and the Bank reflects the economic strength of members in the global economy, as well as to maximise incentives to contribute to capital increases. This economic strength is itself reflected in a formula which embodies *per capita* income and level of imports and exports both in total and as a proportion of total national income.

Not only has the weighted voting system ensured the dominance of the economic superpowers, but in addition there has been a widespread use of more complex special voting procedures, particularly on major issues of policy – e.g. admission of new members, increases in quotas – in order to provide a veto power. This veto power has been of significance to the United States and to the EEC, although it applies equally to the developing countries should they wish to employ it.

Although the rhetoric of developing countries at the United Nations and elsewhere persistently denounces the weighted voting system of the IMF and the Bank, the reality of economic power has to be recognised in financial matters just as the reality of political-military power is recognised in the veto powers of the Security Council. This reality of economic power is particularly recognised by the ministers of finance and planning and central bank governors who comprise the Boards of Governors of the Fund and the Bank. Their recognition can be contrasted with the attitudes of ministers of foreign affairs and their representatives in the United Nations. The contrast is most glaring when negotiations for the replenishment of the resources of IDA are underway. While developing country economic ministers laud the virtues of the World Bank in general and IDA in particular, and are widely mobilized to argue the case for a high IDA replenishment before governments and legislators of developed countries, foreign ministers of developing countries are frequently and simultaneously denouncing the Bank as a tool of colonialism, and in other similar ways, in the United Nations. Needless to say, these 'stabs in the back' do not pass unnoticed by the opponents of IDA in the developed world (especially in the United States).

While the reality of economic power, reflected particularly in the weighted voting system, can be – and has to be – accepted by developing countries, the substance and style of the use of this power can vary in order to make this acceptance more or less 'grudging'. Considerable dismay was caused, not only among developing countries but also in some developed countries, by the hardening of attitude under the Reagan Administration and the arrogant manner in which the US government has used and even flaunted its power – with full encouragement from the US Congress and often supported by the British, West German and Japanese governments.

For instance, in the absence of more idealistic schemes for replenishing IDA from autonomous revenue sources such as an SDR-link or a tax on arms trading, the reality is accepted that donors will determine the level of the three-year replenishment; and that it is unrealistic to expect donors to contribute to a replenishment determined by simple majority vote in which developing countries have the power but developed countries have the money. The seventh replenishment of IDA in 1985 began with a figure of $16 billion presented by the Bank, but this was soon reduced to $12 billion. The latter was the figure acceptable to most donors and would have kept the real flow of IDA roughly unchanged in real terms. However, the United States proposed a $9 billion replenishment and was unwilling to be persuaded even by other donors to raise this figure to $12 billion or thereabouts. It is the degree of arrogance of the Reagan Administration and its unwillingness to demonstrate any spirit of co-operation on such matters, even with its close allies, that has alarmed its friends and many governments in the richer as well as the poorer countries of the world.

The arrogance shows up in the Bank and the Fund where there has been a considerable weakening of the collegial atmosphere among executive directors which had prevailed before. It could be argued that this collegiality was in any case artificial and in particular that executive directors of developing countries were too prone to accept the realities of the weighted voting system and of economic power in general, rather than resisting these realities. However, by means of quiet persuasion they could often modify the positions of developed countries and avoid outright confrontation. Executive directors recognised more strongly then that they had a responsibility not only to the governments they represented but also to the IMF and the Bank. This collegial spirit has been eroded owing to the overbearing style and narrow national focus of the United States in the two institutions. This is particularly unfortunate because the voices of more moderate opinion on the weighted voting system were beginning to be heard. These voices have now been drowned. This more moderate opinion was best expressed in the 1983 Report of the Study Group appointed by the Finance Ministers of the Commonwealth countries and chaired by Professor G. Helleiner, entitled *Towards a New Bretton Woods: Challenges for the World Financial and Trading System*.[2] This Report recognized that, on matters of broad policy, a weighted voting system is the only acceptable and realistic system. This is so particularly when it is a matter of size of quotas, SDR allocations, IDA replenishment, IBRD capital increases and so on. However, the Report argued that when day-to-day operational matters are being determined, the weighted voting system is less relevant. The Report focused in this respect particularly on the question of the appropriate policies and programmes which countries should be following in order to remain eligible for funding – i.e. the question of conditionality. This recommendation could be extended to the question of whether certain countries should be eligible for funding at all – as in the notoriously controversial cases of Vietnam and Ethiopia.

## Executive Heads

The President of the Bank and the Managing Director of the IMF are appointed for five-year terms and have typically been reappointed for second and sometimes subsequent terms. They have the dual responsibilities of managing the staff and operations of the two organisations and acting as Chairmen of the two Boards of executive directors which represent the member governments. Therefore both their formal terms of appointment and their substantive responsibilities give them very considerable power. They are in this respect very similar to the Executive Heads of other Specialized Agencies – the so-called 'feudal barons'.

In other respects, the President and Managing-Director are markedly different from the Agency Heads. To begin with they are

2 Published by the Commonwealth Secretariat, London.

by convention nationals of the United States in the case of the President of the Bank, and of a European country in the case of the Managing-Director of the Fund. In the case of the Bank's President, in particular, the appointment is almost one of patronage. It certainly carries the initial support of the US government, although a gulf increasingly developed between it and Robert McNamara,[3] and the same happened with A.W. Clausen.[4] Nevertheless, whatever their reservations about particular aspects of Bank and IMF policies being pursued by the President and the Managing Director, developed countries generally have the confidence of knowing that the institutions are being led by people from the group of countries providing most of the money. This is, however, a 'tight-rope' act. On the one hand, the President and Managing Director must not lose the confidence of the rich countries who provide them with the money to help the poorer countries; this is most obvious in the case of the Bank, whereas the IMF assists richer countries as well although since the mid-1970s, with the exception of Britain in 1976, its operations have been limited to developing countries. At the same time, both institutions – again, this is especially true of the Bank – have to speak up for the developing countries when the rich countries of the world are pursuing policies which are inimical to their growth – e.g. industrial protection policies (even though this might trespass on GATT preserves, EEC agricultural policies, high interest rates etc). McNamara moved from his original position of being regarded with suspicion by most developing countries to being lauded by them as their most outspoken and effective advocate.

The power of the chief executives of the IMF and the Bank clearly comes in the first place from the volume of resources which they control – the Bank has $12 billion of commitments per year and the Fund about half this amount in the 1980s. But their power also comes from the fact that they influence decisions by other financial institutions – commercial banks, bilateral donors and so on. This is sometimes through formal co-financing activities but more generally through informal understandings agreed to at consultative groups, meetings of creditors and so on. But the power of the chief executives comes, secondly, from the combination of this money with the technical work which they command. This leads on to the whole question of the quality of the IMF and Bank staffs and the quality and usefulness of their analytical work – i.e. the non-financial activities of the two institutions.

3  President of the IBRD, 1968–81.
4  President of the IBRD, 1981–6.

## IMF and World Bank non-financial activities

Although the IMF and the Bank are financial institutions, it is probably in their non-financial activities that they have developed their strongest comparative advantage. Commercial banks, bilateral aid agencies, regional banks, OPEC agencies, the EEC and so on can provide money to the developing world, but none of these institutions can provide the same wide range or high quality of non-financial activities. These activities represent all stages of the project-cycle including pre-appraisal and ex-post evaluations; analytical and programme formulation work at the sectoral level, of which the World Bank/UNDP Energy Assessment and Implementation Studies are the most well known; work at the national level on macro-financial/balance of payments issues (IMF and World Bank) and on growth/developmental/poverty alleviation issues, which are regularly made available to countries and to the development community in the form of country economic reports; work on region-wide issues of which the Bank's three reports since 1981 on Sub-Saharan Africa are the most obvious example; and finally, work at the global level (e.g. the IMF's Annual Economic Prospects and the World Bank's Annual World Development Report).

Clearly the analytical work in these areas has many shortcomings; moreover, it is controversial. Nevertheless, whatever its shortcomings, these non-financial activities – and particularly those of the Bank – have acquired a high reputation. Even the Bank's critics – both official and non-official (e.g. academics) – will agree, in personal conversations if not in public utterances and papers, that the Bank's project, sectoral, national, regional and global work is unique in terms of its combination of operational and policy relevance, analytical quality, and willingness to state issues sharply rather than blandly. In all these respects the Bank's non-financial work stands out in marked contrast to that of almost all other parts of the United Nations.

Why is this? It has arisen partly from the quality of the leadership of the Bank and the IMF; partly from the semi-autonomous position of the two institutions, particularly their 'distance' from day-to-day political control and interference (at times indeed they act like technocracies out of control); and partly from the quality of their staffs. It is difficult to estimate how important this latter factor is and, if it is important, whether the absence of national quotas in staff selection has been critical in determining staff quality. Are the staff of the Bank and Fund 'better' than in the United Nations generally, or is it simply that staff of the same average ability are able to perform at a higher level in the Bank and the Fund because of a more supportive and congenial 'atmosphere' for undertaking serious analytical and technical work? Does the 'arrogance' of the two institutions generate self-confidence and high morale at the level of the individual staff member, resulting in better performance? These questions are critical but difficult to answer. Although national quotas do not apply to staff selection in the Bank and the Fund, both affirmative action programmes in respect of regional groups (e.g. Africans) and ceilings on the recruitment of certain nationals (e.g. those of the United States and the United Kingdom) have moved them in this direction. Bank and Fund managements assert that this has been achieved without any lowering of standards of entry, and hitherto there has been no reason to doubt this assertion.

# CHAPTER XV

# THE UN DEVELOPMENT PROGRAMME: EXPERIENCES OF THE DECADE 1975–1985

We have already referred many times to the UN Development Programme (UNDP). Chapter VII deals with it as a source of funds to the Specialized Agencies, while Chapters IV and IX discuss its role as an instrument for ensuring a better co-ordination of Agency activities and as a supervisor of technical assistance in the field. Since the publication of the Jackson Report in 1969, very little about the UNDP has appeared in the press or learned periodicals. Nevertheless, acquaintance with its policies and problems is as necessary as ever to understanding how the UN System works and the possibilities of reform.

It is not possible here to write a detailed history of the UNDP, or to give a full expose of all its financial and administrative policies since 1970.[1] What will be attempted below is a brief examination of the principal problems encountered by the UNDP since the Jackson Report, why these have occurred, what solutions have been worked out to meet them and what may be the lessons for the future. This will be done against the background of what was said in Chapter VII about the Non-assessed Voluntary Expenditure of the UN Agencies and the scale of Technical Assistance Expenditure passing through the UN System, especially the table on page 90.

## *The UNDP's declining share in financing UN technical assistance programmes*

One of the main recommendations in the Jackson Report – and one which apparently received the endorsement of donors and recipients in the General Assembly (although outside there were doubters) – was that in future the UNDP should become the principal channel for technical assistance funds passing through the

---

1 Those seeking more information on the operations of the UNDP from year to year are recommended to consult the annual report of the administrator of the UNDP to his Governing Council on the UN System – Regular and Extrabudgetary Technical Co-operation Expenditures. The references for the five years up to the time of writing are DP/1985/65, DP/1984/66, DP/1983/57, DP/1982/63 and DP545 for 1981. The information in these reports on the sources of funds available to the UN System and their distribution by sectors has become much clearer in recent years.

UN System. In 1968, the year before Jackson reported, UNDP funds represented some 65% of the total; by 1980, however, they had sunk to some 39%, admittedly of a larger total. The Table on page 90 shows that over the years 1981-4, UNDP central resources and UNDP-administered resources averaged some 47% of the total. Most of these funds came from the principal donor countries represented on the Development Assistance Committee (DAC) of the OECD who had endorsed the Jackson recommendations; but the DAC statistics in the table below show how, nevertheless, their contributions to UNDP declined as a percentage of their total multilateral expenditure (i.e. from 13.5 to 6.8%) in the post-Jackson years.

Why, despite the donor governments' acceptance of the Jackson recommendations in 1970, has the trend been in the opposite direction? Part of the reason lies in the lack of consistent policy among all governments – donor and recipient alike – in dealing with the UN System. They claimed, in the discussions on Jackson, that they wanted a system of technical co-operation, operated through the United Nations and centrally financed. Their subsequent actions belie the claim. There are various reasons why in practice their policy changed. The first is that since 1970 the UN System has been fractionalised even more than it was previously by an increase in the number of Specialized Agencies, Special Funds, Committees and Programmes, with a corresponding increase in the number of governing bodies. This has greatly complicated the task even of

## TOTAL MULTILATERAL FUNDS FROM O.E.C.D. DONORS, 1971-84

|  | Amounts of contributions to individual agencies (US$ millions) | | | | Percentages of these contributions to total multi-lateral funds | | | |
|  | 1971-2* | 1977-8* | 1983 | 1984 | 1971-2 | 1977-8 | 1983 | 1984 |
|---|---|---|---|---|---|---|---|---|
| UNDP | 258 | 506 | 525 | 612 | 13.5 | 8.1 | 7.6 | 6.8 |
| UNICEF | 49 | 102 | 135 | 172 | 2.6 | 1.6 | 2.0 | 1.9 |
| UNRWA | 53 | 97 | 109 | 125 | 2.8 | 1.5 | 1.6 | 1.4 |
| WFP | 55 | 312 | 444 | 538 | 2.9 | 5.0 | 6.5 | 6.0 |
| UNHCR | 12 | 29 | 192 | 230 | 0.6 | 0.5 | 2.8 | 2.6 |
| UNFPA | – | 64 | 113 | 135 | – | 1.0 | 1.6 | 1.5 |
| Other UN | 108 | 303 | 397 | 484 | 5.6 | 4.8 | 5.8 | 5.4 |

* Averages.

*Source:* Table IV-1 of OECD Report, *'Twenty-five Years of Development Co-operation – A Review'*, 1985.

*Note:* This table shows payments by DAC governments to the multilateral funds. The table on page 90 shows payments by the funds to recipients.

those governments who genuinely wished to pursue a consistent line across the board in dealing with these organisations. It has become easier than ever for the delegates to the governing bodies to pursue their own line, representing their own institutional interest or speciality regardless of their government's declared policy on the wider issues. The politics of inter-Agency rivalry which have already been referred to then take over.

There is another contributory cause which is seldom referred to. It is part of the UNDP philosophy that it should rely on the recipient government's decision about its economic and social priorities in deciding the allocation of the technical assistance funds allocated to individual countries. This does not mean that the UNDP accepts uncritically every government proposal, but simply that it is not tempted to give more weight to some extraneous interest in the way that bilateral donors do. In practice donor governments, though repeatedly maintaining that choice of priorities is the prerogative of a recipient government, take other factors into account, such as matters of commercial or political interest to the donor rather than of advantage to the recipient. As a result, donor governments have themselves admitted that although they have every confidence in the UNDP as a channel for their multilateral technical assistance funds, they nevertheless do not like to see the resources they provide lost in the general pool of multilateral funds, where they can have little say in how the money is used and get little credit for their contribution. This latter factor in particular has led some donors to respond favourably to appeals from some Agencies for trust fund allocations for particular sectors or projects, especially where donors believe that UNDP funds are not likely to reach those sectors or countries to which they attach priority. In short, one factor leading to the decline in the UNDP's share has been that donors, when put to the test, were not wholeheartedly in favour of using the UNDP as the principal channel for their multilateral technical assistance funds because they were not wholeheartedly in favour of multilateralism.

There has been another important element, namely that the size of the multilateral cake has been declining in real terms at the very moment when the number of potential consumers (Funds, Agencies and Programmes) has been increasing. Furthermore, several major donors, while they have become increasingly sceptical about the value of aid in general, have become especially sceptical over the merits of multilateral aid. Some aspects of this question have been examined earlier, but one additional element is the declining public support for multilateral aid for *development* purposes. This does not capture the popular imagination as easily as multilateral relief aid, a point well taken by Bob Geldof and his supporters in the wake of the African famine crisis of 1985.

## UNDP direct financing and execution of technical assistance projects

One of the important features of the Jackson recommendations was that not only should the UNDP become the prime channel for multilateral technical assistance, but also that it should use the UN Specialized Agencies as its main executing agents on its projects. The difficulties which have arisen since Jackson, both in the quality of some of the technical assistance provided through the Agencies and in the lack of success in persuading Agencies to co-operate in the execution of country development programmes, have led to suggestions that the UNDP should do more in executing projects direct, rather than through the Specialized Agencies.

The UNDP indeed has an office for this very purpose, established since the time of Jackson: the Office for Project Execution (OPE). During the 1980s the OPE used 5–7% of the UNDP's funds in direct project execution. From the outset there has been strong opposition from the Specialized Agencies to OPE's activities, since the Agencies argue that it deprives them of their legitimate business (to say nothing of the 13% administrative expenses which they take on all UNDP projects executed by them). They even use the activities of the OPE as a justification for seeking Trust Funds on their own account. Of course, by turning themselves into both funding and executing institutions in this way, the Specialized Agencies are guilty of the very practice of which they complain in the UNDP. Moreover, the UNDP has never pretended that it could offer a complete alternative to the Agencies' technical co-operation services.

In consequence, although the OPE's activities have been a modest part of the UNDP's total programme, they have excited more than their share of criticism from the Agencies. Nevertheless, the experience of the OPE has provided some useful lessons on the delivery of technical assistance through UN channels. For one thing, in about 90% of its projects, the OPE uses the sub-contract approach through competitive bidding with consulting firms and specialist institutions. This contrasts with the usual Specialized Agency procedure, which is to use the individual recruitment of experts as their primary method of project implementation, with sub-contracting used only in about 10 or 20% of their projects (varying with the Agency). The reason for this is alleged by the Agencies to be that they prefer to use technical headquarters staff to supervise and monitor field personnel recruited individually.

Experience shows that the OPE method is often more successful in delivering services quickly and with higher expertise, though possibly less successful in training local 'counterpart' staff to take over. Moreover, OPE sub-contracts specify precisely the technical requirements and the work to be performed, with detailed tasks and objectives. This makes them much easier to monitor and evaluate. There is much less need for extending project implementation time, which frequently happens with Agency projects (and even worse with Programmes), and which causes cost over-runs and waste of resources. On the other hand, it is fair to say that the OPE concentrates its executing activities on projects which would be especially suitable for sub-contracting.

Another technique used by the OPE has been valuable to recipient governments. On technical projects, it has made its services available to governments to assist them in executing suitable UNDP-funded projects, with the governments rather than the UNDP retaining responsibility for management and supervision, including the normal supervision of sub-contractors. These procedures have not been in operation long enough for general conclusions to be drawn; in any case, results must depend almost as much on the competence of the government as on the OPE's techniques. The Specialized Agencies also arrange for government management and execution of projects, although in practice they seem less enthusiastic about these methods. But given the right circumstances and the right kind of project, this looks likely to be a valuable technique, having the advantage of backing up the indigenous resources of governments; and the number of projects handled in this way must continue to increase.

In the face of Agency criticism of the OPE, the UNDP has steadfastly maintained that not only is it valuable in itself but that the UNDP needs to experiment with new methods of executing technical assistance projects so that recipients should have as many choices as possible. Moreover, in the UNDP's view, the OPE has demonstrated the value of using sub-contractors in the right circumstances as a quicker and marginally cheaper variant of the usual method. Most Agencies, however, still regard the OPE as trespassing on their preserves. They maintain that the UNDP's sole function should be to provide funds and not to execute projects itself. They also argue that the UNDP lacks what is known in the jargon of the multilateral business as 'backstopping capacity', i.e. access to the technical knowledge to appraise the merits of a project and to monitor its execution adequately. The UNDP recognises that the Agencies possess a large fund of knowledge and technical expertise and that the UNDP must so conduct its operations as to make this expertise available to developing countries. In consequence the vast bulk of UNDP projects – at least 90% of the total – will continue to be executed by the Agencies. It is generally accepted that this is as it should be.

## Agency salesmanship

As has already been pointed out, Agency Salesmanship was one of the principal targets of the Jackson Report, and more than fifteen years later it is still very much with us. Every UNDP Resident Representative has his private catalogue of 'atrocity stories' of Agency salesmen persuading sectoral ministries to sponsor the submission of projects to UNDP regardless of their impact on their own government's stated development objectives. Indeed, because of the increase in the number of funds and Agencies, competition is probably fiercer today than ever before, and so is Agency pressure on governments. Agency field offices are more numerous, and they all compete in urging recipient governments to favour one sector rather than another. Moreover, as circumstances change and new problems become paramount, the Agencies show great ingenuity in advertising their wares on any bandwagon which may start rolling. Thus when rural health became (rightly) one of the fashionable sectors for development in Africa, the ITU – normally one of the more responsible Agencies – saw nothing incongruous in circulating posters in Africa proclaiming 'International Communications for Rural Health Week.'[2]

Nevertheless, many Resident Representatives do claim to have had some success in persuading the recipient governments to put Agency proposals into the perspective of the priorities in their development plans. This process has been helped where the country's development plans are themselves the work of UNDP personnel or UNDP-funded consultants. However, the UNDP country policy guidelines issued to Resident Representatives and governments in December 1985 made it plain that the intention was not only to ensure that recipient government priorities are properly respected but also that the Agencies are given a proper say in each country's

2  A variant of this phenomenon was seen in the British bilateral programme in the 1970s when 'Rural Development' became the fashionable policy. Some argued that constructing airports should be classed as 'rural development' because airports are often built in green fields. People who make their living constructing airports can, easily and genuinely, come to believe that the best way to end rural poverty is to bury the world under concrete and winking lights. Sectoral enthusiasms of this kind are useful up to a point, but not when they sacrifice a country's development priorities in favour of building up an Agency's bureaucratic empire.

programming process when sectoral issues are discussed. If this procedure can be made to work, it ought to bring with it better discipline and greater inter-Agency co-ordination, since the Agencies will be forced to judge their own sectoral proposals in the context of the government's priorities.

Moreover, the UNDP has experimented with a number of devices directed to the same end, or participated in devices run by others. Thus they have led Needs Assessment Missions and organised Round Tables for the poorer countries or taken their full part in the Consultative Groups run by the World Bank.[3] In December 1985[4] the Project Development Facility (PDF) was announced, its purpose being to 'finance field missions of specialized consultants and/or UNDP technical staff *prior* to the approval of projects' in cases of 'complex, innovative or controversial projects, especially those where difficult technical issues arise'. One aim of the PDF facility is to give governments a second opinion on difficult projects at the project identification stage. For that reason it has already encountered some opposition from the Agencies, which regard it as one more attempt to poach on their preserves. The UNDP's intention, however, is to give governments another option and to ensure to donors and recipients alike a better chance of choosing the best project and executing it in the most cost-effective way.

Indeed, although anecdotal evidence – supported to some extent by JIU reports and other studies – suggests that Agency salesmanship is as persistent as ever, there are signs of improvement, thanks largely to the whole planning process having improved since the 1970s in many government machines (a movement in which UNDP technical assistance has played an important role). Central co-ordinating bodies in many governments are being strengthened, not least by the fact that they are the bodies with which the UNDP Resident Representatives deal directly.

## The UNDP's financial management since Jackson

The problems in financial management which the UNDP has faced since Jackson may offer useful lessons for the future. The conditions on which the UNDP is forced to manage its affairs would be totally unacceptable to any of the world's great business houses as a foundation for commercial operations. The UNDP has faced three

3  For a brief discussion of the co-ordination issue and much factual information see pp. 200–9 of the OECD Report *25 Years of Development Co-operation* (Nov. 1985).
4  There is no reference number on this document, but it was circulated to Agencies and Governments on 4 Dec. 1985.

main difficulties. The first is that although, ever since the consensus in 1970 on Jackson, the donor countries have claimed to have every confidence in the UNDP as a central funding instrument for technical assistance throughout the UN System, in practice their actions have not matched their words. The second is that donors' financial contributions have often not matched the expectations which their encouraging promises originally aroused. Finally, there has been the general financial uncertainty of the early 1980s, when the future dollar value of pledges in other currencies was hard to determine; this made forward planning of expenditure very difficult. This was accompanied by a decline in the proportion of multilateral expenditures among most donors in the 1980s after a rapid expansion in the 1970s.[5]

Dealing first with donor practices on funding UN technical assistance, one problem associated with all forms of multilateral funding is that of 'burden-sharing'. For a variety of reasons, some donors have always been more willing than others to see their funds disbursed by international organisations. Sometimes this springs from a genuine belief in the virtues of internationalism, sometimes it is due to the donor not having the administrative machinery or the specialised knowledge to run aid programmes bilaterally in developing countries. These factors have produced a big discrepancy in the percentage of aid funds which each donor is prepared to spend through multilateral channels. For example, in 1984 France spent only 9.4% of its Official Development Assistance multilaterally compared with Japan's 35.5%, Britain's 28.9% and West Germany's 19.6% (these figures exclude the amounts spent through the EEC). Because of these differences in donor performance, governments which in principle support multilateral funding have in practice been reluctant to see their contributions disappear into a common fund such as the UNDP for which they can get no credit and whose policies they cannot influence commensurately with their contribution. Irrational factors have also influenced the outcome: some donors show preferences for some multilateral funds rather than others, which may be due to no more than the influence of some Agency head on the minister who controls the finances from which the contributions are made.[6]

The results are shown statistically in the table on page 168.

5  As a percentage of their ODA, DAC donors' contributions to multilateral agencies increased from 13.4% in 1965 to 24.3% in 1974. This increased to 26.9% by 1983, but this was due to increases from Canada and Norway. The rest declined (see Table IV-3 of OECD Report on *25 Years of Development Co-operation*).
6  On this issue see pp. 146–8 of the OECD Report on *25 Years of Development Co-operation*, 1985.

One has been the steady increase in expenditures financed from Agency Regular Budgets from 1980–3. Another has been that in every year except 1982, Agency Regular Budgets and extra-budgetary resources combined have exceeded the UNDP's resources. Even of the funds under the UNDP's control, the amount of Special Funds administered by the UNDP has grown from 2% to nearly 6% of the total. Although this is contrary both to Jackson's principles and to the UNDP's best interests (which in the long term lie in the steady growth of core resources), the UNDP has had to make the best of it. For this purpose they have developed a number of what are known in the United Nations as 'modalities' to try to match donor priorities with recipient needs. They have set up, and manage, a number of Trust Funds which, apart from some accounting complications, involve much the same procedures as the other main device used – that of cost sharing (under which projects are not wholly funded by the UNDP but executed jointly with other donors). In 1986 the UNDP introduced a new device known as Management Services Contracts which will permit the UNDP to help even *bilateral* programmes by using its field office capacity for a percentage of the cost. By these compromises the UNDP has managed to acquire additional funds at a time when its central funding role was being reduced. This has been done at the cost of some administrative complications but without detriment to the UNDP's objectivity and sectoral impartiality. The UNDP has also retained its capacity to influence donors to respect the wishes and priorities of the recipients.

Account must also be taken of the fact that over the period 1975 to 1985 the UNDP has gone through two periods of financial difficulty in both of which its credibility with recipients has been damaged. Both have stemmed in part from the UNDP's inherent difficulty in managing its programmes – the unpredictability of its resource levels. Even if the UNDP manages to predict accurately what donors will pledge at their annual conference, there is no guarantee that they will deliver – especially in the case of the biggest donor of all, the United States. Indeed, during the 1980s the unpredictability has been twofold. It has not been known either how much donors would contribute in terms of their national currencies or how much those contributions would be worth once the currencies came to be used. Indeed, the period 1975–85 saw two crisis periods, each of a different origin. The first, in 1975–7, was a liquidity crisis, due in varying degrees to a shortfall of $42 million on the expected US contribution, an increase of $54 million in the programme over a forecast made early in 1975, debts outstanding to UNDP of some $72 million, and inadequate reserves (amounting to only $150 million). In so far as these difficulties were created by management shortcomings, it is understood that they have been put right, although the inherent difficulty remains of managing a programme in which the value and timing of incoming contributions is unpredictable, while project commitments have to be made for a number of years ahead.

The problems of the 1980s are due essentially to the fact that donor governments have not lived up to the expectations of fixed percentage increases raised by their own delegates to the UNDP Governing Council. The Governing Council in 1980 had led both the UNDP and recipient governments to expect that a growth of resources of 14% a year would be acceptable. Resolutions to that effect had been adopted by 'consensus'. In fact, however, a number of governments had no intention whatever of acting on such a resolution. Although this time, through careful management, in 1982 and 1983 there was no liquidity crisis, the UNDP's credibility with recipients was seriously damaged. Eventually the Indicative Planning Figure[7] announced to governments on the basis of a 14% growth rate had to be considerably reduced – to about 55% of the figure originally fixed.

## The UNDP's relations with the IBRD and the IMF

The Bretton Woods institutions – especially the IBRD and the IMF – have always been regarded, both by outsiders and by themselves, as the aristocrats of the UN System. Indeed they have on occasion tried to distance themselves from it (the IMF still tries to do so). Relations between them and the UNDP have sometimes been strained, not least because the UNDP by the nature of its business is believed to be more sympathetic to the developing countries' aspirations than are either the IBRD or the IMF. Nevertheless, from the outset Jackson, Paul Hoffman[8] and Robert McNamara all saw the activities of the UNDP and those of the IBRD as complementary, on the basis that the latter would supply the capital while the former supplied the technical assistance to go with it and (it was hoped) paid for the feasibility studies on which the capital investment would be based. This happy division of labour when put to the test was some-

7  The IPF is a target figure which the UNDP gives to each recipient government as a basis for that government's preparation of its programme plan for four years ahead. It was introduced post-Jackson as an alternative to the 'full funding' procedures which had operated before and in accordance with which funds had to be available for the whole cost of a project before it could be started. The IPF procedure has always had many critics, who in particular maintain that it encourages Agencies and governments to spend beyond the resources available.
8  Head of the UNDP, 1966–72. Formerly an Administrator of the Marshall Plan.

times found to have underestimated the differences in approach between an institution primarily looking for 'bankable' projects and one looking more to an improvement in the absorptive capacity of developing countries through an improvement in technical skills.

## The UNDP and the sectoral approach

It was one of Jackson's tenets, to which many have paid lip-service since, that, to be effective, technical co-operation should not be planned and operated on a purely sectoral unintegrated basis. This is still a major source of conflict between the Agencies and the UNDP. The Agencies by their very nature are bound to put sectoral interests first, while the UNDP is equally bound to encourage recipient governments to adopt an integrated approach. Moreover, through the influence of its Resident Representatives as well as through the power of the purse, the UNDP can be in a good position to ensure that its advice carries weight. As against this, the Agencies are the source of sectoral expertise, whereas the UNDP has none 'in house'; so this is a conflict in which there are weapons on both sides. In practice, many projects are not amenable to sectoral treatment. Many, especially in such areas as rural development, demand an integrated approach; moreover, even a sectorally well balanced pro- gramme must have its size adjusted to the limited available resources – especially resources in trained people and funds, both of which are scarce, most of all in the poorest countries. The UNDP, through the activities of its representatives in the field, is in a strong position to stimulate and organise an integrated approach. What it needs is more encouragement from donors and stronger support from recipients.

However, it would be fair to say that over the years, the relations between the IBRD and the UNDP have grown both more complex and more cordial, especially since 1982. The IBRD has always been a valuable executing Agency for the UNDP. More recently, UNDP Resident Representatives have become more closely involved in the IBRD's Consultative Groups in identifying the entire technical assistance needs of particular countries on behalf of the UN System as a whole. In the parallel Round Table process which is organized for the poorest countries, where the UNDP has always had a primary role, the UNDP has gone out of its way to involve the IBRD more and more – with considerable success. In addition, in 1985 the UNDP, in conjunction with the IBRD, conducted a technical assess- ment co-operation mission in Somalia and may undertake similar missions elsewhere in Africa (these are in addition to the National Assessments of Technical Co-operation and Programmes which the

UNDP is already conducting in Africa). The UNDP, through its Office for Project Execution (OPE) also offers management services for Bank-funded technical assistance projects. There are training programmes for Bank staff at UNDP headquarters, and UNDP staff participate in IBRD training courses in Washington. There are also exchanges of staff at working level. Working relationships in the field between the staffs of the two organisations are said to be excellent. In short, both organisations seem to be taking a more positive approach to each other's activities than in the past. Even so, the IBRD is still at pains to emphasise its distinctiveness from the UNDP; for example, it appoints its own representatives in developing countries and would not ask the UNDP Resident Representative or Co-ordinator to act on its behalf (although it keeps him informed of its activities).

Unfortunately, relationships with the IMF are much more 'at arm's length'. IMF missions to developing countries seldom make contact with UNDP field representatives; this may well suit the UNDP in practice, since, in the eyes of developing countries, too close a contact with IMF representatives could compromise it.

## Resident Representatives and Resident Co-ordinators

In January 1986, the UNDP maintained 115 Field Offices looking after programmes in 150 countries. The Resident Representatives are the backbone of the UNDP. Their reputation with donors and recipients alike is high, and their importance and that of their offices has grown steadily over the years. Recipient governments respect them for their impartial advice, sought and often given on a daily basis. They have an unparallelled knowledge not only of the UNDP's own operations but also of where else to seek funds and expert advice.

Resident Co-ordinators, where they have been appointed by the UN Secretary-General, are in effect Resident Representatives backed by the authority of the UN General Assembly. Following the Restructuring Resolution of 1977, the General Assembly determined that there should be a single official responsible for the co-ordination of all UN System activities at country level and that this should normally be the UNDP Resident Representative. The first Co-ordinators were appointed in 1981. The arrangements have proved their value. Resident Co-ordinators have provided a better basis for collaboration between both bilateral and multilateral donors; they have been able to organise effective follow-ups to the Round Table process; their role as co-ordinators in emergency situations has been effective; and they have given valuable assistance to all governments in mobilising fresh sources of technical assistance. Donors and recipients have responded positively to their appointment, as have most other multilateral aid donors and the Non-Governmental Organizations. By all accounts, however, the same cannot be said of some of the Agencies from whose representatives UNDP officials often find it harder to secure co-operation than they do from non-members of the UN 'family'.

The picture which emerges more than fifteen years after Jackson is one in which the reforms he prescribed have in several important respects not been implemented. A large part of the technical assistance funds channelled by the UN System is not going through the UNDP. Agency salesmanship may be as bad as ever, and so is Agency resistance to attempts at an integrated approach to country development programmes. Nevertheless in practice, despite appearances to the contrary, progress is slowly being made in securing a more effective collaboration between all involved in the development process. The prestige of UNDP Resident Representatives has risen and so has their experience. Their influence over many developing country governments is growing, and with it has come an increase in the determination of those governments to impose their own pattern of priorities even on some of the more obdurate of the Agencies. Experience has shown that the principles underlying the Jackson reforms were mainly correct.

The setbacks in the implementation of the principles have led some to contemplate more drastic solutions, such as abolishing the technical assistance role of the Agencies altogether and confining them to one of information-gathering and standard-setting. This is both unrealistic and undesirable: unrealistic because the Agencies would never stand for it, and undesirable because it might be difficult in any other way to harness for development purposes the considerable bodies of knowledge and expertise that the Agencies have in their specialist fields. Moreover, to continue to give staff field experience in technical assistance programmes is an important way both of keeping their knowledge up to date and of testing its relevance to the real world.

The way ahead is to improve the ability of the UNDP – and the resources available to it – to assist governments to impose the necessary discipline on the Agencies whose knowledge and expertise they all need. This of course is a long way from the ideas in the Jackson Capacity Study, which envisaged fusing all the funding organizations (UNDP, UNFPA, WFP etc.) into a single UN Development Authority which would use the Agencies as contractors in conjunction – or sometimes in competition – with outside consultants and contractors, This would still be the ideal solution if the level of expertise available to the UNDP to manage development funds were to match that of the World Bank, and if the contributors to these funds would tolerate this degree of centralisation. In the actual circumstances, however, patient improvement of co-ordination on the ground is the best way to progress.

# CHAPTER XVI

# THE BERTRAND REPORT

While this study was being prepared, a report was published in Geneva by the Joint Inspection Unit (JIU) of the United Nations, which is highly relevant to the subject. It is entitled *Some Reflections on Reform of the United Nations*.[1] Its importance arises not simply from its being wide-ranging in scope and lucidly written, but also from the fact that its author Maurice Bertrand was for many years a member of the JIU. We have already referred several times to M. Bertrand's work as the instigator of programme budgetting in the UN System. As he rightly points out in the introduction to his report, the JIU is normally concerned with partial reforms in specific areas of the UN and its System. However his 1985 *Reflections* go much further than this and are concerned with examining 'a radical reform of the actual framework of the institutions or of the System as a whole' (Foreword, p. 1), and it is important that we both look at M. Bertrand's analysis in so far as it relates to our present subject matter, and discuss his conclusions.

M. Bertrand begins by stating that 'criticism alleging mismanagement of the UN and some of the organisations of the UN System has now reached the status of a political phenomenon.' Although much of it comes from the developed countries (both market economy and Socialist) and manifests itself mainly by demands for budgetary stringency or threats of withdrawal, members of the Group of 77 have also raised the question of 'ways and means of escaping from the cul-de-sac' following the failure of global negotiations on the New International Economic Order. M. Bertrand makes the valid point, however, that the resulting frustration of both rich and poor countries is directed as much at UN performance in political and disarmament matters as in the economic and social sphere, with which we are concerned here. All are agreed, however, that 'it is as if North and South were both seeking a new type of dialogue.'

'The logical conclusion of this type of frustration', M. Bertrand argues, 'is of course the idea of reform.' But he admits that there is widespread scepticism on this subject, based on the limited success

1 Published as JIU/REP/85/9. Those interested in M. Bertrand's views should also see JIU/REP/84/7 of 1984 entitled *Reporting to the Economic and Social Council*, and his book *Refaire l'Onu! Un programme pour la paix*, Geneva: Editions Zoë, 1986. After this Chapter was prepared, a good review of M. Bertrand's ideas by A.F. Ewing, entitled 'Reform of the United Nations', appeared in the *Journal of World Trade Law*, vol. 20, no. 2 (1986), pp. 131–41.

of the partial reforms tried in the past. He therefore suggests not a wholesale change based upon some radical redrafting of the UN Charter and the Constitutions of all the Specialized Agencies, nor yet a continuation of the old pattern of partial reforms directed at improving the operations of the existing machinery, but changes directed to 'a greater realism' and a better adaptation of the System to present circumstances. 'The need [is] for an organisation that is more efficient and fulfils useful functions', rather than the more utopian schemes usually invented by those in favour of reform (Chapter I).

What exactly does M. Bertrand mean by reform which is at once 'radical' but 'realistic' and yet not based upon 'utopian' formulae? The starting point of his proposals is his analysis of the 'shortcomings' of the existing system. These he considers are not 'managerial' but 'structural' (Chapter II), and the structural complications contribute powerfully to the absence of 'co-ordination' and of any proper system of 'priorities', the establishment of which have over the years been the object of so many reforming efforts of the United Nations and the Agencies. So complex are the structures that among those acquainted with the United Nations 'knowledge of the System is a sort of palpable professional skill.' The structural complexity is shown not simply in the operations of the principal organisations and Agencies but also within the Agencies themselves, especially in the number of independent entities attached to each organisation – 20 for the WHO, 18 for the FAO, 10 each for UNESCO and the ILO, 13 for the UNDP, and 15 for the UN itself, making about 100 in all. Moreover, 'this impressive list gives only an approximate idea of the real complexity' (para. 13). He maintains however, that 'the degree of co-ordination and hierarchical structure varies within each organisation, but in most cases it is extremely feeble' (which, in spite of what M. Bertrand, says, appears to argue that both structural complexity and managerial weakness exist, the one indeed leading to the other).

The second major shortcoming, he argues, is 'the inordinately ambitious content of the various programmes' (para. 15) both of the Agencies and of the United Nations itself. To judge of their wording, nothing is beyond their scope; indeed they deal with 'all the questions dealt with in the national administrations of the individual countries: trade, industry, natural resources, food and agriculture, fisheries, science and technology, education, labour, social security, health, culture, human rights, the rights of peoples, general development problems, nuclear energy and all the sectors which can be subsumed under each of these fields'. This very varied range of interests causes much overlapping between the various organisations and 'an extreme fragmentation of the resources available', especially of qualified staff. This fragmentation of effort is in turn reinforced by the way the operations are funded through a variety of programmes ranging from the UNDP to UNICEF, the World Food Programme and others. In consequence, 'this system of allocation of funds means that in a single country which is a recipient of aid, about 15 different organisations intervene simultaneously to organise their projects there', plus up to 13 bodies directly attached to the UNDP. 'The aid channelled through the United Nations System can thus be proposed to one and the same country by some 30 bodies of the most varied types and completely independent' (para. 18). The resulting complexity weakens the capacity of all governments to control the activities of all these Agencies and organisations effectively, and greatly strengthens the positions of the Executive Heads, who in consequence may strongly influence the decisions taken by Executive Boards in defining the Agency's objectives and priorities, and allocating financial resources to programmes. Further, 'the dictatorial power at [the Head's] disposal in relation to staff and recruitment increases still further his scope for influence.' M. Bertrand maintains that in this the Agencies differ from the United Nations itself, where 'delegations have organised a measure of parliamentary power which is exerted even in the administrative field' (para. 23).

The situation is made worse because all the organisations have, over the period of their autonomous existence, acquired an individual character with different philosophies and different approaches to the same problems. M. Bertrand maintains that this cannot 'be rectified by better management methods' (para. 25), and this explains why 'the attempts at co-ordination which culminated in the establishment of an extremely complex machinery in the 1960s and 1970s with such extraordinary perseverance produced no results'. (para. 29). Indeed, 'the notion of an integrated approach to development, although adopted by the General Assembly and ritually repeated . . . , has remained for the United Nations System an empty formula.' Moreover, 'this useless effort at co-ordination has over the last 15 years gone hand in hand with a parallel effort towards planning, programming, monitoring of the implementation of programmes and evaluation', in which admittedly some 'progress has certainly been made on paper.' Nevertheless 'these formal exercises', although they have made it possible to provide a better description of the activities, '. . . have not been used for the purposes for which they were originally intended, namely a better definition of priorities; definition of accessible objectives; examination of alternative solutions; concentration of means of action on a few prime objectives; better organisation and better division of labour between executants; and utilisation of the lessons to be drawn from success and failure with a view to establishing better programmes' (para. 31).

This is a savage indictment of the way the System, or at least parts of it, have been operating, and it is a key passage if reforms are to be considered. However, these faults – i.e. the failure to fix proper priorities etc. – would generally be regarded, whatever M. Bertrand may say, as failures of management not of structure. However, the true position is that the complexity of the structure – combined with the constitutional forms of the organisations which comprise it, especially the position of the Executive Heads and the methods they employ to keep the support of developing countries – encourage these faults of management and frustrate attempts to remedy them.

Be that as it may, M. Bertrand makes it plain that the results in projects, publications and reports are frequently mediocre. He identifies many other reasons for this mediocrity, including the fact that 'with some exceptions the average quality of the staff is inadequate', and their qualifications are poor (paras 33–40). These staff weaknesses are most noticeable in the higher grades, where 'appointments are often made without concern for qualifications or professional and administrative experience.' M. Bertrand argues powerfully that in the United Nations itself some effort has been made to improve the situation through a better recruitment policy and the setting of career prospects; 'but these measures, which have not so far been adopted by the other agencies, have so far remained half-hearted and have not even been properly applied.' Across the board, M. Bertrand maintains, 'resistance to any improvement is very strong, and when formal measures are taken, they are implemented in such a way that they do not bring about the results intended by Member States' (para. 41). Hence it is important that all aspects of mismanagement by the organisations within the System should be brought home to public opinion and to political leaders within governments and parliaments, so that pressure can be exerted to bring about improvement (which is indeed one of our purposes in this book).

Despite this powerful indictment of the administrative performance of the organisations within the System, M. Bertrand further contends that although remedies need to be found for these defects of structure and management, they are not the main cause of the problem. This lies, rather, in the fact that governments worldwide lack a proper 'concept of the World Organisation' (para. 43). They see it much more as a stage for exerting diplomatic influence and securing the appointment of the maximum number of their nationals to the available jobs, than as an instrument to render an efficient service to member states on a wide range of issues. Thus there is a need to remove 'the current vagueness as to the role of the UN'. This cannot be removed by 'a perusal of the texts, resolutions or documents' which established the existing pattern of organisations (para. 46). There is a 'hiatus between hard facts and mere talk' in the basic instruments of these bodies which give them 'terms of reference which are totally unrealistic'.[2]

The vagueness of these broad aims is made even worse by the imprecision of the 'thousands of resolutions adopted every year, the planning and programming documents describing the objectives and strategies of the organisations' which do not supply 'an appreciably greater amount of correct information'. Instead, the System is 'the whole time throwing out a smokescreen to conceal' the fact that its mandates are defined 'in an unreal fashion'. Above all, the smokescreen helps to maintain 'a permanent state of confusion between the functions of negotiating or seeking a greater consensus on the one hand and the functions of management on the other'. 'Real discussion of the problems and the give-and-take of vested interests' (which is the essence of negotiation) is replaced by mere 'verbal consensus'. M. Bertrand condemns 'resolutions that set forth basic principles or truisms to which it is all the easier to subscribe in that there is no follow-up to them'. Many of them are not only over-ambitious but impractical.[3]

The over-ambitious character of these vaguely worded objectives, applied by the Agencies on a world-wide scale but on a strictly sectoral basis, divorces them from reality. The use of the same format to describe the objectives of activities as diverse as those of disarmament, education, agriculture, science, labour law, health and a host of other things besides, adds to the unreality of the resulting programmes. On top of everything else there are a number of conflicting conceptions in circulation, among both governments and public opinion, about the very nature of the world organisation and the purposes it should serve. In the West, among the section of

2 E.g. 'to achieve international co-operation in solving problems of an economic, social, cultural or humanitarian character' (UN Charter); or 'promoting collaboration between and among the nations through education, science and culture in order to further universal respect for justice, for the rule of law and for human rights and fundamental freedoms' etc. (UNESCO Constitution).

3 As an example, M. Bertrand cites para. 12 of the latest International Development Strategy which recommends member governments 'to end without delay colonialism, imperialism, neo-colonialism, interference in internal affairs, apartheid, racial discrimination, hegemony, expansionism and all forms of foreign aggression and occupation, which constitute major obstacles to the economic emancipation and development of the developing countries' (para. 49).

public opinion which takes an interest in these matters, there is a tendency to believe that any shortcomings can be remedied by strengthening the powers of the United Nations. Among these circles in the West, 'in the area of development, views vary between a relatively favourable assessment of the results of operational activities and the irritation at the political or ideological debates, the purpose of which is very little understood.' On the other hand, 'in the socialist countries . . . the World Organisation appears rather as an institution which should serve peace and disarmament and enable support to be given to the claims of developing countries. Socialist countries make similar allegations of extravagance and mismanagement as the West.' 'For the nationals of the developing countries, again, the Organisation is above all a forum where it has been possible to strive successfully for decolonisation and which should make it possible to improve the present international economic order,' as well as 'provide a certain amount of technical assistance' (para. 57).

In so far as these different views of the United Nations and its Agencies converge, the basis is a mistaken view in East and West, North and South, about the reality of the world organisation. This takes two forms. First, there is the belief that the UN and the Agencies are the most important international bodies through which relations between governments are conducted at the end of the twentieth century. This is simply not true. Not only are the most important international issues dealt with bilaterally, but there has also been a steady growth in the number of international organisations outside the UN aegis altogether, many of which have more power and play a more important role than any UN organisation in many of the very areas and sectors with which the UN and its Agencies are supposed to deal. 'The system of international relations has thus been built up in a way which tends to reduce considerably the role of the United Nations and its system. The functions entrusted to the latter have thus with exceptions been confined either to narrow or marginal fields or to partial contributions to tasks carried out by other organisations or by other means' (para. 62).

The second major error, Bertrand argues, is a mistaken view of what the nature of the United Nations and its Agencies ought to be. It lies in a popular misunderstanding that the main purpose of these institutions is to manage the implementation of policies universally agreed upon, at least by a world majority, whereas in fact their main task ought to be to initiate a measure of consensus in areas in which policies have not yet been agreed. The confusion springs from regarding the assemblies of these bodies as the equivalents of national legislatures and the secretariats as the equivalent of national administrations executing policy. The confusion is made worse by the fact that, to a very limited extent (about 20% of the total funds employed, according to M. Bertrand's estimate) UN institutions are indeed executive Agencies in this sense (as, indeed, are some of the Specialized Agencies). Over most of their activities, however, this is not the case. Instead, 'the normal function of a World Organisation is . . . to work with extreme tenacity for a better consensus or a different type of consensus in order to enable more progress to be made in the direction of the distant goals laid down in their Charters and Constitutions' (para. 70). Unless this is clearly understood, 'the observer will come up against many obstacles in trying to understand' what he sees in the UN System. Reformers therefore ought to concentrate not so much on seeking 'better management' or more effective 'decision-making', but on 'increasing the yield of negotiation methods'. The clue to understanding both the System as at present devised and its shortcomings lies in appreciating that it is trying 'to manage activities which would presuppose a level of consensus which is far from existing among member states'.

Of the present situation, M. Bertrand argues that the world organisation we possess is 'an ensemble of four very different types of activity'. The first is that involved in the compilation of information and its distribution, and functional co-operation and technical standardisation in such fields as transport, telecommunications, meteorology, statistics and health, together with those dealing with certain humanitarian subjects such as refugees. The second activity of the world organisation is to contribute to or organise the search for peace and security. The third activity is the worldwide promotion of 'development', economic and social. The fourth is that of providing a forum for identifying, elucidating and if necessary negotiating on specific points of world concern or interest such as human rights, population, international law or the law of the sea. (We should note in passing that the group of organisations dealt with in this book is involved in varying degrees in all but the second of these activities.)

M. Bertrand maintains that it is only the first of these four activities (the compilation of information etc.) which involves 'management' in the proper sense of the word. The last three (the search for peace, the promotion of development and the forum for discussion) involve negotiation; and only if the methods and structures of the world organisation can be reformed in a way which recognises this fact, and the fact that these three activities are very different from each other, will it be possible to make any progress. These are what M. Bertrand calls 'the three main objectives', and he examines the three separate and different strategies for attaining them (Ch. IV of the Report). What he has to say about the first of the three – collective security and the search for peace – need not detain us, since it is only marginally relevant to our main theme. On the second – the search for development – M. Bertrand has much more to say of relevance to this study; indeed it is this which leads him to some of the main conclusions of his 'reflections' (paras. 84 ff.). His aim remains the same throughout: to produce a greater measure of world consensus, leading later to negotiation, although – as he admits at the outset – 'ideas concerning development strategies are extremely diverse and are still in the throes of confrontation and evaluation.' 'The respective virtues of planning, industrialisation, priority to agriculture or to this or that other sector' are all the subject of vigorous debate and are likely to remain so. 'The very concept of development is understood differently according as we look at it from the point of view of general application of the Western model or concentrate on preserving and enriching existing culture' (para. 89).

The absence of international consensus on method is reinforced by the fact that the paramount importance of national sovereignty means that the prime responsibility for dealing with each country's problems, in whatever sector they present themselves, is a national one and not one for the international community. In so far as other countries are prepared to help, it is from a desire to maintain their differing zones of influence. (M. Bertrand's views on this point are characteristically French, and it is doubtful if they would be shared by, say, the Scandinavians.) 'Aid is first and foremost a means of exerting influence; in the political or economic rivalries between North and South, the developing countries represent a stake' (para. 93). One result of this is that 'fragmentation and competition between bilateral aid schemes . . . create for the developing countries difficult problems of co-ordinating the whole mass of external aid,' made worse by the 'tied' nature of so much of it, and by the absence of any coherent system of long-term aid from either bilateral or multilateral sources. 'In the face of such a situation it might have been thought that the role of the UN and its System should have concentrated first and foremost on problems of co-ordination. What has happened is exactly the opposite: the UN System has developed a sectoral approach which has aggravated the fragmentation of aid and has added to the existing complexity' (para. 95).

Further complications are introduced by each organisation within the UN System which is engaged in operational activities having its own particular outlook. Thus each has its own 'theory on development and on the goals which should be pursued by the recipient government'. In general it means enhancing the importance of the sector for which each organisation is responsible (industry in the case of UNIDO, agriculture in the case of the FAO etc.). On top of this sectoral cleavage, there can also be a doctrinal cleavage, such as that which developed at one time between UNICEF and the WHO over concentrating on particular health services for infants versus the 'primary health care' approach. The absence of proper systems of evaluation adds to the confusion (para. 97). As a result, although (according to M. Bertrand) some 70% of the resources available to the United Nations are today devoted to development, 'the sectoralised, decentralised and fragmented structures of the System are the reason for its failure to adapt to the solution of development problems.' Developing countries 'need a World Organisation capable of facilitating syntheses, organising co-ordination, helping to find long-term financial arrangements, and granting many-sided aid to solve the most urgent problems,' in place of the 'series of divergent and contradictory recommendations' offered at present. This calls for a reconsideration of 'the very structure of the United Nations System'.

Before dealing with possible changes of structure, however, M. Bertrand considers the fourth of the world organisation's functions as set out above – as a world forum, with the purpose of identifying, analysing and finally promoting negotiation on problems of world interest or concern (paras 107 ff.). To perform this task successfully, the organisation needs to be able 'to identify the problems which are susceptible to negotiation' – a far from easy task in face of 'difficulties of a cultural, technical, ideological and semantic kind'. It needs also to define the interest groups involved in each issue. M. Bertrand then identifies a number of problem areas which have been or might be susceptible to the 'forum' treatment for either identification, analysis or negotiation. Among them are human rights (economic and social as well as political), aspects of international law, environment and population; on the two last-named, the United Nations has had some success in promoting a degree of world consensus. He argues, however, that the United Nations lacks 'precise criteria for defining problems which have a chance of being taken seriously by the international community as a whole'. (Although M. Bertrand does not say so, one such criterion would appear to be that the problem should be one of interest to both developed and developing countries, but on which the developed countries have a positive interest in securing the agreement of the developing – witness environment and population).

Among these problem areas of special interest to us in this study is that of economic and financial problems (including the

North/South dialogue), where the United Nations and its Agencies have so far had small success in promoting a world consensus. M. Bertrand's accusations on this score are severe. He considers that 'economic, financial and monetary problems have only been dealt with very superficially in the discussion and negotiating bodies belonging to the United Nations System. They have only been approached descriptively or ideologically, which has led either to bemoaning the crises or the difficulties that exist or to discussing the claims of developing countries.' The forums provided by UNCTAD, ECOSOC or the General Assembly have served only to debate the role which the Group of 77 would *like* to play in the discussions between industrialised countries or to criticise the policy of the IMF (para. 129). He maintains that whereas between the United States, Japan and Europe the questions of complementarity of economic policies are the subject of much research and of almost continuous negotiation between the governments concerned, 'the UN System provides no analysis of the place which could or should be occupied in these matters of concern by the developing countries, and puts forward no theory of economic complementarity which they would find useful' (para. 130) or, as he might have added, which carries any conviction with the governments of the West.

Major policy documents such as the International Development Strategies, to which a great deal of effort is devoted, reflect in their superficial character the inadequate equipment of the United Nations in the sphere of economic and sociological thought. . . . The apathy of member states towards any serious discussions of these problems in the United Nations is explained largely by the fact that the industrial countries prefer to discuss among themselves the vital problems, namely balance of external trade flows, currency, credit, investment etc. and to keep the developing countries out of these discussions. This situation, prejudicial to the developing countries, is likewise prejudicial to the international community as a whole (para. 133).

Earlier, in discussing the North/South dialogue, M. Bertrand had brought out an important point: the absence of any agreement in the analysis of the issues raised. He rightly points out that the dialogue itself stems from the theories which hold the developed countries, especially the former colonial powers, responsible for the poverty of the Third World, and which claim that this is perpetuated through the domination by the developed countries of the mechanism of the markets with consequent disadvantage for the developing countries in the international division of wealth (para. 120). However, he also points out that 'the tenets of the New International Economic Order are challenged by theoreticians of the right and the left, the former maintaining that its planned economy and protectionist aspects contain nothing new and merely attempt to prevent the laws of the market from functioning properly, and the latter arguing that the machinery proposed merely tends to increase the dependency of the developing countries and benefits only an infinitesimal fraction of their population' (para. 123), the alternative being to delink the developing country economies from those of developed countries.

What then does M. Bertrand propose as the way to reform? First, he suggests that we have to get rid of three fallacies: that the maintenance of peace in the modern world can be brought about by an institution; that development of poorer zones can be brought about by a sectoral and non-integrated approach; and 'that negotiations to improve or alter world consensus can be conducted without prior definition of negotiation structures accepted by all the participants' (para. 138). Thereafter, in Chapter V of his Report, he proposes a series of fundamental reforms which should be studied in full. His aim is to make the institutions of the UN System accord more with political and economic realities in both their structure and their operations, so that they can, first, produce a great degree of consensus on a selection of world issues, and thereafter negotiate a series of solutions to particular problems which will lead to effective action, mainly by individual governments and principally on a regional basis.

The structural reforms would involve getting away from the present type of UN organisation (Assembly/Executive Board/ Secretary-General) and moving towards an EEC-type structure, 'which might be referred to as the 'Council-Commission', plus launching of joint ventures' (para. 152). The aim would be to secure 'greater cohesion in respect of precise objectives', so that action could go ahead on precise tasks with measureable results. They would also involve, in the end, establishing processes of negotiation by representative groups of states working in smaller negotiating fora than the present Councils or Assemblies based upon one State one Vote. The aim would be to negotiate agreements on a range of particular issues rather than to pass generalised resolutions by majority vote to which no one would subsequently pay any attention. Finally the United Nations itself should be reconstructed to create an 'economic United Nations' (para. 178). At its head should be established an 'Economic Security Council' corresponding in these new arrangements to the Council of Ministers in the EEC. This Council would have to be small to provide an effective negotiating forum, and yet it would also have to provide worldwide coverage. This would be achieved by representing countries by groups depending upon their GNP, population and region, so as to produce a Council of no more than 37 members – preferably smaller. They would be supported by a comparatively large secretariat, and it would be essential to make this inter-disciplinary so that issues could be properly identified and agreed solutions to problems negotiated (paras 181–4).

M. Bertrand envisages no sudden sweeping reform, but a programme of steady change in the directions he proposes over a comparatively long transition period. The changes would include: continued pressure to eliminate the most flagrant shortcomings in the present system as identified in the JIU reports and in the Jackson Study (many of them in staffing policy); transfer of resources and staff from the present operational aid structures (i.e. in UNDP, WFP, UNFPA, UNICEF etc.) and most of the technical co-operation services of the main agencies to regional development agencies to deal with regional problems on a regional basis; reorganisation of the secretariats of the United Nations and the larger Agencies (UNESCO, the FAO, the ILO, the WHO) 'so as to concentrate and develop the economic and interdisciplinary services in the UN and to organise the relations of this central service with the sectoral secretariats'; and reorganisation of the intergovernmental machinery so that ECOSOC, UNCTAD and the intergovernmental organs of the main Agencies are converted into institutions for the negotiation of solutions to economic and social problems, and transformation of the ACC into machinery for inter-agency co-operation on economic problems (para. 190).

M. Bertrand's proposals deserve the most thorough investigaton both by member governments and throughout the UN System, but the indications as we go to press are that they will not get it. Within weeks of their public appearance 'a senior UN official in New York' was reported as saying that M. Bertrand 'was out of touch with the political realities of the institution'.[4] As for member governments, they may prefer instead to have a frustrating wrangle over the consequences of Kassebaum.

Public pressure must ensure that more attention is paid to M. Bertrand. It is not necessary at this stage to accept the totality of his criticisms of the UN System, though they are widely echoed in many quarters. All that is necessary is that his proposals for reform should be examined in the light of experience, both in the United Nations and in international organisations outside the United Nations,

4  *The Guardian (London)*, 1 Oct. 1985.

preferably those from outside the System which have no vested interests to serve.

As for the role of the United Nations System in the economic and social field, there are four major questions to be examined before any serious programme of reform can be embarked on. The first is: do member governments really want reform, or are they content with the present situation? The present situation is broadly that, in relation to many economic and social questions, the United Nations, together with part of its System, is little more than a glorified international debating society, voicing the concerns of many nations but one to which most of the world pays little attention. The true desires of governments over these questions will probably be discovered not in their public pronouncements but only by discreet soundings behind the scenes either by a person of international eminence such as the UN Secretary-General or by some individual government, or group of governments, willing to take a lead.

If the response to the first question is positive, then the next question to be decided is to what end should a programme of reform be directed? In so far as the UN System is providing services of a functional kind, it must be expected that most governments would want them to be provided as efficiently as possible. The more important question, however, is whether governments want the United Nations and its System to become an effective negotiating forum on a range of economic and social issues of global or regional concern – and; if so, on which questions. Or, alternatively, do governments want the UN System and its secretariats to play a role with other bodies outside the United Nations, both public and private, in preparing issues for negotiation, identifying the alternative solutions, and establishing the parameters of agreement? Or, as a final possibility, are governments content with the *status quo*, when they have resort to parts of the UN System (notably, for developed countries, the Bretton Woods Institutions) simply when it suits their purpose and when its activities can be controlled in a way that would produce no radical changes in the present economic arrangements? In which case, it follows that they are prepared to see the parts of the System which do not fall into this category become moribund.

The third question to be considered is: what can be learned from past experience both inside and outside the System? This is a more difficult question than is apparent at first sight. Where different arrangements from those prevailing in the UN System seem to have had more success, the reasons need to be carefully analysed. For example, when one examines M. Bertrand's suggestion that the 'Assembly Executive Board Secretary-General' structure in the System should be replaced by a 'Council/Commission' structure like that of the EEC it is necessary to take account of the fact that the EEC machinery serves a small group of countries with a 'community' of interests. It operates within the framework of a Treaty (of Rome), of which Parts II and III spell out the policies to be implemented with some precision (indeed Title III, on agriculture, spells them out in considerable detail).[5] The essence of the Economic United Nations, as envisaged by M. Bertrand, is that it would mainly be exploring new areas of policy. Moreover, the EEC, through its Council, involves the constant attention of ministers with a competence in particular subjects. Could ministers afford such attention to a world body – even if representation on it were divided up on a regional basis in order to keep it compact? Next, it should be noted that even though the EEC has a more successful record for practical negotiation than the United Nations, it is still a wasteful system in terms of administrative time. The Commission elaborates many initiatives which in practice get no nearer to being negotiated, let alone achieving practical results, than being translated into nine languages. It would be frustrating to the world community if this result were repeated on a world scale; it would not increase international goodwill, nor would it improve the performance of functional Agencies. M. Bertrand's proposal therefore needs some elaboration.

Above all, however, the EEC machinery downgrades the role of the 'Assembly' and with it the function of public debate in the process of political decision-taking. True, the Community has its 'Parliament' but it is a legislature so deprived of powers that it is as likely as the General Assembly to adopt 'resolutions which have no practical consequences' (or, in Brussels terminology, to 'indulge in gesture politics'). This point needs further thought. At first sight it would seem that the repeated passage of resolutions which have no practical effect, most of them hostile to the developed countries, has over time simply bred irritation in the developed and frustration in the developing countries. However, it would be wrong to assume from this that it has been without any practical effect. On the contrary, it has had some effect in inducing ministers in market economy countries to make concessions which they would not otherwise have contemplated, and in inducing pressure groups in developed countries to agitate for them. Moreover public debate can reveal ·where the problems are arising in any situation. Some 'assembly' element, therefore, must be retained. Moreover, if it were clear that the ultimate aim is 'negotiation' worked out by an effective Council Secretariat machine, it could make the 'assembly' debates much more effective.

5  M. Bertrand himself recognises this point in footnote 54 to his report.

A final question which needs examination is whether the balance of activity which has emerged between the information-gathering, standard-setting and technical assistance functions of the Agencies is justified by the results. The question needs to be examined Agency by Agency as well as in relation to the System as a whole. On technical assistance, the examination would need to show how the sectoral approach was affecting development plans in the countries which are major recipients of assistance. On information-gathering, the examination should determine how this role can best be related to identifying problems of global or regional importance and where negotiation between governments is indicated. The same should apply to standard-setting, although this is usually less problematical.

Whatever happens, those who are concerned about the United Nations and its System should ensure that M. Bertrand's report and proposals continue to receive public attention. He has precisely identified too many of the skeletons in the cupboards of the System. If they are not removed and given a decent burial, the ghosts of their former owners will continually return to haunt the proceedings.

# PART THREE: THE FUTURE

# CHAPTER XVII

## THE PROBLEM IN PERSPECTIVE

In Chapter I it was stated that the UN System of Specialized Agencies was undergoing severe strain. In subsequent Chapters we have examined the areas in which this strain is being felt. We now look at the general considerations which affect possible remedies.

### The strain in the UN System is not uniform

The fact that the strain is not being felt uniformly throughout the System is almost certainly due to the fact that the System itself is not uniform. Those areas of it which are running services or exchanging technical information of importance to a large number of countries, regardless of their economic standing or political complexion, are functioning normally and providing a useful service, much of which could only be provided internationally. The difficulties which these parts of the System encounter are mostly inherent in any large organisation, increased by the fact that these are 'international' organisations with all the additional administrative difficulties which that entails. Strains and even international disagreement arise at times from the effort to keep them efficient, but this is in no way unusual. Typical of these organisations are the UPU, the IMO, the WIPO, the ITU and the WMO. Occasionally, as illustrated in Chapter V, extraneous political issues have intruded (e.g. into the debates of the WMO, ICAO, the ITU, the IAEA); but these have been in the general debates of the organisations, and their ordinary work has not been much affected. Nor have they suffered much from the confrontations which have taken place elsewhere in the System between rich and poor on economic issues and other matters connected with the New International Economic Order. Indeed their role in relation to the development of developing countries has not been primary. Moreover, their staff have maintained a higher level of professional competence – probably from sheer necessity – than has been displayed elsewhere in the System, where professional and, even more, administrative competence has tended to decline (for reasons shown in Chapter XI).

Another group of organisations which perform a comparatively non-contentious role with reasonable efficiency, despite some allegations to the contrary, are the humanitarian organisations (e.g. those dealing with refugees and disasters), with which we have chosen not to deal in this study. They face special problems simply because of the nature of their work. Much of this work inevitably consists of providing emergency relief, and much of it involves solving logistical problems in physical and political circumstances of very great difficulty. Much of it, too, is of a pioneering character and a lot is constantly being learned about the best way to carry it out. Thus there is a need to keep the performance of these organisations under constant scrutiny; but their operations, combined with those of a whole range of voluntary organisations, have undoubtedly contributed greatly to the alleviation of misery in the twentieth century, and they need to be continued – and continued *under the United Nations* because, despite all the UN's weaknesses and decline of prestige, this affords them a measure of protection in the difficult circumstances in which they work, as well as doing something to enhance the standing of the United Nations itself.

Contrasted with these few groups of institutions, carrying out tasks of functional importance which need to be performed globally, or tasks of humanitarian relief, there are three other groups whose situation, for various reasons, is different. The first are the financial and commercial institutions – the IMF, the IBRD, the GATT and the more recently created IFAD. The second are UNESCO, the WHO, the FAO and the ILO – traditionally known as the 'Big Four', although they have now been joined by a fifth (UNIDO) – whose major concern has become that of providing technical assistance on a sectoral basis to Third World countries. (We refer to the group henceforth as the Big Five.) The third are a miscellaneous batch of programmes, funds and institutions – some general like the UNDP and some specialised like UNICEF or the WFP – and one major standing conference (UNCTAD). It is in these last three groups of organisations that the strain has mostly appeared, although again not uniformly throughout all three. Their common feature – and the common source of strain – is that they play an important role in the relationships (especially economic) between developed and developing countries.

In the first group, classed as 'financial', the sources of strain are threefold. First is the shortage of real resources – the shortage of capital funds in the case of the IBRD and IFAD, the inadequacy of reserves in the case of the IMF, and the unwillingness to make trade concessions in the case of the GATT. Secondly, and probably more important, the successful implementation of the policies these institutions pursue demands structural adjustments, especially in developing countries but also to a lesser extent in developed countries too. Structural adjustments demand sacrifices – by groups, interests or countries – and are therefore highly charged matters politically: political tension arises from genuine policy differences over the scale and use of resources in a prescribed area of activity. The third source of strain arises from the purpose of these Bretton Woods institutions, which was to secure the better operation of 'market forces'. Many governments outside the West pursue policies based on a different economic and political theory, which also forms the basis of the ideas embodied in the New International Economic Order. But despite these sources of strain, the institutions are competently administered, in contrast to other parts of the UN System; their constitutions ensure that they are little affected by extraneous political issues although, exceptionally, friction has developed between a major donor and a developing country such as Vietnam, Ethiopia and Nicaragua. These financial institutions have played, and continue to play, an important role in world economic relationships, as is shown not least by the developing countries wanting a greater say in running them.

The major strains within the UN System arise in relation to the second group of organisations – the Big Five Specialized Agencies – and to some of the Miscellaneous Funds and programmes in the third category – especially the Standing Conference, UNCTAD. As we pointed out in Chapter I, the Big Five Specialized Agencies have the same kinds of functions as their less contentious fellows successfully operating in technical areas (such as the WMO, the UPU etc.), namely to exchange information, set standards and channel technical assistance to developing countries. In all of them, however, standard-setting and channelling technical assistance have achieved greater importance than the exchange of information; and, except in the ILO, providing technical assistance to developing countries has become the paramount function. Although the Big Five have not become the major source of funds to any developing country (not even of technical assistance funds), they are an important source of money which they can distribute with little control being exercised by those who provide it. It is the technical assistance role of these Agencies, and to a less extent their standard-setting role, which have indirectly created most of the difficulties.

The reasons for this are not far to seek. First, it is the technical assistance monies which make these Agencies operationally active in developing countries. However, they are active on a strictly sectoral basis, even when they try to poach on each other's preserves; the sectoral distribution of effort they thereby achieve may not be the best for the development of a country's resources or for bettering the conditions of its people. Moreover, it is difficult to run a large technical assistance programme in an important sector of a country's economy without making judgements about that economy as a whole. In some instances, an Agency pursuing its sectoral aims may even recommend policies which in the wider context turn out to be positively disadvantageous to the economic development of a developing country (e.g. African countries which established expensive systems of primary education in the 1960s as the result of external advice when, in the view of many competent judges, they might have done better economically to put more resources into adult literacy campaigns).

Secondly, the concentration on technical assistance has created rivalry between the Agencies. It has given their heads a source of funds from which, if they want to, they can 'buy' support; and sometimes the technical assistance given is not of the highest quality (some allege that this is increasingly so). Moreover, to the detriment of the developing countries themselves, in some of the Agencies it is detracting from the performance of the first of the Specialized Agencies' functions – the accumulation and supply of information. Data is still being accumulated on a vast scale, but it is not being properly analysed nor is the attention of the world being drawn to its policy implications. (Thus, although the data about the deteriorating food situation in Africa in the early 1970s and early 1980s was being accummulated by the FAO, the task of analysing what the world and African governments should do to help was carried out by the World Bank,[1] stimulated by a meeting of African heads of state which produced the Lagos Plan of Action, and not by either the FAO or the World Food Council.)

In two organisations only – the ILO and UNESCO – have serious difficulties arisen over the standard-setting functions. This is because in the ILO and UNESCO these functions themselves, though dealing with matters which are primarily 'social', (such as human rights, trade unions and 'cultural' development), relate to subjects with a high *domestic* political impact in member states. The difficulty is compounded by the fact that those who drafted the constitutions of these organisations conceived of them as being based on 'liberal' principles, whereas the majority vote in these organisations now belongs to groups of states who do not necessarily accept such

---

1 See *Accelerated Development in Sub-Saharan Africa* (Berg Report), IBRD, 1983, and *Towards Sustained Development in Sub-Saharan Africa*, 1984. Admittedly the policies advocated by the Bank created controversy (on which see 'Sub-Saharan Africa: Getting the Facts Straight', *IDS Bulletin*, no. 16, July 1985). But they have helped to promote action, multilateral and bilateral, on a bigger scale than before.

principles, and indeed adopt a 'collectivist' approach, especially in relation to trade unions, 'culture' and human rights. This is a major source of strain whenever these issues are debated in such fora between democratic and other groups of states.

The third group of organisations within the System to be considered is that consisting of the Standing Conference (UNCTAD) and the Funds and Programmes. UNCTAD (possibly contrary to the wishes of its founders) has played a key role in generating the present strain within the UN System. This is, first, because its ideas and philosophies on economic issues have underlain many of the resolutions at the General Assembly and other UN bodies including the Specialized Agencies. They have therefore become embodied in the resolutions establishing the Development Decades and similar documents. These resolutions can hardly be reconciled with the economic philosophies which now predominate in the 'market economy' countries of the West. Secondly, UNCTAD was bound by its mandate to concern itself with major structural adjustment within the world economic system, with repercussion that would be widespread both in relations between countries and within the domestic economies of countries. Therefore its proposals could not but be highly charged politically. This, paradoxically, would have mattered less if both sides in the argument had had real bargaining power; instead, one side – the South – effectively lacked it. The result, unhappily, has therefore been confrontation rather than negotiation. What is needed now, as both sides recognise, is some basis for real negotiations between developed and developing countries on a range of economic issues of importance to both, aimed at producing effective agreements. Substance apart, UNCTAD procedures – i.e. a Group system which no longer corresponds to economic realities – have not been conducive to succesful negotiation.

The Funds and Programmes present a different picture from that shown by other parts of the System, simply because most of them are voluntary. Where donors have lacked confidence in their management or their policies, they have not contributed. Thus the major donors have contributed to the UNDP, UNICEF and the World Food Programme, but mostly not to the UN Capital Development Fund, the Vienna Programme of Action on Science and Technology for Development, and a number of others whose administration and policies did not inspire them with confidence. Hence there has been little strain between any of these organisations and member states, except the sort of strains that spring from shortage of funds. The unsuccessful Funds or Programmes add to the complexities of the System and probably waste scarce resources on administrative overheads that are not justified by results. Otherwise they do little harm, and survive in the Micawberish expectation that someday something – including some donors – will turn up to justify their existence.

## *The UN System and other forms of international co-operation*

The second general matter which needs to receive some attention is the fact that the UN System of Specialized Agencies, Programmes and Funds, as it has developed since the Second World War, is only one part – and no longer the most significant part – of a complex of international organisations which have sprung up, largely over the same period, many operating also in the social and economic sphere. Most of these organisation have some form of consultative or observer status with the United Nations. Some, like the Common-wealth, the OECD, the OAS or the OAU, are mainly consultative; others, like the EEC or EFTA, have real executive and even legislative power. Others, like OPEC, ASEAN, the Andean Group, the Caribbean Community (CARICOM), the Pacific Commission or the South Pacific Forum, have exerted or could exert real economic power and influence. Yet others echo, on a less than world scale, activities or organisations which already exist within the UN System. Thus the Colombo Plan, as a mobiliser of technical assist-ance and capital aid, duplicates some of the efforts of the UNDP and other UN bodies. The four regional development banks operate on much the same basis as the World Bank and its adjuncts. Looked at from another angle, some of the efforts of the United Nations to set up regional organisations[2] merely duplicate on a less adequate scale other regional organisations which are outside the UN 'family'. Thus ECLA has a more limited range of activities over a more limited geographical area than the OAS – which, with its Councils for Education, Science and Culture, its Functional Committees and its specialised organisations dealing with Agriculture, Health, Women's Affairs and so on, sometimes seems to duplicate the whole range of the UN System.

In addition to these intergovernmental organisations, there is a range of worldwide non-governmental organisations covering many aspects of social, economic, scientific, cultural and even religious

2 There are five such bodies: the Economic Commission for Africa (ECA), the Economic and Social Commission for Asia and the Pacific (ESCAP), the Economic Commission for Europe (ECE), the Economic Commission for Latin America (ECLA) and the Economic Commission for Western Asia (ECWA).

activity globally or regionally, of sufficient importance for the United Nations itself to set up an office to deal with them. Some of them, like the International Confederation of Free Trade Unions, the World Confederation of Trade Unions and the World Confederation of Labour, are active as non-governmental organisations in an area which is in the purview of a Specialized Agency (in this case, the ILO). Their problems are discussed in Appendix C.

Several conclusions can be drawn from this multiplicity of international organisations. Some would argue that it is merely a symptom of the growing appetite among bureaucrats everywhere for foreign travel, but such a complex phenomenon is not susceptible to so simple and cynical an explanation. It is much more likely to be because those responsible for dealing with the consequences of rapid economic and social change find international contacts more of a help than a hindrance – despite the many strains and frustrations entailed by any form of co-operative effort, whether local, national or international. Therefore if, because of failure to remove some of its shortcomings, any of the existing institutions of the UN System were to disappear, some alternative form of organisation would almost certainly be created, or at least some alternatives would be found to provide the same services to the international community, perhaps through existing organisations outside the UN System. What would be weakened, in this case, is the authority of the United Nations itself; it would mean that the United Nations and its member states had shown themselves incapable of carrying out reforms in organisations within their System which are nevertheless providing services the members needed.

## How successful has post-war international co-operation been?

After a prolonged examination of the shortcomings of international organisations as catalogued in many academic studies, UN reports, Joint Inspection Unit reports or ECOSOC or General Assembly debates, it is easy to fall into an unjustified despair. They create a picture of maladministration by overstaffed, incompetent bureaucracies, paid for from inflated budgets, engaged mainly in building up their own empires; this is the picture which the press likes to paint, when it takes any notice at all. Unhappily, participation in some of the governing bodies of these organisations does not entirely dispel this impression. Nevertheless it is far from being the whole truth. Many of the staff are very able people devoted to their subject and to the cause of international co-operation. Moreover, the results of all the international effort since 1945 do not jutify the pessimism.

This can best be illustrated by looking at the progress of economic change worldwide since the 1950s – from which it is clear that during this time the rate of economic growth, though geographically uneven, has been universal and on a scale without precedent in human history. In developing countries as a group it was 3.4%, annually *per capita* in 1950–75; in developed countries it was 3.2% (compared with an annual growth rate in nineteenth century Britain of 1.3% *per capita*.). Furthermore, this has been accompanied by an increase in social welfare. Taking the developing countries as a group, life expectancy increased in the three decades from 1950 from 43 to 58 years; child mortality dropped from 28 to 12 per thousand; and the literacy rate rose from 33% to 56%. These improvements have been seen in low-income as well as middle-income countries, and in all parts of the world.

International organisations have played a major role in promoting these changes. Even where external aid has been supplied bilaterally (as most of it has), it has been internationally stimulated. Much of it has been multilaterally organised, often by Agencies within the UN System. The reduction in child mortality owes much to the WHO and UNICEF, and the improvement in literacy to UNESCO. The World Bank has succeeded both in mobilising capital resources for development and in fostering an enlightened debate on how best to use them. Most countries have benefitted at some time since 1945 from the growth of world trade stimulated by the GATT, and from the fairly orderly processes of exchange rate adjustment organised by the IMF. The UNCTAD-organised General Scheme of Preferences has played a useful role which could expand in any future growth in world trade.

It has to be admitted that in the mid-1980s the prospects for the poorer countries were less favourable than previously. Since the 1970s some have even shown signs of regression: GDP diminished between 1973 and 1983 in Chad, Uganda, Ghana, Zaire, Jamaica, Nicaragua and El Salvador. However, a larger group (including such a diverse array as Egypt, Tunisia, Paraguay, the Yemen Arab Republic, Congo, Cameroon, Indonesia, Thailand, Burma and the People's Republic of China) continued to show an annual growth rate over the same period of between 6% and 8.8% per annum.[3] This is no small achievement at a time of world recession, two major oil crises and a staggering international debt problem. Moreover, natural disasters apart, the difference in performance between countries has been due more to civil war and domestic mismanagement than to any failure by the United Nations

3 *Source*: World Bank, *World Development Report 1985* (Appendix, Table 1).

or its Agencies, or indeed by any other group of international organisations.

It has to be concluded, therefore, that the huge international co-operative effort that has taken place since 1945 in the economic and social fields has been a success, not a failure. Moreover, the relative success has been such that if there were a break-down in the UN System as a whole or in any part of it (say in an organisation like UNESCO), some other means would be found of performing many of the same functions. The relationships between countries at the end of the twentieth century are such that it is no longer possible to conduct them with the techniques of bilateral diplomacy alone.

The things that have gone wrong in the economic and social parts of the UN all concern relationships between the Third World and the developed world, and relate to three major areas. At the top of the list, there has been the attempt to use the machinery of the United Nations, especially the General Assembly and UNCTAD, to appear to *negotiate* major new economic arrangements between developed and developing countries (a process summarised in the demands for a New International Economic Order, and codified in the Resolutions establishing the Development Decades). Since the procedures involved were not devised for *negotiating* solutions binding on participants but only for making recommendations, they have not resulted in binding agreements. The effort has been sustained only by the pretence (a pretence which has begotten great frustration) that the General Assembly, and even possibly UNCTAD, was some kind of Parliament of Mankind which could legislate for the world. This they are not; and developed countries, whether market economy or Socialist, would never permit them to become so – too many of their economic interests, domestic and international, would be placed in jeopardy if they did. Nor are developing countries, with their continual insistence on 'national sovereignty' inclined to tread that path. At the same time, the demands in UN Resolutions concerning the New International Economic Order do clearly indicate the need to negotiate – within the proper machinery – new economic arrangements between states or groups of states. Ways in which this might be done will be suggested later.

The second major area causing concern is in the middle of the system: the abuse of power by some (not all) Executive Heads and their Secretariats; their concentration on increasing the importance of their organisations and the sectors in which they operate rather than on promoting the development of recipient countries; their maladministration; and their lack of budgetary restraint. Because of their autonomous constitutional position and their past history, this is the.hardest part of the problem to tackle, but suggestions will be made later.

The third area lies within member states. The Group of Experts who produced the proposals which led to the last great attempt to reform the UN System from the top down (embodied in General Assembly Resolution A 32/197 of 1977) rightly commented: 'Most of the structural deficiencies of the United Nations system are the result of actions by its member states, and the correction of these deficiencies will require action by the same states.'⁴ In other words, member states have got the UN System which they deserve. This problem is usually described as being one of securing better co-ordination within the administrations of developing countries – a defect which the appointment of Resident Co-ordinators in some of the least developed countries was designed to help put right. But this is only part of the story; some of the blame lies with developed countries as well – not, as a rule, in any weakness in their domestic arrangements for 'co-ordination', but in their failure to devote the right diplomatic and intellectual resources to making the System work.

All reforms of the System, including those of 1977, have rightly seen the key to reform as lying in these three areas. These reforms, especially those of 1977, have even produced some marginal improvements. However, they have mainly failed for three reasons. First, they have not considered what conditions are necessary for successful *negotiations* on major economic issues. Secondly, they have not been prepared effectively to tackle the problems of disciplining the Executive Heads of the Agencies, nor the related problems of securing effective co-ordination between them. And thirdly, out of respect for the susceptibilities of national sovereignty, they have not given enough attention to the role of member states and how to improve their performance in relation to the System.

It is on these three fronts that future progress must be sought. Some suggestions follow. But before considering them, a final word of warning is necessary. Despite the criticisms which have been made of the UN System both from inside and outside and from countries pursuing very different economic policies around the world, changing it will be extremely difficult because so many of the participants are well content with the *status quo* and because so many of

4 For a valuable account of the 1977 reforms, see an article by Davidson Nicol and John Remminger in *Third World Quarterly*, Jan. 1982, p. 89.

those who want change are not united on what change they want. It is not just a question of overcoming the inertia inherent in the reform of any large organisation. For example, many of the developed countries are well content with it because they have perfected the techniques of 'damage limitation' and of ignoring the System when it so suits their purpose. At the same time, the financial cost of continuing it, though irritating, is not unduly burdensome. Developing countries, on the other hand, will go along with it because, although they are frequently disappointed with its results, it is sympathetic to their aspirations and it provides them with a limited source of additional funds. Many of those working within the System go along with it for a variety of reasons, ranging from a genuine belief in its efficacy to more mercenary considerations. In these circumstances, the United Nations and its System could continue for many more years without great change. However, it would be like other great institutions in the past which have suffered from schism – impressive in appearance, good in parts, a source of prestige and lucrative employment for a limited class of people, and steadily losing influence, credit and credibility.

# CHAPTER XVIII

# NEGOTIATING ECONOMIC ISSUES

It was argued in Chapter XII that there are many more important reasons for finding solutions to the world's economic problems than that of reducing the difficulties of the Specialized Agencies. Nevertheless, these issues are central to the work of the most important of them, and have some relevance to most of the others, especially since the United Nations as a whole – including the more important of the Specialized Agencies – has made Third World concerns one of its primary considerations. It was also argued that to make progress on these issues three things were necessary: some agreement on aims and methods; machinery to work out the details; and adequate resources. However, it should be made plain at the outset that the range of economic issues is so complex that progress does not depend *solely* on action within the United Nations and its Agencies. If it did, the prospects would be dim, because unfortunately the prestige of the United Nations has fallen so low, and its record in dealing with economic issues is not good. The question is rather: how can the United Nations and its Agencies best contribute to negotiations on economic issues wherever they take place, i.e. even in fora outside the United Nations?

The second point to be borne in mind – although UN procedures have often disregarded it – is that in economic negotiations, agreement on aims does not necessarily entail agreement on methods or on policies for achieving them; nor will agreement on aims and methods necessarily ensure provision of adequate finance or other resources. All require patient negotiation, preceded by careful analysis. It is not a simple matter of 'political will'.

## *The prospects for consensus on economic issues*

Agreement on aims and methods of economic policy and on the role of international co-operation in achieving it is probably more difficult to attain now than at any time since 1945. Between 1950 and 1970 there was broad agreement between developed and developing countries: first, that the aim of economic policy was economic growth – indeed such growth was considered synonymous with 'development' – and secondly, that government policies played a major role in achieving growth through economic planning and state action to stimulate and direct it. This agreement covered in broad terms both the domestic policies to be pursued and the international policies to support them. For developing countries it was believed that the way to 'development' lay through import substitution and the planned removal of constraints and market imperfections through state intervention. As for the techniques to be employed, President Kennedy and the World Bank alike encouraged the idea of a satisfactory state development plan as a precondition for external assistance long before the creation of UNCTAD; indeed the technique was part of the accepted wisdom of the day. The importance of the price mechanism and of market solutions to the problems of development was played down, and parastatal enterprises of all kinds were favoured. After 1970 these theories tended to be replaced, but what replaced them was a new agreement broad enough to establish a fresh consensus around the idea that the main aim of development was not simply to produce growth but also to satisfy 'basic needs' and contribute to the relief of inequality and poverty. Although the idea of state intervention as an instrument was retained, 'Redistribution with Growth' became the aim. Promoting subsistence-level agriculture rather than industrialisation became the technique.

In both the interventionist and the distributive phases of development theory just stated, there was a broad consensus among developed and developing countries both on the internal policies and on the need for some centrally regulated adjustment in external economic relations between groups of countries, though only a limited agreement on how to attain it. Against this background, negotiations designed to reach agreement on particular issues were possible, and some even had a measure of success. After 1980 there was a shift in opinion which produced a marked divergence of view between most developed countries outside the 'Socialist' bloc and most developing countries. This was over the efficacy or otherwise of market and competitive forces as instruments both of economic growth and for the allocation of scarce resources even in developing countries. The advent of conservative governments in the United States, West Germany and Britain made this the dominant view among developed countries. This view was not shared by most developing countries, so that for the first time in four decades there was a marked absence even of general consensus as to how best to promote 'development'.

Nevertheless, as was shown in the 1984 World Bank Report *Towards Sustained Development in Sub-Saharan Africa*, there has been a shift of opinion in developing countries which *could* provide a fresh consensus and the basis for new negotiations. In their domestic policies, more and more developing countries are recognising that medium-term planning as practised in the 1960s and 1970s has not worked. They are beginning to admit that parastatal enterprises in developing countries have generally proved inefficient. Many approve the shift in the 1970s of the balance away from industrialisation and the move towards agriculture. Some admit that the fear of multinational corporations has in many cases been overdone with results harmful to the economic growth of a number of developing countries. Many developing countries recognise that they did themselves damage by disregarding the benefits of staying open to competition in world markets and by over-valued exchange rates which discouraged exports and aggravated the foreign exchange constraint on development. The recognition that all people – no matter what the stage of their development or under what political or economic regime they live – are responsive to price incentives is now more widespread.[1]

Unhappily there have been fewer signs of a consensus among developed countries on their role and their responsibility for helping progress. Consequently, by 1984 dialogue between the two groups and *negotiations* on development issues had almost ceased . The rhetoric of the United Nations and the 'pseudo-consensus' of the New International Economic Order have some responsibility for this. Developed countries – especially those with a market economy philosophy – are very reluctant to enter into serious negotiations on economic issues in a forum in which, even before detailed negotiations start, they are called upon to forgo all reciprocity from all developing countries in tariff negotiations, to reduce freight rates in shipping to developing countries, to minimise all insurance costs, to accept time-bound programmes for increasing foreign aid, to control their transnational corporations and force them to transfer their technology to developing countries 'on equitable and favourable terms', 'to ensure that developing countries can import the necessary quantity of food without undue strain on their balance of payments', and at the same time to 'make appropriate adjustment in their economies so as to facilitate the expansion and diversifaction of imports from developing countries', and much else besides.[2] Moreover this was to the accompaniment of speeches designed to demonstrate that *all* the economic ills of developing countries are due to the policies of 'colonialism, apartheid and neo-colonialism' fostered by the market economy countries of the West. Even if the arguments

---

1  On this whole subject see an article by Dr Tony Killick, Director of the Overseas Development Institute, entitled 'Twenty-Five Years of Development', *Development Policy Review*, Vol. IV, no. 2 (June 1986).
2  These are all demands embodied in the Resolutions of the Sixth Special Assembly, Resolutions 3201 and 3202.

were true and all the remedies soundly based, it would be bad tactics for developed countries to try to 'negotiate' from such a starting point, or to try to conduct the *negotiation* through machinery in which such arguments had become unquestioned items of faith; in practice, none of them is now prepared to do so.

At this point we must distinguish more clearly between aims and methods, as UN resolutions on Third World economic problems often fail to do. For example, few would quarrel with the aims of the International Development Strategy for the Third UN Development Decade (Resolution 35/36 of 1980), which includes the elimination of hunger and malnutrition (para. 28), the 'rational development, management and utilisation of natural resources' (para. 32), the 'strengthening of the scientific and technological capacities of developing countries' (para. 36), and 'the reduction and elimination of poverty and a fair distribution of benefits of development' (para. 43). Many, however, would question its methods; for example, is 'the elimination of hunger and malnutrition' best assured by a substantial increase in 'the share of developing countries in world exports of food and agricultural products' (para. 28)? Or is 'the strengthening of the scientific and technological capacities of developing countries' best promoted by the implementation of the Vienna Programme of Action on Science and Technology for Development (paras 117–125)? It is because these documents are such a mixture of virtuous aims and debatable methods that they have lost their usefulness as bases for *negotiation* on these issues.

Equally, however, some of the critics of the United Nations appear to have fallen into the same confusion of aim and method in considering UN resolutions. Many condemn the resolutions because the means they propose are excessively 'dirigiste' and do not rely sufficiently on 'market forces'. Thus Douglas Bandow[3] expresses hostililty to them because 'the United Nations has become a vehicle for a global assault on the liberal international order. Repeated Third World demands for a NIEO are more than just rhetoric, they are part of a concerted effort to impose global management over a host of natural, financial and technological resources, as well as to regulate world business activity.' He is probably right in thinking that this describes the intention of some of those who drafted these resolutions, but so far they have been very unsuccessful in imposing 'global management' because – regardless of their intentions – the machinery at their disposal is not equal to the task. This is one of the

3 Douglas Bandow, *Unquestioned Allegiance*, London: Adam Smith Institute, 1986, p. 27.

causes of the present disillusionment with the United Nations which has led some to suggest that a different technique needs to be employed – i.e. the isolation of particular issues and their analysis and negotiation piecemeal in particular fora as appropriate. But world economic issues are so interrelated that they are frequently not susceptible to such treatment.

The problem must be seen in context. Because dialogue between North and South on economic issues *under the aegis of the United Nations* has for the time being broken down, often on points of general economic principle, it does not follow that there is no need for such dialogue. Relations between all countries and groups of countries in the economic sphere are as important as ever. Conditions in any one country are even more dependent on economic conditions and policies in other countries than they were previously. The need for dialogue therefore remains. But it is now clear that the form of dialogue promoted by the United Nations since 1960 is no longer suitable for promoting international co-operation in the solution of economic problems. If progress is to be made and the United Nations and its Agencies are to make a contribution to restarting the dialogue in a way which will lead to real negotiation on real issues, then a different approach based on new concepts is needed.

A number of authors, such as Maurice Bertrand, have stressed that progress will only be made by detailed negotiation on particular issues; but for this to be proposed on a satisfactory basis it is desirable to have international consensus, on broad issues at least, as wide as that which existed in the 1960s and 1970s; furthermore the United Nations and its Agencies can have a role in creating it – despite developments in the 1980s. However, this consensus must be based on the economic realities of the 1980s and not on some economic theories current in the 1930s – and even earlier. What sort of consensus might emerge as a basis for negotiations on particular issues? The following is put forward as a possible scenario. No doubt there are others.

## The basis for consensus [4]

It might be possible to secure a broad international consensus on three general propositions which might then form a basis for nego-

---

4  On this range of issues, see *Towards a New Bretton Woods* (1983) and *The North South Dialogue: Making it Work* (1982), both produced by the Commonwealth Secretariat. In them a number of these ideas are amplified and alternatives discussed. It is a symptom of the breakdown in the North/South dialogue that these publications have not received the attention they deserved.

tiation on individual issues. These do not cover all aspects of the
world economy, but they all concern government policies which
would be helped by international co-operation. In addition, they all
relate to Third World problems which the United Nations has made
its special concern.

The first proposition is that the economic history of the period
since the mid-1970s – recession, the rise and fall of the oil price,
changing population patterns, the growing debt burden of some
developing countries – has clearly created a need for economic
*adjustment* worldwide. All countries have been called on to make
great sacrifices to meet such adjustments, but developing countries
are being called on to make greater sacrifices than are demanded of
developed countries; moreover, some developing countries are being
called on to make even greater sacrifices than others (so that
different sections of the Group of 77 now have different interests).
This is where the real injustice in the present situation occurs, rather
than in any past evils of colonialism. Perhaps, in accordance with
theories about economic development now current in some circles,
such adjustments *might* be left solely to 'market forces'. However,
in making such adjustments among themselves, developed countries
do not rely solely on market forces but use instead a whole range of
international 'interventionist' machinery from the EEC to the
Group of Five. They should therefore recognise that it might be
reasonable to consider whether adjustment between themselves and
developing countries might be helped by some measure of agreed
central regulation, rather than relying entirely on market forces, if
only to ensure 'policy compatibility'. The fact that market forces are
given a greater role in the domestic policies of some developed and
some developing countries than they have been in the past does not
mean that they are the *sole* remedy in the case of *all* countries and all
adjustment programmes, domestic and international. Are not
special measures – and measures additional to those now being
undertaken – necessary to assist developing countries to play their
part in the world processes of adjustment which all agree are
required?

The second object of the search for consensus would be to get
agreement on a list of substantive issues on which international co-
operation worldwide *might* promote beneficial action. Such a list is
not likely to be of startling originality – it would include such
matters as debt, commodities, monetary matters and various aspects
of international trade, although it might include others, such as
world unemployment and energy, which have not so far featured
prominently. Its importance would become clear in the next phase,
namely that of identifying in each case the conditions in which

negotiations might take place, the subjects the negotiations would need to cover and the possibilities of reaching agreement on international co-operative action (on which see below).

The third object of the search for consensus would be to get agreement on which geographical areas, or classes of country, need special treatment, and to review this list as circumstances change. The least developed and the Sahel zone would certainly be on any current list. But a stronger formal recognition by the international community that some classes of country, not by any means synonymous with the whole of the Group of 77, require special help (in ways to be identified as precisely as possible) from all countries capable of giving it and not just from developed countries, would be an important point of consensus.

## Devising the methods and the machinery

Having established these triple pillars of consensus, the next phase would be to establish a suitable basis for negotiations on individual issues. It would probably help to avoid the special pleading which goes on now when issues for negotiation are selected, if this process could take place in the first instance by quiet diplomacy outside the United Nations and its Agencies, between representative groups of developed and developing countries. The Commonwealth Secretariat or the EEC/ACP machinery in Brussels might be suitable for this purpose.

Once issues had been selected for this treatment, the next step would be to set up expert teams drawn from the Secretariats of *all* appropriate international organisations, whatever the economic bias of the institution and whether part of the United Nations or not, supported as necessary by outside expertise. Their task would be to analyse issues in detail, to establish the parameters of agreement and disagreement, and to set out the policy options and the possibilities of reaching agreement between the different interested parties. If this analysis was sufficiently encouraging, the next phase would be inter-governmental negotiation. Generally, the aim should be to make this at ministerial level. Initially, it would be useful to keep the groups as small as the nature of the subject permitted; therefore ministers would have to represent the interests of a group as well as their own government;[5] larger numbers could be involved as the negotiation proceeded.

One point should be stressed regarding the involvement of inter-

5  On this point see paras 4.22 *et seq*. of the *North South Dialogue* by the Commonwealth Secretariat, op. cit.

national organisations in the analytical phase. The teams must be inter-organisational and interdisciplinary (depending on the nature of the issue). This in itself ought to help avoid some of the difficulties which have arisen from excessive use within the UN System of the sectoral approach (so rightly castigated by M. Bertrand). Selecting these official teams for the analytical role could well be the task of the UN Director-General for Development and International Economic Co-operation. One organisation might be allotted a lead role depending on the nature of the subject, provided that this could be objectively justified by the nature of the task and not by some new process of Agency salesmanship.

## Identifying the resources to implement agreements

It should be made plain from the start that one of the purposes of these negotiation processes would be to identify – and ultimately agree upon – the resources available to implement the conclusions; and the provision of resources should normally form an integral part of any agreements reached. This would avoid the frustrations which arise when the conclusion of 'agreements', often embodied in resolutions, is followed by appeals for funding which are never met. It would be necessary to make it plain to participating ministers that ultimately they must be able to commit the necessary resources on behalf of their governments.

If some confidence is to be restored in the processes of international co-operation to promote economic and social welfare in developing countries, it will be necessary to focus on *negotiation* of particular issues. But for this to proceed successfully, it is necessary to establish some broad consensus on which issues might be negotiable in the light of current fashions in economic theory and economic policy worldwide, both among developed and developing countries. In these processes the United Nations and the Agencies – and above all their staffs – have a part to play, but to be useful they must be more realistic than in the past and they must work closely with competent organisations outside the United Nations.

However, it will probably be necessary to adopt this new approach gently and discreetly. It is not essential that it should immediately replace the UN procedures which have been followed since 1960 of passing generalised resolutions on the world economic and social situation. For one thing, developing countries are hardly likely to forgo the advantage they believe this gives them in drawing attention to their grievances. Moreover, such resolutions can even serve a useful purpose in identifying the problems which need consideration and even in generating some of the 'political will' required for their solution. What must end, however, is the pretence that such rhetoric is a substitute for serious negotiation on detailed measures related to clearly identified particular issues, which alone can offer prospects of real progress; and participants must stop using it to stimulate the spirit of confrontation which has hitherto been the principal fruit of UN debates on economic issues.

# CHAPTER XIX

# THE INTERNAL PROBLEMS OF THE SYSTEM

It was argued in Chapter XVII that the second major area causing concern was internal to the System: the absence of adequate control over the Executive Heads, the lack of co-ordination between the Agencies, inadequate control over the Agency budgets, overstaffing and maladministration.

This area has always been the primary concern of the System-wide reformers, and because of the intransigence of vested interests it will be the hardest one in which to make progress. Some of the attempts at reform have been described in earlier Chapters (notably Chapter IV). General Assembly Resolution 32/197 of 1977 marked their culmination, and its indifferent results have led many to despair of this kind of approach. Nevertheless a retrospective look at both the content and the consequences of Resolution 32/197 make a good starting point for considering the prospects of internal reform.

## The relevance of Resolution 32/197 to reform

Such approaches are attempts to produce order in the System from the top downwards. Thus the Annex to Resolution 32/197 starts with the General Assembly, which it describes as 'the supreme organ of the UN system in the economic and social fields', and which it calls upon 'to function as the principal forum for policy-making and for the harmonisation of international action' on international economic, social and related problems. It goes on to exhort the Assembly to 'concentrate on the establishment of over-all strategies, policies and priorities for the system as a whole in respect of international co-operation, including operational activities, in the economic, social and related fields. It may assign to other forums within the UN System, as necessary, the responsibility for negotiating and submitting recommendations for action in specific areas.' The General Assembly has been trying to do this – or something like this – at intervals since 1960, and the task has been shown to be altogether beyond its capacities. It may be beyond the capacity of any human institution at this time because divisions between nations over economic and social affairs are too great. However, this is not to argue that there is no need for a world body to consider some economic and social problems; by their very nature some of them are global (population, for example), and it can be a means of ensuring that various institutions co-operate properly in their solution.

The next level of activity tackled by Resolution 32/197 is that just below the General Assembly – namely the Economic and Social Council, which it exhorts 'to serve as the central forum for the discussion of international economic and social issues of a global interdisciplinary nature and the formulation of policy recommendations thereon addressed to Member States and to the UN system as a whole'. Thereafter ECOSOC is instructed to 'monitor and evaluate the implementation of all strategies, policies and priorities established by the General Assembly in the economic, social and related fields' as well as 'to ensure the overall co-ordination of the activities of the organisations of the United Nations system' in all these fields. The rest of the recommendations on ECOSOC are procedural and structural, for example on the biennial formulation of programmes of work, the streamlining and discontinuance of various subordinate committees and change in the membership of ECOSOC's committees. These structural changes apart, the role envisaged for ECOSOC in Resolution 32/197 is not radically different from that which it was supposed to have been performing previously. The great weakness of these recommendations is that few people – whether inside or outside the UN System – would be prepared to take them seriously. The people really responsible for the major decisions affecting the world economy would not be prepared to see ECOSOC become the 'major forum' even for their discussion, let alone for their negotiation. Nor do the Specialized Agencies show much sign of being willing to accept ECOSOC as having a major responsibility for ensuring 'overall co-ordination' of their activities. Constitutionally and structurally ECOSOC is not equipped to perform this role. Unless ECOSOC's role is changed radically as part of some fundamental reform of the UN System, such as that envisaged in Chapter V of the Bertrand Report (which might involve revising Chapters IX and X of the Charter), the prospects for making it more effective are not good, particularly since revision of the Charter requires the agreement of all five permanent members of the Security Council, never an easy goal to achieve.

At a third level, Resolution 32/197 deals with 'other UN forums for negotiation, including UNCTAD and other UN organs and programmes, the Specialized Agencies, the IAEA and *ad hoc* World Conferences'. These bodies it urges 'to co-operate in whatever measures are necessary for the effective discharge of the responsibilities of the General Assembly and the Economic and Social Council'. It states in particular: 'In carrying out their respective mandates, all UN organs and programmes, agencies and *ad hoc*

World Conferences should be similarly guided by the overall policy framework established by the General Assembly and the Economic and Social Council, taking fully into account the needs and requirements of the developing countries.' This is very much a counsel of perfection, which has so far produced no change in the practices of these bodies, because the General Assembly Resolutions express no real policy consensus between the member states.

The fourth level is that of regional organisations where improvements are suggested for the structures of regional and inter-regional co-operation. They are urged to 'exercise team leadership and responsibility for co-ordination at the regional level'. The principal means proposed for improving their discharge of this task are 'to strengthen and, as appropriate, expand existing arrangements for the continuous exchange between them of information and experience'. These, even more than some of the earlier recommendations in Resolution 32/197, are the suggestions of bureaucrats at their wits' end as to what to do next, and resorting instead to platitudinous generalisations which in practice will produce little change from previous performance, whereas they ought to be making very specific suggestions. In fact the possibility of securing more effective co-ordination through regional organisations deserves some serious and detailed examination. It might, in particular, be easier to negotiate constitutional changes which would give the regional organisations a co-ordinating role *vis-à-vis* the Agencies than it would be to negotiate changes in the Charter itself.

However, a modest level of success has rewarded the fifth level of changes suggested by Resolution 32/197, concerning the operational activities of the UN System. This was 'the achievement of optimum efficiency and the reduction of administrative costs with a consequent increase in the proportion of resources available to meet assistance requirements of recipient countries' – surely a laudable objective. Two reforms were urged, both of which have been adopted. The first dealt with the voluntary funds and programmes, and suggested that instead of all these funds and programmes soliciting their annual contributions separately, there should be held a single annual United Nations' pledging conference for all UN operational activities for development.[1] This arrangement has been introduced; at the pledging conference held on 30 June 1985 just over US$1 billion was pledged to the twenty-three funds participating in

1  Detailed descriptions of all the funds covered by the pledges for 1986 are given in the Annex to the UN Secretary-General's Circular FI 323/4(9) of September 1985. The full pledges made for 1985 are given in General Assembly Document Note by Secretary-General A/Conf. 126/2 of 18 September 1985.

these arrangements. They ranged all the way from the UNDP, to which US$636 million was pledged, to the UN Trust Fund for the Transport and Communications Decade in Africa which attracted only US$18,000. The arrangements have certainly proved administratively tidier than those which previously existed, and they are more convenient to governments. However, there is not yet any evidence to suggest that they have been more successful in raising additional funds for the UN programmes. As long as the present multiplicity of funds and programmes is retained, the single pledging session is a good idea because it emphasises the inter-relationship between these sources of finance, but any expectation that it might increase the general level of funding is likely to be disappointed. Furthermore, the arrangement is not an adequate substitute for the Jackson proposal to channel the major part of voluntary funds through the UNDP.

The second set of recommendations at this level go back in origin to Jackson. These are that 'overall responsibility for and co-ordination of operational activities for development carried out at country level should be entrusted to a single official . . . who should be responsible for evolving at country level a multidisciplinary dimension in sectoral development assistance programmes.' This is the origin of the proposals for 'Resident Co-ordinators' who, as previously explained, are beginning to enjoy a modest success (reinforced by the new form of co-ordinating group known as the 'Round Table').

The sixth level dealt with in the Resolution concerns planning, programming and co-ordination. It concerns the responsibilities of the Committee for Programming and Co-ordination where the Resolution tries to simplify procedures. It states that 'measures should be taken to improve the effectiveness of internal evaluation procedures in respect of programme implementation' – as indeed they certainly should, but the Resolution does not suggest how this might be done. It exhorts all the Agencies to 'intensify their efforts to develop harmonised budget presentations' to improve their processes of programme budgeting and to secure greater co-operation between the Committee for Programme and Co-ordination and the ACABQ. The recommendations are highly bureaucratic and not very specific. It is understood that those parts of them which could be implemented by the UN Secretariat have been reasonably successful, but have hardly produced a revolution. It has done little to produce greater co-operation from the Agencies.

The seventh level addressed by the Resolution ought to be the most critical of all – at least from the point of view of the problems we are dealing with in this volume. This is the level of inter-Agency Co-ordination. It treats two areas of activity – the intergovernmental and the inter-secretariat. The intergovernmental, it declares, should 'be governed by the policy guidelines, directives and priorities established by the General Assembly'. In the inter-secretariat area, co-ordination should 'centre on the Administrative Committee on Co-ordination under the leadership of the Secretary-General', and should be responsible for 'preparing, in compliance with the relevant general and specific legislative directives, concise and action-oriented recommendations for consideration by the inter-governmental bodies concerned'. This part of the resolution's proposals seems to have produced some tidying up in the machinery but not much change in the performance – largely because they cannot impose the necessary discipline on the Agencies.

Finally, at the eighth level are proposals for changes in Secretariat Support Services which have been implemented and which have produced some beneficial results. In particular, the Secretary-General was invited to appoint a Director-General for Development and International Co-operation 'at a high level . . . who would effectively assist him in carrying out his responsibilities . . . in the economic and social fields'. Included in his terms of reference is 'exercising over-all co-ordination within the system in order to ensure a multi-disciplinary approach to the problems of development on a system-wide basis'. This appointment has been made, and has had some success at least in identifying where some of the problems lie and giving publicity to them. However, there has been little sign up to the present that he has been able to impose fresh discipline on the Agencies.

### The possibilities of further reform

Although its success in securing improvements in the System has been no more than modest at best, Resolution 32/197 does make it possible to identify most of the points where improvements need to be sought.

The first thing to be considered is whether there is any need for a System at all. Those who drafted the UN Charter deliberately made the Agencies so independent in their sectors that it is necessary to ask whether combining them in the present loose System under the United Nations adds anything to their performance or merely increases the general complexity of both the UN and the Agencies' bureaucracies.

The answer is that some measure of central regulation – and therefore of 'systematisation' – is necessary. For this there are four main reasons. The first lies in the nature of the process of 'development'. Although the Agencies are organised on a sectoral basis for professional reasons, development takes place in societies as a whole. What happens in one sector affects whole economies and societies. Sectors interact, and unless this fact is recognised in the way public business is organised, the result is friction and a waste of resources; this is exactly what has been happening in the UN System. The second reason is that the basis on which most of the Agencies were set up and have operated since 1945 is Chapter IX of the UN Charter. Under Article 58 of the Charter, the United Nations is charged with making 'recommendations for the co-ordination of the policies and activities of the specialized agencies'. If the attempt to make this Article work is abandoned, it is yet one more blow to the Charter as a whole; while not mortal, it will certainly not help the cause of international co-operation. Thirdly, unless some system of international taxation can be found for financing the Agencies, they must continue to look for their support to member government contributions – whether assessed or voluntary. Such funds are bound to be limited, and the Agencies are bound to be in competition for them. Some central control is necessary to regulate this struggle for funds as well as to monitor how they are spent. Finally, if the United Nations and its Agencies are to be considered a 'family', some uniformity is desirable in their staffing arrangements and terms of service, if only in the interest of securing good staff management.

## The problem of centralised regulation

What then has gone wrong in the attempts up to the present to systematise the operations of the United Nations and its Specialized Agencies? The first clue is provided by Resolution 32/197 when it calls on the General Assembly to concentrate on 'overall strategies, policies and priorities for the system as a whole'. All attempts to do this so far have failed, and the reason is not far to seek. It lies in the very procedures of the United Nations itself as they have developed since 1960. The aim of most General Assembly debates is to reach agreement on a form of words in a Resolution which most member states will vote for, or at least not vote against. This is particularly true of economic issues on which it is very difficult to negotiate firm agreements because they usually involve some sacrifice of real interests. This is what most members mean by 'consensus', whereas what the word ought to mean if their votes are to produce some concerted action is 'general agreement on how the constituent parts of the United Nations are to work together to achieve a common purpose'. Under such an interpretation of 'consensus', the UN

General Assembly would not be called upon to pass its Resolutions on strategy and priorities until patient preliminary diplomacy had established that there was, on the face of it, a good chance of acceptance by a sufficient number of parties to make the Resolution work. The UN General Assembly does not possess the authority, by virtue of either its constitution or its past history, to impose strategies or priorities, even on the organisations in its own 'family'. Until a different view of the General Assembly's method of operation in determining global economic and social strategy begins to prevail, there is little hope of securing a better orchestration of the operations of the System.

## More radical solutions?

Some will argue that the modest level of the results obtained from Resolution 32/197 is due to its not having been radical enough. This is somewhat hypothetical. In any event, the weakness of radical solutions is that they would require major reforms of structure, which in turn would require great changes in constitutional instruments calling for years of complicated negotiation, with little prospect of success if these involved revision of the UN Charter. Moreover, there would be no guarantee of real improvements at the end of it, because the weaknesses of the present System lie in the fact that too many member governments have connived at its abuses and may wish to continue so doing. Most of the abuses can be reformed without changes in the present constitutional instruments; the way to achieve this is for a sufficient number of member governments to press consistently over time for their replacement by better *practices*. Furthermore, it is highly desirable that the governments pressing for these reforms should.be from both developed and developing countries. The financial crisis facing the United Nations because of the Kassebaum Amendment and other factors could be an excellent moment to begin this process.

However, it is important to note that much of the present trouble arises because it is much too easy for those with a vested interest in maintaining the existing shortcomings to play developing countries off against developed countries. If both groups could recognise the extent to which they have a common interest in reform, progress would be possible. Machinery for identifying this common interest may not be easy to find; especially since, for tactical reasons, it would be desirable to look for it *outside* the United Nations. The Commonwealth Secretariat again suggests itself as a possibility, especially if a Commonwealth initiative could be organised by two such countries as Canada and Kenya.

There is a possibility of more limited reforms, in favour of which pressure might be exerted. One such reform (not reflected in Resolution 32/197 for diplomatic reasons) would aim at ensuring that the Executive Heads of Agencies are more concerned with giving an effective service to the international community in their specialist functional field than with building up the importance of their organisation within the System. This, obviously, is more easily said than done. As was pointed out earlier, the Headships of the Specialized Agencies are regarded as prestige appointments, not just for the individual holder but also for the country from which he comes. The holders are elected to office, and their election entails intense political lobbying, not only for the successful candidate but also against his rivals. It is a process likely to produce somebody more renowned for his political acumen than for professional skills or managerial ability in the specialist field required. Unless the governing body concerned gives a strong lead in the direction of functional efficiency (as some of them do, including some of the better known), he will be more concerned with issues such as maintaining his personal position or the prestige of his organisation, or (which can be worse) with being re-elected to office, than with the technical performance of his Agency. He may endorse policies which favour sectional or regional interests because they support him electorally, rather than through any consideration of the broader interests of developing countries or of the international community. A major step forward would be to limit the term of office of Executive Heads to, at most, two terms; this would be practicable, even where the constitution permits otherwise, if a sufficient majority of member states were to agree. However able, most Agency Heads have run out of ideas after two terms, and from then on they are clinging to office for other reasons.

There is a corollary to the extension of the terms of office of Executive Heads which deserves more attention than it usually receives. This is the almost automatic continuation of certain programmes of work in some Specialized Agencies without any independent outside evaluation of their usefulness or their results. The preservation of such programmes can easily become another vested interest to a Secretariat, with tasks incompetently performed and rendering no real service for the international community – a situation likely to continue as long as any evaluation of such programmes is either not done at all or only done 'in house'. Member governments, if they combine, can produce important changes in this area which will have wholly beneficial effects on Agency performance.

## Co-ordination

Another area in which only member governments can produce improvement – or sustain the improvement already attained – is co-ordination. There are three weaknesses in present arrangements which have been evident since the 1950s. First, there is no directing authority at the centre of the System to allot tasks and insist on a reasonable degree of co-operation. Secondly (and despite some recent improvements), at the point where planning inputs are made into any country's development programme, some of the bilateral donors for political or commercial reasons will not provide the necessary information about their plans and intentions. And thirdly, there are recipient governments whose administrations are not up to the task of planning and co-ordinating external aid – this is especially notable in those very countries which most need external assistance.

Short of constitutional changes in the United Nations which would introduce a more hierarchical structure into the whole System, almost the only way of achieving progress at the top is for the Secretary-General or possibly the holder of the Office of Director-General for Development and International Co-operation, by steady pressure and with the support of important groups of member states, to acquire greater influence over the Agency Heads. Member states should give the holders of both offices every encouragement, and the necessary resources, to exert this sort of influence; but it will be a long haul.

On the question of achieving better co-ordination by collective planning of the inputs either into an interdisciplinary programme or into a country, the ideal desiderata have long been recognised: an agreed analysis of a country's or region's economic situation; an agreed plan for mobilising the necessary external capital resources; planning how to match these with locally mobilised resources; and agreed schemes for furnishing the necessary technical assistance. All this has been tried with modest success in the Consortia and the Consultative Groups of the World Bank on behalf of the bigger countries such as India, and more recently in the 'Round Tables' organised by the UNDP on behalf of the least developed countries. However, the ideal pattern tends to disintegrate for a variety of reasons: sometimes because the recipient countries are less than wholehearted in their co-operation, but more often because the providers of the inputs, both bilateral and multilateral, often for reasons of political or commercial interest, are less frank than they should be about their intentions. The principal cure for this situation lies with the bilateral donors. They discussed the question at ministerial level in the DAC in 1983 and arrived at an admirable set of platitudinous conclusions[2] which seem to have made little difference in practice, and are hardly likely to do so as long as the more important of the donors concerned remain wedded to policies of '*crédits mixtes*' and aid-tying.

The best hope of effective co-ordination remains at country level, but here we should give a word of warning. Failure to achieve it is sometimes depicted as some kind of moral delinquency on the part of developing countries, but this is unfair. Effective co-ordination is time-consuming and resource-consuming, and its achievement requires the personal attention of somebody with both ability and authority, as well as the necessary machinery. Such persons are usually to be found, not among ministers but among the abler officials in developing countries who are, however, usually over-worked already on other more immediately important tasks. Before any form of co-ordination at country level is insisted upon, its cost-effectiveness in terms of accelerated development must be constantly monitored by all concerned – including those who insist on it. It must be made worthwhile to the recipient country. Only donor poli-cies can ensure this.

## Staffing and administration

There is also the question of administration and personnel, analysed in some detail in Chapter XI. The remedy for the situation which has developed lies in a return to the principles of Article 101.3 of the Charter: 'The paramount consideration in the employment of the staff and in the determination of the conditions of service shall be the necessity of securing the highest standards of efficiency, com-petence, and integrity. Due regard shall be paid to the importance of recruiting the staff on as wide a geographical basis as possible.'

The main reason why this principle has been breached is that in relation to the Specialized Agencies, for a variety of reasons, most of them misguided, the Western countries gave up the struggle to main-tain it. They must resume it if they think that the UN System as a whole is valuable, and they must encourage developing countries to support it. This does not mean that they have to campaign for the appointment of their own nationals, some of whom have not always lived up to the highest possible standard, but merely that they should insist on the 'highest standard of efficiency, competence, and integrity' as the first criterion for whoever is appointed. This is now going to be a long uphill journey, but when the United States has

2  See DAC Chairman, *Annual Report for 1983*, Paris: OECD.

withdrawn from UNESCO and when the Kassebaum Amendment is about to take effect – i.e. while everyone is still in a state of shock – is probably the right moment to start.

## Budgetary control

Budgetary controls that are internal to the System have probably attained as good a level as can be devised. This is thanks to a number of procedures ranging from the processes of internal audit to the general supervision of the ACABQ and of the Fifth Committee. However, they need to be sustained. The weaknesses come from governing councils who approve extravagant programmes, often on the advice of misguided secretariats, in the knowledge that they can force the resulting expenditure on those who lack the voting power to resist. Again Kassebaum, regrettable as it is in many ways, might in this instance have a salutary effect. In the mean time, the Geneva Group are probably right in many cases to insist on 'zero real growth'. Where they are wrong is to try to insist on this across the board, regardless of the usefulness of the programmes being undertaken and the effectiveness of the Agency carrying them out. Indeed this blanket limitation is a measure of the lack of seriousness with which the Geneva Group countries have come to treat the System; their object has become one of damage limitation, not of improved performance. This attitude needs to change if the System is to be both preserved and improved. We will examine this question further in the next Chapter.

# CHAPTER XX

# ACTIONS BY MEMBER STATES

We argued earlier that the member countries have the UN System which they deserve. The weaknesses which have allowed the Executive Heads of some Agencies to become over-powerful, and some administrations to become swollen with staff of doubtful competence spending money on programmes of questionable utility, lie mostly in the attitudes with which governments have approached the work of these Agencies. In debate among UN *aficionados* about reform of the System, there will doubtless continue to be much discussion of structural reform and management techniques. Although these are important, the situation will remain much as it has been without some change in the attitudes of member governments. It naturally cannot be pretended that such a change will of itself be sufficient to produce reform, but it is a necessary precondition if there are to be any lasting reforms.

But before any progress can be achieved, it is desirable to arrive at a degree of broad agreement across the North–South divide on the nature of the changes both sides would like to see. These are changes *in practice, without changes in the existing constitutions* of the Agencies. A government, or a small group of governments would need to take the initiative, but before any detailed proposals are launched, the issues must be carefully examined. If governments were to agree, this would be a suitable task for a body like the Commonwealth Secretariat or for a group of outside experts, suitably supported. For the objectivity of such an exercise to be guaranteed it would be essential in the first instance for it to be undertaken outside the UN ambit, and preferably involving a small group representing both North and South. Before any proposals are formally launched, ministers should be involved; the matter should not simply be left to officials, otherwise this could become just another academic exercise to join many others on library shelves. Some possible objectives for these discussions are suggested below. The overriding purpose would be, first, to make the UN System more effective in rendering services in its functional specialities to all states, with special reference to the problems of the developing countries. Secondly, it would propose how the United Nations and its machinery could be better employed and organised to negotiate economic and social change globally.

Meanwhile, there are several steps which might be taken immediately by member states to lessen strain within the UN System. For example, there should be some self-denying ordinance on raising contentious political issues in fora where they are marginal to the terms of reference of the organisations concerned or outside them altogether. This point needs to be clarified. There should be no question of avoiding contentious issues which are clearly *within* the mandates of the organisations simply because they are contentious; however, there should be agreement to limit those on which, in the light of experience, no progress is likely to be made in the organisations concerned. Intensive efforts should be made elsewhere to resolve intractable issues of this kind. Otherwise some agreed procedural changes, limiting the number of contentious political issues per session, might help to improve the atmosphere and leave more time to concentrate on functional performance. All states, however, should make it plain that where contentious issues are raised in any forum – whether or not they are clearly within its mandate – they will 'fight their corner' and stand up for their principles. They render a disservice to their cause and to the System in the long run if they let their case go by default on the ground that voting procedures are so loaded against them that the argument is not worth the effort. This applies particularly to voting on human right issues in UNESCO, or to labour issues in the ILO, on which some delegations in the past have been too ready to adopt a 'low profile' for the sake of peace and quiet. It is the argument, not the voting, that is important. All countries should recognise that one of the main purposes of the United Nations must be to help them to live together in amity, despite their deep divisions of interest and opinion which there is no point in disguising while they exist.[1]

Another area in which agreement might be sought is that of a return to the principles in Article 101 of the Charter on the appointment of staff, to which reference was made in the last Chapter. It ought to be universally accepted that it is in everyone's interest to ensure that the UN System does not become a dumping ground for incompetents recruited 'on as wide a geographical basis as possible'. In the past there have been two difficulties about implementing the principles of Article 101. The first is that the rest of the world has silently acquiesced in the Soviet bloc's view that adherence to Communist principles is more important than 'efficiency, competence and integrity' in the staff they send to international

---

1 Some of the damage in UNESCO has been caused by the United States not defending its position sufficiently vigorously at an early stage of discussion on the World Information Order but instead exhibiting what the *Wall Street Journal* of 5 December 1978 castigated as 'a kind of crazed cheefulness in the face of yet another erosion of liberal values'.

organisations. The second has been the difficulties of developing countries which have had staff of sufficient 'efficiency, competence and integrity', but have wanted them in their own government service and not serving in an international organisation. This last situation is changing, as the experience with staffing IFAD has shown. Perhaps the governments of all countries should consider whether the time is ripe for a change of policy in their nominations to the United Nations and the Agencies, and how all their interests would be served by the nomination of more competent staff.

Where member governments, in discussion between themselves, might seriously examine the possibility of progress is the joint area of decision making and fund raising. This will probably be more difficult than the first two, but it is worth a trial, especially in the light of the experience with IFAD and the provisions in the constitution of UNIDO about the Programme and Budget Committee. In fact the Kassebaum Amendment will make some reconsideration of this question essential. The problem may in part be one of assessed budgets and voluntary funds as sources of Specialized Agency expenditure; but it is now more widely accepted than previously that there has to be some trade-off between majority control and minority funding, if the minority are to be persuaded to provide the funds which the majority want. Equally, the majority ought to be given a bigger say in the policies on which funds are to be spent. A continuing attitude of 'stand and deliver' on the part of the developing countries will get nowhere. A response from the developed countries which stresses nothing but cost-efficiency and has no regard for the wishes of the developing countries concerning the programmes to be undertaken will breed continuing frustration. Some kind of weighted voting, decided organisation by organisation or, more probably, programme by programme, might make more funds available, ensure their cost-efficient disbursement, and make them more relevant to the needs of developing countries. Again, the Kassebaum Amendment might help to clarify thinking on this issue. However, before those who want weighted voting press for it, they must give other countries firm assurances that more resources will be forthcoming as a reward.

If some modest programmes of advance along these lines could be agreed internationally among a limited group of countries across the North-South divide, they could then be discussed in other groups of countries such as the OECD and the DAC, the EEC, the OAS, the OAU, CARICOM, ASEAN and other groupings – again, preferably outside the aegis of the United Nations to begin with. The points at which groups of governments have a common interest in the reform of performance (reforming constitutions or systems might be too difficult) might then emerge, and they could press them consistently in governing bodies and back them with funds once they were satisfied with the changes taking place.

Meanwhile, there are a number of reforms 'in house' which all governments should consider. First, developed countries should reconsider whether their present attitude of 'damage limitation' towards the Specialized Agencies (especially the Big Five) best serves their interests. Obviously some form of budgetary restraint is to be insisted upon in circumstances where those who pay the piper do not call the tune; but if the System is to continue working, it is necessary for the principal paymasters to give more attention to the content of programmes and their relevance to the attainment of the agreed objectives of these organisations, rather than exclusively to the volume of expenditure; this, in turn, must entail a better dialogue with developing countries about the content of programmes.

One of the troubles is that, in developed countries, policies towards the Specialized Agencies are too often determined either by ministries of finance (which are concerned with limiting expenditure) or by ministries of foreign affairs (which are primarily concerned with maintaining cordial foreign relations). Neither are well equipped to make a constructive contribution to a debate on functional issues, or even to recognise their significance. Yet within a number of developed countries – notably in Western Europe, Japan and the United States – as well as in some developing countries, there are considerable bodies of knowledge and skill which could make a significant contribution to evaluating many Specialized Agency programmes, thereby greatly improving the quality of Agency debates and the contribution they can make to evolving sound development policies in the Third World. Indeed, the nuclear accident at Chernobyl in 1986 demonstrated that it is not simply the Third World which can benefit from these processes. There are whole areas of public policy worldwide where new knowledge is having an impact and where all governments can benefit from the freer exchange of information and of knowledge about its applicability which the Specialized Agencies can provide. Such an approach, however, has a corollary. Governments that want to make the UN System more effective have to realise that this will demand more than a different diplomatic skill and funds to finance programmes run by the Agencies. It demands from each participating country a continuing intellectual input which will cost real resources to mobilise, the more so since most of the programmes deal with tropical countries while much of the intellectual input must come from the temperate zone.

Developed countries are not unaware of these possibilities.

Indeed, most OECD countries and the EEC itself now have policies and machinery to mobilise knowledge and research at all levels – basic, strategic, applied and adaptive research – to meet the needs and problems of developing countries, as well as other problems of a global rather than exclusively national character. Sometimes, as in Japan, this machinery is relatively new. Sometimes, as in France and Britain, much of it is of very long standing. What seems to be lacking in some developed countries, however, is any attempt to relate such policies and machinery to those of the Specialized Agencies.

Another change which, if made in all countries, would contribute usefully to a more effective System is a recognition that diplomacy conducted through the multilateral Agencies, whether inside or outside the United Nations, requires different techniques and skills from bilateral diplomacy through which most of the world's intergovernmental business is still done. This fact and its implications need to be appreciated by two different sets of people when dealing with the Specialized Agencies. The first set are the professional diplomats, whose styles and expectations are often geared to the give-and-take of bilateral *negotiation* between governments. This is not what is happening much of the time in the governing bodies of Specialized Agencies. The game that is being played there is partly that of general debate on broad issues, with conclusions that are simply recommendations (often not very precisely formulated); and partly that of administering technical business, with whose subject-matter the diplomat is probably unfamiliar. The techniques for performing in this environment have been studied,[2] and they can be taught. Some delegations are better at it than others. The second group who need to be educated in the facts of life in Specialized Agencies are the technocrats. They often get so carried away by their specialist enthusiasms that they have little regard for the consequences of their decisions on wider aspects of Specialized Agency diplomacy and indeed on their own governments' interests. They must be taught to take such matters into account.

Finally, all countries need to make a greater effort to improve their internal machinery for co-ordinating their policies towards the Agencies within the UN System. It is ironic that so many of them castigate the UN System for lack of co-ordination while at the same time, through failures in domestic organisation, they contribute to the confusion. This is not to say that, in dealing with something as

2 See, for example, Johan Kaufman, *Conference Diplomacy*, Dobbs Ferry, NY: Oceana, 1968.

diverse and wide-ranging as the UN System, co-ordination is easy; it is not, especially for developing countries. But if it can be improved, and if it can be accompanied by a willingness by all countries to use the Agencies more constructively than in the past, then the results in a few years could justify the effort.

# CHAPTER XXI

# CONCLUSIONS

We began by describing the United Nations System as being 'under strain'. We must conclude by describing it as being probably in a state of 'crisis'. The strain was the culmination of certain factors which have long operated: the use of Specialized Agency forums to discuss subjects not clearly related to their functional reponsibilities; the lack of co-ordination between the Agencies based on lack of authority in the United Nations; declining standards among the staff; voting procedures unrelated to national strength or to financial contributions; and, above all, profound differences of view among the members of the United Nations about the aims and methods of economic and social policy.

The trigger for the crisis as it manifested itself in the spring of 1986 came from the United States in the form of the Kassebaum Amendment, reinforced by the Gramm-Rudman Act. This crisis is not purely financial. Once the legislation begins to bite, it will force a major world power – one of the principal founders of the United Nations and its Specialized Agencies – into a breach of its treaty obligations under the Charter. Moreover, it will do so not as a result of a policy decision by the government but by the will of an elected legislature. This betokens a lack of popular support in a major world democracy for the United Nations and its Agencies which is serious – not least because a similar trend can be seen in other Western democracies.

It is not possible to foresee at the time of writing what solutions may be found to the difficulties produced by Kassebaum and Gramm-Rudman. Indeed a long period of growing embarrassment and confusion for the United Nations and the Agencies will probably ensue without any tidy solution being found at all. Muddle and dissension are more likely to be the consequences of Kassebaum and Gramm-Rudman than either major reform or total collapse. The reason for this is that to attempt major reform would reveal so many wide differences between governments and groups of countries that it would probably only widen the dissensions. On the other hand, few governments would be willing to see a total collapse of the UN System. All of them have benefitted at some time from the operations of parts of it; none of them can foresee when and in what circumstances they may need to resort to it again, as was shown by the role which the IAEA played in 1986 in the aftermath of the Chernobyl accident. Moreover, few governments would be in favour of the blow to international co-operation which such a breakdown would entail.

This reluctance to see the demise of the UN System seems to be manifested even by the 'free enterprise' school of its critics, represented by the Heritage Foundation in New York and the Adam Smith Institute in London. Thus, Douglas Bandow recommends simply that 'the United Kingdom, after forty years in the United Nations, should initiate a complete review of the UN Agencies to which it is affiliated.[1] The purpose of this review would be to 'investigate the activities and the excesses of each UN agency . . . assessing their impact on Britain's interests and their success or failure in promoting liberal social and economic institution on which genuine future progress depends'.[2] These suggested terms of reference are obviously more than somewhat 'loaded', but clearly they aim at an evaluation of the UN System according to certain criteria and not at its abolition.

Assuming therefore that the majority of governments throughout the world will wish to see the Specialized Agencies continue their work, what can be done to improve their performance and the climate in which they operate? We summarise below the conclusions which emerge from earlier Chapters.

## Recognising the historical context

It would help to reduce the strains which have arisen in the UN System if all concerned would recognise that – despite particular incidents such as the withdrawal from UNESCO or the Kassebaum Amendment – they result from a secular crisis in the relationships between the Third World and the West. What is done to reduce the strain will largely depend on how governments – on both sides – see these relations, what importance they attach to them, and what sacrifices they are prepared to make to see them improved.

This observation applies with special force to two particular aspects of the problem. One is that of debating 'political' issues in fora where they are – in the view of some powerful governments – outside the 'competence and mandate' of the organisation concerned. The second is that of the economic relations between North and South, and the demands summarised in the resolutions setting out the New International Economic Order. Both these aspects of the problem raise very difficult issues. International

1 Douglas Bandow, *Unquestioned Allegiance*, London: Adam Smith Institute, 1986, p. 28.
2 Ibid.

relations generally would be helped if all governments would recognise that some issues are not yet ripe for negotiation either inside or
outside the UN machinery; and if they would refrain from raising
them in forums where they are not relevant to the main operations
and where there are other matters to be discussed on which negotiations are possible, with results that would benefit international co-
operation and be of practical service. All governments need to
recognise that in our world we must live together, and *work together*,
despite our differences, however profound. Within the UN
machinery there are forums where every international issue,
however contentious, can be properly discussed. Governments
should recognise this fact. Such self-denial will not be easy to
achieve; but it can be done at no cost to any government and at no
disadvantage to any cause.

Economic issues are in a different category; they are contentious
and deeply divisive, because they are in fact disputes about the division of real resources; but they are also both a major element in relations between the West and the Third World and relevant to the work
of the Specialized Agencies. Thus commodity arrangements are
relevant to the work of FAO; balance of payments policies affect
employment and hence the work of the ILO and UNIDO; arrangements for technology transfer can affect many agencies from IAEA
to the WHO. Until more progress can be made on these issues, the
UN and its System will continue under strain.

Before progress can be made, however, countries must recognise
that much of the UN machinery is inadequate for the serious
bargaining which must accompany negotiation on these economic
issues. General Assembly resolutions and their counterparts in the
Specialized Agencies may have their uses for purposes of agitation;
they are poor instruments for negotiation. In consequence their
effect on the real world in economic matters is slight. This suits those
who are well content with the economic *status quo*. Curiously, it also
suits many of those who profess to want change, because it substitutes the rhetoric of resolutions for serious thought about the
methods and implications of change.

At the same time, within the components of the UN System there
are both considerable deposits of information about the world
economy and people with talent for analysing it and relating it to
issues which might be ripe for negotiation. There are also considerable bodies of information and talent *outside* the System which
equally have a contribution to make. If enough governments across
the North/South divide would agree, all this talent could be
organised to identify and analyse issues which appear ripe for negotiation so that some progress can be made piecemeal in organising

the processes of economic change and adjustment in a way which would contribute to worldwide prosperity.

## Co-ordination and the sectoral approach

The problems of co-ordination among a group of autonomous agencies, each pursuing its sectoral interests, have been present from the outset of the UN System. A seemingly disproportionate amount of effort has been devoted to the subject over the years, resulting only in minimal improvements. The need for some form of co-ordination remains. It is suggested that the time has come to learn from past experience and to rethink the problem as it relates to the UN System.

What should co-ordination try to achieve in so vast a collection of diverse operations as those undertaken by the UN System?

First, it should provide a better definition of priorities as between sectors while leaving priorities *within* sectors largely to the Agencies. This, however, is very difficult to do worldwide or to apply universally. Although the task has seemingly been attempted in UN resolutions, the result has not been a serious definition of priorities but an emphasis on whatever happened to be the development panacea fashionable at the time (e.g. industrial development and import substitution in the 1960s, agriculture in the 1980s); or else a ragbag of proposals designed to gratify all vested interests. All concerned need in future to be more realistic. Broad priorities between sectors can be defined provided everybody accepts the limitations on the accuracy of the forecasts on which such broad planning must be based (e.g. in population growth or food production). Real sectoral priorities must be built up on a country basis and revised on that basis as the situation changes; therefore the attempt to settle world development priorities on a global basis, either by UN resolution or by action of the UN Secretariat, must have severe limitations. The fact that these limitations are exploited by empire-building Agency secretariats for their own ends does not mean that they will be overcome by strengthening 'New York' against the Agencies. They will be overcome by better processes of decision making at country level by individual governments. Better co-ordination does not mean more centralisation.

The second object of co-ordination in the UN System has been to define more accurately what objectives of policy are attainable in Third World development and what alternative means might be used to reach them. The UN System's efforts in this direction have produced few results. The account given in Chapter XIII of UN efforts in the field of scientific research shows something of what has gone wrong as well as the possibility of alternatives. There is a bias in UN organisations towards relying exclusively on sources of information available within the System and for establishing objectives which will add to the bureaucratic complexity of the System rather than providing solutions to the problems with which the System is intended to deal. The Agencies need to become more open, especially to the possibilities of working better on clearly specified tasks with organisations outside the System – both public and private – likely to produce results of benefit to all, but especially to developing countries. They need also to consider better arrangements for relating their vast stores of information to appropriate programmes of action whether or not such programmes originate within the UN System.

The third object of co-ordination has been that of preventing overlap and promoting a better division of labour between the System's component parts. Failure to make progress in this area is a serious scandal, which brings the entire System into disrepute every time it occurs. The main problem is not one of machinery but of bringing it home to those responsible that they do themselves, their organisations, their clients and the System great damage every time overlap occurs. It ought not to require changes in Charter provisions to deal with it (e.g. through the strengthening of ECOSOC). It ought to suffice to secure changes *in practice* which would enable the UN Secretary-General to arbitrate in cases of dispute and allocate lead roles to those best able to perform them. Press exposure of scandals of overlap together with continued pressure from member governments ought to produce a more satisfactory situation *de facto* over time. There has been some improvement since 1980: there could be more.

Lastly there is one other element of the UN's efforts at co-ordination which must be mentioned – that of some central evaluation of programmes. Evaluation of results so that lessons can be learned and applied elsewhere is an important part of financing all development projects and programmes. However, it is a more difficult process than the non-expert might assume – so much depends on the techniques used, the time at which it takes place (i.e. how long after project completion) and the scale of resources devoted to it. In the UN System, however, the worst defects could be removed by evaluating *programmes*, especially those which have run for some years without any proper outside independent examination, and which are continued simply as a result of some vested interest, often in the Secretariat. Member governments, through their representatives on governing bodies, should press for this more effectively. What has clearly failed is the attempt to secure better co-ordination directly through using a single financial channel like the UNDP. This failure is probably largely due to the fact that even where UNDP controls the money, it has not got enough technical know-how to decide what activities to spend it on; for this it depends on the resources of the Agencies. It has far fewer professional resources 'in house' than has the World Bank, and in view of the wide spectrum of its operations in the technical assistance field, this situation must continue. The idea that the UNDP should orchestrate the UN development effort by being the sole channel or even the principal channel of the technical assistance funds in the UN System has suited almost nobody – neither donors, nor recipients, nor Agencies – whatever lip-service they may have paid to it. In that form it should be abandoned. What should continue are the efforts to make the UNDP the largest single channel of technical assistance funds. Its skills in administering such funds should continue to be built up, including those of seeking the best technical advice outside as well as inside the Agencies. Its efforts to secure better co-ordination on the ground in co-operation with local administrations, on a country-by-country basis, should be increased.

## Finance, voting and related matters

Every large organisation or group of organisations faces difficulties over finance – its adequacy, its division among the different operations, its cost effectiveness and the prospects for future flows of resources. The organisations within the UN System are no exception; within that System efforts to deal with these problems by maintaining the levels of funding and improving its administration have been constant. They need to be sustained and improved (as they do everywhere else), and the machinery for doing so exists. However, the UN System, faces special problems not present elsewhere. The major one as a source of the recent strains is the discrepancy between financial contribution and voting power. The Kassebaum Amendment may bring the issue to a head; or, as seems more likely, it could lead to a period of confusion and wrangling.

In these circumstances it will be helpful to remember certain basic facts. The present system, in which finance is provided broadly on the basis of capacity to pay while voting is based on equality between nation states, was a deliberate creation of those who are now its principal critics – the Western states who were the main architects of the United Nations. At the time, it was an expression of international solidarity. The criticism now directed against it is in part a measure of how that sense of solidarity has declined; if the sense of solidarity could be re-created, the importance of the issue would diminish proportionately. Despite Kassebaum, the reaction to African famine and the Chernobyl accident may indicate that this could be happening – an impression reinforced by the 'new realism' that has emerged in the demands of developing countries in the economic field.

It may be that Kassebaum will force some revision of the constitutional provisions relating to budgets throughout the UN System. It might be possible to meet the requirements of Kassebaum simply by reducing the maximum level of contributions from any one country from 25% to 20%, and providing for weighted voting on the *total* level of each budget, or even on the aggregate of all budgets thoughout the System, rather than permitting weighted voting on all items within a budget (still less on all the issues coming before the Agencies). However, this would include among other things making up the 5% shortfall from elsewhere – not easy to do when the only other major source of funds in recent years, the oil producers, are themselves facing severe difficulties. Anyway, Kassebaum relates only to the assessed part of the Agencies' budgets. There is a danger that it will merely reinforce the existing policy of the Western donors on the Geneva Group to press for zero real growth in Agency budgets by making a 5% cut across the board. The fact that this policy is pressed by the major donors regardless of each Agency's programme or performance is a measure of the lack of seriousness with which these governments have come to treat the Agencies. It is bureaucratically simple; it is also uncritical and unconstructive, and could be changed at no great additional cost to the governments concerned.

On the other part of the Agencies' finances – the voluntary contributions to Trust Funds and the UNDP – the donor governments are right to be critical, provided that such criticism is based on sound assessment of such funds' cost-effectiveness, and of the programmes they are intended to finance.

One other problem is faced by the UN and its System in the field of finances: that of persuading the rest of the world to see it in proportion. The press often depicts both the budgets themselves and the waste as gigantic. This is untrue on both scores. The budgets represent a very small share of world public expenditure, and although waste and scandals occur and are to be entirely condemned, they probably occur less frequently than in most national administrations – or for that matter in many private concerns. What is important is that all concerned should take a more critical but constructive look at the cost-effectiveness of the programmes undertaken and their relevance to the welfare of the world.

## The internal problems of the System (including staffing)

Since the 1960s, the United Nations has devoted a great deal of effort to trying to 'systematise its system', extending all the way from the Jackson Report of 1969 to General Assembly Resolution 32/197 of 1977. In effect these efforts have been mainly an attempt to cure the System's shortcomings through greater centralisation. They have failed because constitutionally the component parts already had too much autonomy and the potential centralisers lacked the professional competence for them to succeed. The remedy for this lies in achieving co-ordination without centralisation. This can be done by more effective leadership from the UN Secretary-General, backed by proper support from member governments inside and outside the Governing Councils.

A major stumbling block is that a few of the Executive Heads abuse their very strong constitutional positions. These should be weakened. Their functional effectiveness and that of their Agencies would not be damaged if they were limited to at most two terms of office.

Indeed, the situation throughout the UN System would be improved if all governments would accept that in their policy towards the Agencies the aim should be to secure the highest degree of functional effectiveness in the Agency's sector. All governments stand to benefit by such a policy, not least the governments of developing countries whose welfare the Agencies aim to promote. For the same reason, in their staffing policies all governments ought to support the Agencies in following the principles of Article 101.3 of the Charter, i.e. 'securing the highest standards of efficiency, competence and integrity'. In view of all that has happened, this may be a counsel of perfection; however, to abandon it would be a counsel of despair. In staffing policy, account needs to be taken of the changing pattern of the work of the Agencies, especially the increased specialisation required in an ever-widening range of disciplines, as contrasted with the more generalised skills required for administration. The fact that the operations being undertaken by the System are now so diverse must call in question some aspects of the 'Common System' which has governed the staffing of most of the Specialized Agencies up to the present. What they chiefly call for, however, is new methods of personnel management and recruitment which the international Civil Service Commission would, if properly directed, be best qualified to introduce System-wide. What it needs is better guidance from member governments. Instead the main concerns of member governments in personnel policy are short-sighted and mercenary; namely securing more posts for their own nationals, rather than ensuring the highest level of professional competence, and reducing budgets. Here, as in so many other areas of UN activity, member governments have the international civil service they deserve – indeed a better one than most of them deserve.

## The problem of member states

If the UN System is to be improved so that it can give a better service to the international community, attitudes towards it in member states need to be changed. Indeed, many of its shortcomings reflect the weakening sense of international solidarity worldwide and the increased emphasis on national self-interest, amounting in some cases to a new isolationism.

Much of the strain of recent years has been due to some Specialized Agencies having become arenas of confrontation between developed and developing countries on issues ranging from major international political and economic questions to the levels of Agency budgets. This confrontation has revealed faults and weaknesses on both sides. On the side of the developed countries, the fault has been in trying too often to assume a 'low profile', and in abandoning the argument too easily in favour of 'damage limitation' and a quiet life. As the example of UNESCO shows, this course has not limited the damage or produced the quiet life. As a corollary, developed countries have not been prepared to put enough intellectual resources into their relations with the Agencies, with the aim of improving Agency performance in the functional field. Instead they have preferred to put their energies into pressing for zero real growth in Agency budgets regardless of the comparative values of Agency programmes or their relevance to improving economic and social conditions worldwide. Developing countries on the other hand have likewise tended to pay too little attention to the quality of the Agencies' performance in their functional fields. They have too readily acquiesced in Agency salesmanship; they have found it difficult to organise their government machines internally to cope with the complexities of the UN System; they have been too content to use meetings of governing bodies to air their views on general international matters rather than on the proper performance of the Agency's functions.

The strain which has resulted from the policies of member states can largely be removed without any amendments to the Charter or the Agencies' constitutions, and with no additional financial resources. Changes of attitude – sustained over time and manifested by groups of governments, preferably across the North-South divide – are what is required.

## The prospects for the future

The immediate prospect is of a time of difficulty and frustration, with Agencies having to operate on reduced resources, in the face of doubts about the efficacy of their policies in the development field, general lack of international consensus on economic policy, continued political tensions on insoluble issues, and discontent among staff.

On the credit side, the Agencies and the System have proved their usefulness in many areas of activity, and the world would be a poorer place without them. Most of the defects have been clearly identified and could be removed without too much difficulty, if that were the will of enough governments on both sides of the economic divide. Indeed, changes of attitude among more governments could enable more fundamental reforms to be undertaken such as would lead to an 'Economic United Nations'.

Those who wish to see the System damaged or even destroyed give priority to other interests than those of international co-operation. These are the interests of national prestige, sometimes seen in extremely mercenary terms, or the virtues of certain economic philosophies currently in fashion. The experience of earlier decades in the twentieth century shows the dangers of giving undue importance to such concerns. The many obvious defects of the United Nations and its System reflect the deficiencies of the world in which they have their being. Reform of the System – whether as a whole or in part – can contribute to creating a better and a safer world. Those who are not prepared to contemplate it are the victims of short-sighted despair.

# APPENDIXES

# BUDGETS OF THE MAIN U.N. SPECIALIZED AGENCIES (GENEVA GROUP) AND MEMBER GOVERNMENTS' CONTRIBUTIONS

Table 1.   BUDGETS OF THE MAIN U.N. SPECIALIZED AGENCIES*

| Organisation | Current (approved) budget period | Growth (or decrease) over current (approved) budget period (%) | | Previous (final) budget level | Growth (or decrease) in previous budget period (%) |
|---|---|---|---|---|---|
| ICAO | (1984–5) $72,112,000 | Nominal: | +16.7 | (1982–3) $61,813,500 | (1982–3) (ZRG) |
| | | Real: | – 1.5 | | |
| WHO | (1984–5) $520,100,000 | Nominal: | +10.9 | (1982–3) $468,900,000 | (1982–3) + 2.2 (real growth) |
| | | Real: | – 0.3 | | |
| WIPO | (1984–5) SF42,106,000 | Nominal: | +19.4 | (1982–3) SF35,272,000 | (1982–3) + 4.4 (real growth) |
| | | Real: | ZRG† | | |
| UPU | (1984) SF18,637,500 | Nominal: | +0.2 | (1983) SF18,602,500 | (1983) ZRG |
| | | Real: | ZRG | | |
| WMO | (1984–7) $77,516,400 | Nominal: | +4.2 | (1980–3) $74,400,000 | (1980–3) ZRG |
| | | Real: | ZRG | | |
| FAO | (1984–5) $421,100,000 | Nominal: | +14.9 | (1982–3) $366,640,000 | (1982–3) + 8 (real growth) |
| | | Real: | + 0.5 | | |
| UNESCO | (1984–5) $374,400,000 | Nominal: | – 13 | (1981–3) $625,000,000 | (1981–3) + 6.3 (real growth) |
| | | Real: | + 3.8 | | |
| IAEA | (1984) $97,100,000 | Nominal: | +7.9 | (1983) $88,071,000 | (1983) + 1.2 (real growth) |
| | | Real: | + 2.5 | | |
| ITU | (1984) $43,000,000 (SF90,200,000) | Nominal: | +8.6 | (1983) $41,202,969 | (1983) |
| | | Real: | + 3 | | |
| ILO | (1984–5) $254,700,000 | Nominal: | +16 | (1982–3) $226,329,469 | (1982–3) + 8.8 (real growth) |
| | | Real: | + 2.6 | | |

\* These are the Agencies covered by the Geneva Group.
† ZRG = zero real growth.

Table 2. BUDGETS OF THE MAIN U.N. SPECIALIZED AGENCIES: MEMBER GOVERNMENTS' CONTRIBUTIONS (%), 1985

| | UN | ILO | FAO | UNESCO | ICAO | UPU | WHO | ITU | WMO | IMO[b] | WIPO | IAEA |
|---|---|---|---|---|---|---|---|---|---|---|---|---|
| Afghanistan | 0.01 | 0.01 | 0.01 | 0.01 | 0.06 | 0.09 | 0.01 | 0.03 | 0.04 | – | – | 0.01 |
| Albania | 0.01 | –[a] | 0.01 | 0.01 | – | 0.09 | 0.01 | 0.06 | 0.04 | – | – | 0.01 |
| Algeria | 0.13 | 0.13 | 0.16 | 0.13 | 0.17 | 0.47 | 0.13 | 0.25 | 0.10 | 0.36 | 0.33 | 0.13 |
| Angola | 0.01 | 0.01 | 0.01 | 0.01 | 0.06 | 0.09 | 0.01 | 0.06 | 0.07 | 0.05 | – | – |
| Antigua & Barbuda | 0.01 | 0.01 | 0.01 | 0.01 | 0.06 | – | 0.01 | – | – | – | – | – |
| Argentina | 0.71 | 0.70 | 0.86 | 0.70 | 0.70 | 1.88 | 0.70 | 0.76 | 1.18 | 0.63 | 0.48 | 0.71 |
| Australia | 1.57 | 1.56 | 1.90 | 1.55 | 1.64 | 2.35 | 1.54 | 4.59 | 1.73 | 0.59 | 3.27 | 1.57 |
| Austria | 0.75 | 0.74 | 0.91 | 0.74 | 0.59 | 0.47 | 0.74 | 0.25 | 0.62 | 0.12 | 1.77 | 0.75 |
| Bahamas | 0.01 | 0.01 | 0.01 | 0.01 | 0.06 | 0.09 | 0.01 | 0.13 | 0.04 | 0.21 | 0.16 | – |
| Bahrain | 0.03 | 0.03 | 0.04 | 0.03 | 0.06 | 1.41 | 0.03 | 0.13 | 0.04 | 0.02 | – | – |
| Bangladesh | 0.01 | 0.01 | 0.01 | 0.01 | 0.06 | 0.09 | 0.01 | 0.06 | 0.04 | 0.11 | 0.06 | 0.03 |
| Barbados | 0.01 | 0.01 | 0.01 | 0.01 | 0.06 | 0.09 | 0.01 | 0.06 | 0.04 | 0.04 | – | – |
| Belgium | 1.28 | 1.27 | 1.55 | 1.26 | 1.16 | 1.41 | 1.26 | 1.27 | 1.26 | 0.64 | 3.27 | 1.28 |
| Belize | 0.01 | 0.01 | 0.01 | 0.01 | – | 0.09 | – | 0.03 | 0.04 | – | – | – |
| Benin | 0.01 | – | 0.01 | 0.01 | 0.06 | 0.09 | 0.01 | 0.06 | 0.04 | 0.02 | 0.17 | – |
| Bhutan | 0.01 | 0.01 | 0.01 | 0.01 | 0.06 | 0.09 | 0.01 | 0.06 | 0.12 | – | – | 0.01 |
| Bolivia | 0.01 | 0.01 | 0.01 | 0.01 | 0.06 | 0.09 | 0.01 | 0.13 | 0.04 | – | – | – |
| Botswana | 0.01 | 0.01 | 0.01 | 0.01 | 0.06 | 0.09 | 0.01 | 0.03 | 0.04 | – | 0.15 | – |
| Brazil | 1.39 | 1.38 | 1.68 | 1.37 | 1.53 | 2.35 | 1.36 | 0.76 | 1.35 | 1.42 | 2.09 | 1.39 |
| Bulgaria | 0.18 | 0.18 | 0.22 | 0.18 | 0.14 | 0.28 | 0.18 | 0.25 | 0.31 | 0.34 | 0.48 | 0.18 |
| Burkina Faso | 0.01 | 0.01 | 0.01 | 0.01 | 0.06 | 0.09 | 0.01 | 0.03 | 0.04 | – | 0.15 | – |
| Burma | 0.01 | 0.01 | 0.01 | 0.01 | 0.06 | 0.28 | 0.01 | 0.13 | 0.10 | 0.05 | – | 0.01 |
| Burundi | 0.01 | 0.01 | 0.01 | 0.01 | 0.06 | 0.09 | 0.01 | 0.03 | 0.04 | – | 0.10 | – |
| Byelorussian SSR | 0.36 | 0.36 | – | 0.36 | – | 0.28 | 0.35 | 0.13 | 0.47 | – | 0.04 | 0.36 |
| Cameroon | 0.01 | 0.01 | 0.01 | 0.01 | 0.06 | 0.09 | 0.01 | 0.13 | 0.04 | 0.02 | 0.28 | 0.01 |
| Canada | 3.08 | 3.05 | 3.72 | 3.04 | 2.93 | 4.70 | 3.02 | 4.59 | 2.72 | 0.97 | 2.41 | 3.09 |
| Cape Verde | 0.01 | 0.01 | 0.01 | 0.01 | 0.06 | 0.09 | 0.01 | 0.03 | 0.04 | 0.02 | – | – |

| | | | | | | | | | | | | |
|---|---|---|---|---|---|---|---|---|---|---|---|---|
| Central African Rep. | 0.01 | 0.01 | 0.01 | 0.01 | 0.06 | 0.09 | 0.01 | 0.03 | 0.04 | – | 0.16 | – |
| Chad | 0.01 | 0.01 | 0.01 | 0.01 | 0.06 | 0.09 | 0.01 | 0.03 | 0.04 | – | 0.16 | – |
| Chile | 0.07 | 0.07 | 0.08 | 0.07 | 0.15 | 0.47 | 0.07 | 0.25 | 0.29 | 0.16 | 0.18 | 0.07 |
| China | 0.88 | 0.87 | 1.06 | 0.87 | 0.56 | 4.70 | 0.86 | 2.55 | 3.09 | 2.00 | 0.11 | – |
| Colombia | 0.11 | 0.11 | 0.13 | 0.11 | 0.21 | 0.28 | 0.11 | 0.25 | 0.26 | 0.13 | 0.04 | 0.11 |
| Comoros | 0.01 | 0.01 | 0.01 | 0.01 | – | 0.09 | 0.01 | 0.03 | 0.04 | – | – | – |
| Congo | 0.01 | 0.01 | 0.01 | 0.01 | 0.06 | 0.09 | 0.01 | 0.13 | 0.04 | 0.02 | 0.16 | – |
| Cook Islands | – | – | – | – | – | – | 0.01 | – | – | – | – | – |
| Costa Rica | 0.02 | 0.02 | 0.02 | 0.02 | 0.06 | 0.09 | 0.02 | 0.06 | 0.08 | 0.02 | 0.06 | 0.02 |
| Cuba | 0.09 | 0.09 | 0.11 | 0.09 | 0.10 | 0.28 | 0.09 | 0.13 | 0.22 | 0.27 | 0.30 | 0.09 |
| Cyprus | 0.01 | 0.01 | 0.01 | 0.01 | 0.06 | 0.09 | 0.01 | 0.06 | 0.04 | 0.78 | 0.36 | 0.01 |
| Czechoslovakia | 0.76 | 0.75 | 0.92 | 0.75 | 0.56 | 0.94 | 0.75 | 0.51 | 0.90 | 0.13 | 2.22 | 0.76 |
| Denmark | 0.75 | 0.74 | 0.91 | 0.74 | 0.65 | 0.94 | 0.74 | 1.27 | 0.72 | 1.21 | 2.22 | 0.75 |
| Djibouti | 0.01 | 0.01 | 0.01 | 0.01 | 0.06 | 0.09 | 0.01 | 0.03 | 0.04 | 0.02 | – | – |
| Dominica | 0.01 | 0.01 | 0.01 | 0.01 | – | 0.09 | 0.01 | – | 0.04 | 0.02 | – | – |
| Dominican Rep. | 0.03 | 0.03 | 0.04 | 0.03 | 0.06 | 0.28 | 0.03 | 0.13 | 0.08 | 0.02 | 0.30 | 0.03 |
| Ecuador | 0.02 | 0.02 | 0.02 | 0.02 | 0.06 | 0.28 | 0.02 | 0.13 | 0.08 | 0.11 | – | 0.02 |
| Egypt | 0.07 | 0.07 | 0.08 | 0.07 | 0.16 | 1.41 | 0.07 | 0.25 | 0.35 | 0.20 | 0.51 | 0.07 |
| El Salvador | 0.01 | 0.01 | 0.01 | 0.01 | 0.06 | 0.09 | 0.01 | 0.06 | 0.04 | 0.02 | 0.04 | 0.01 |
| Equatorial Guinea | 0.01 | 0.01 | 0.01 | 0.01 | 0.06 | 0.28 | 0.01 | 0.03 | – | 0.02 | – | – |
| Ethiopia | 0.01 | 0.01 | 0.01 | 0.01 | 0.06 | 0.09 | 0.01 | 0.03 | 0.04 | 0.02 | – | 0.01 |
| Fiji | 0.01 | 0.01 | 0.01 | 0.01 | 0.06 | 0.09 | 0.01 | 0.06 | 0.04 | 0.02 | 0.06 | – |
| Finland | 0.48 | 0.48 | 0.58 | 0.47 | 0.42 | 0.94 | 0.47 | 1.27 | 0.52 | 0.61 | 2.22 | 0.48 |
| France | 6.51 | 6.46 | 7.86 | 6.43 | 5.97 | 4.70 | 6.39 | 7.65 | 5.08 | 2.54 | 5.54 | 6.52 |
| French Overseas Territories | – | – | – | – | – | – | – | – | 0.04[c] | – | – | – |
| Gabon | 0.02 | 0.02 | 0.02 | 0.02 | 0.06 | 0.09 | 0.02 | 0.13 | 0.04 | 0.04 | 0.16 | 0.02 |
| Gambia | 0.01 | – | 0.01 | 0.01 | 0.06 | 0.09 | 0.01 | 0.03 | 0.04 | 0.02 | 0.04 | – |
| German Democratic Rep. | 1.39 | 1.38 | – | 1.37 | – | 1.41 | 1.36 | 0.76 | 1.38 | 0.45 | 2.73 | 1.39 |
| Germany, Federal Rep. of | 8.54 | 8.47 | 10.31 | 8.44 | 7.08 | 4.70 | 8.39 | 7.65 | 5.81 | 1.88 | 5.45 | 8.55 |

Table 2  (continued)

| | UN | ILO | FAO | UNESCO | ICAO | UPU | WHO | ITU | WMO | IMO[b] | WIPO | IAEA |
|---|---|---|---|---|---|---|---|---|---|---|---|---|
| Ghana | 0.02 | 0.02 | 0.02 | 0.02 | 0.06 | 0.28 | 0.02 | 0.06 | 0.10 | 0.08 | 0.10 | 0.02 |
| Greece | 0.40 | 0.40 | 0.48 | 0.39 | 0.47 | 0.28 | 0.39 | 0.25 | 0.31 | 8.33 | 0.68 | 0.40 |
| Grenada | 0.01 | 0.01 | 0.01 | 0.01 | 0.06 | 0.09 | 0.01 | 0.03 | – | – | – | – |
| Guatemala | 0.02 | 0.02 | 0.02 | 0.02 | 0.06 | 0.28 | 0.02 | 0.06 | 0.08 | 0.02 | 0.04 | 0.02 |
| Guinea | 0.01 | 0.01 | 0.01 | 0.01 | 0.06 | 0.09 | 0.01 | 0.03 | 0.04 | 0.02 | 0.16 | – |
| Guinea-Bissau | 0.01 | 0.01 | 0.01 | 0.01 | 0.06 | 0.09 | 0.01 | 0.03 | 0.04 | 0.02 | – | – |
| Guyana | 0.01 | 0.01 | 0.01 | 0.01 | 0.06 | 0.09 | 0.01 | 0.06 | 0.04 | 0.02 | – | – |
| Haiti | 0.01 | 0.01 | 0.01 | 0.01 | 0.06 | 0.28 | 0.01 | 0.03 | 0.04 | 0.02 | 0.10 | 0.01 |
| Holy See | – | – | – | – | – | – | – | – | – | – | 0.16 | 0.01 |
| Honduras | 0.01 | 0.01 | 0.01 | 0.01 | 0.06 | 0.09 | 0.01 | 0.06 | 0.04 | 0.07 | 0.04 | – |
| Hong Kong | – | – | – | – | – | – | – | – | 0.04 | 0.49 | – | – |
| Hungary | 0.23 | 0.23 | 0.28 | 0.23 | 0.16 | 0.94 | 0.22 | 0.25 | 0.46 | 0.07 | 0.75 | 0.23 |
| Iceland | 0.03 | 0.03 | 0.04 | 0.03 | 0.06 | 0.09 | 0.03 | 0.06 | 0.08 | 0.06 | 0.48 | 0.03 |
| India | 0.36 | 0.36 | 0.43 | 0.36 | 0.52 | 2.35 | 0.35 | 2.55 | 1.46 | 1.46 | 0.59 | 0.36 |
| Indonesia | 0.13 | 0.13 | 0.16 | 0.13 | 0.31 | 0.94 | 0.13 | 0.25 | 0.51 | 0.48 | 0.30 | 0.13 |
| Iran | 0.58 | 0.57 | 0.70 | 0.57 | 0.45 | 0.47 | 0.57 | 0.25 | 0.45 | 0.48 | 0.30 | 0.58 |
| Iraq | 0.12 | 0.12 | 0.15 | 0.12 | 0.19 | 0.47 | 0.12 | 0.06 | 0.09 | 0.40 | 0.30 | 0.12 |
| Ireland | 0.18 | 0.18 | 0.22 | 0.18 | 0.19 | 0.94 | 0.18 | 0.51 | 0.25 | 0.10 | 2.22 | 0.18 |
| Israel | 0.23 | 0.23 | 0.28 | 0.23 | 0.33 | 0.28 | 0.22 | 0.25 | 0.26 | 0.21 | 0.65 | 0.23 |
| Italy | 3.74 | 3.71 | 4.52 | 3.69 | 3.21 | 2.35 | 3.67 | 2.55 | 2.59 | 2.42 | 3.33 | 3.75 |
| Ivory Coast | 0.03 | 0.03 | 0.04 | 0.03 | 0.06 | 0.28 | 0.03 | 0.25 | 0.08 | 0.06 | 0.28 | 0.03 |
| Jamaica | 0.02 | 0.02 | 0.02 | 0.02 | 0.06 | 0.09 | 0.02 | 0.06 | 0.08 | 0.02 | 0.04 | 0.02 |
| Japan | 10.32 | 10.23 | 12.46 | 10.19 | 9.03 | 4.70 | 10.14 | 7.65 | 4.45 | 9.67 | 4.93 | 10.33 |
| Jordan | 0.01 | 0.01 | 0.01 | 0.01 | 0.12 | 0.09 | 0.01 | 0.13 | 0.04 | 0.02 | 0.01 | 0.01 |
| Kampuchea | 0.01 | 0.01 | 0.01 | 0.01 | 0.06 | 0.09 | 0.01 | 0.13 | 0.04 | 0.02 | – | 0.01 |
| Kenya | 0.01 | 0.01 | 0.01 | 0.01 | 0.06 | 0.28 | 0.01 | 0.06 | 0.04 | 0.02 | – | 0.01 |
| Kiribati | – | – | – | – | 0.06 | – | 0.01 | – | – | – | 0.03 | 0.01 |
| Korea, Rep. of | – | – | 0.22 | 0.18 | 0.59 | 0.94 | 0.18 | 0.25 | 0.18 | 1.46 | 0.30 | 0.18 |

|  | | | | | | | | | | | | |
|---|---|---|---|---|---|---|---|---|---|---|---|---|
| Korea, Dem. People's Rep. of | – | – | – | – | – | – | – | – | – | – | – | – |
| Kuwait | 0.25 | 0.25 | 0.30 | 0.25 | 0.33 | 0.94 | 0.24 | 0.25 | 0.17 | 0.61 | – | 0.05 |
| Lao People's Dem. Rep. | – | – | – | – | – | – | – | – | – | – | – | – |
| Lebanon | 0.01 | 0.02 | 0.01 | 0.02 | 0.17 | 0.09 | 0.02 | 0.06 | 0.08 | 0.13 | 0.51 | 0.02 |
| Lesotho | 0.01 | 0.01 | 0.01 | 0.01 | 0.06 | 0.09 | 0.01 | 0.03 | 0.04 | – | – | – |
| Liberia | 0.01 | 0.01 | 0.01 | 0.01 | 0.06 | 0.09 | 0.01 | 0.06 | 0.04 | – | – | 0.01 |
| Libya | 0.26 | 0.26 | 0.31 | 0.26 | 0.23 | 0.47 | 0.25 | 0.38 | 0.14 | 14.88 | 0.48 | 0.26 |
| Liechtenstein | – | – | – | – | – | 0.09 | – | 0.13 | – | 0.29 | 0.17 | 0.01 |
| Luxembourg | 0.06 | 0.06 | 0.07 | 0.06 | 0.06 | 0.28 | 0.06 | 0.13 | 0.09 | – | 0.22 | 0.06 |
| Madagascar | 0.01 | 0.01 | 0.01 | 0.01 | 0.06 | 0.28 | 0.01 | 0.06 | 0.04 | 0.04 | 0.28 | 0.06 |
| Malawi | 0.01 | 0.01 | 0.01 | 0.01 | 0.06 | 0.09 | 0.01 | 0.03 | 0.04 | – | 0.10 | 0.01 |
| Malaysia | 0.09 | 0.09 | 0.11 | 0.09 | 0.18 | 0.28 | 0.09 | 0.76 | 0.30 | 0.38 | – | 0.09 |
| Maldives | 0.01 | 0.01 | 0.01 | 0.01 | 0.06 | 0.09 | 0.01 | 0.03 | 0.04 | 0.07 | – | – |
| Mali | 0.01 | 0.01 | 0.01 | 0.01 | 0.06 | 0.09 | 0.01 | 0.03 | 0.04 | – | 0.16 | – |
| Malta | 0.01 | 0.01 | 0.01 | 0.01 | 0.06 | 0.09 | 0.01 | 0.06 | 0.04 | 0.22 | 0.16 | 0.1 |
| Mauritania | 0.01 | 0.01 | 0.01 | 0.01 | 0.06 | 0.09 | 0.01 | 0.06 | 0.04 | 0.02 | 0.15 | – |
| Mauritius | 0.01 | 0.01 | 0.01 | 0.01 | 0.06 | 0.09 | 0.01 | 0.06 | 0.04 | 0.02 | 0.10 | 0.01 |
| Mexico | 0.88 | 0.87 | 1.06 | 0.87 | 0.94 | 1.41 | 0.86 | 0.25 | 0.86 | 0.41 | 1.61 | 0.88 |
| Monaco | – | – | – | – | 0.06 | 0.09 | 0.01 | 0.06 | – | – | 0.22 | 0.01 |
| Mongolia | 0.01 | 0.01 | 0.01 | 0.01 | – | 0.09 | 0.01 | 0.06 | 0.04 | – | 0.04 | 0.01 |
| Morocco | 0.05 | 0.05 | 0.06 | 0.05 | 0.10 | 0.47 | 0.05 | 0.25 | 0.15 | 0.11 | 0.51 | 0.05 |
| Mozambique | 0.01 | 0.01 | 0.01 | 0.01 | 0.06 | 0.09 | 0.01 | 0.06 | 0.07 | 0.02 | – | – |
| Namibia | – | – | – | – | – | – | 0.01 | – | – | – | – | – |
| Nauru | – | – | – | – | 0.06 | 0.09 | – | 0.03 | – | – | – | – |
| Nepal | 0.01 | 0.01 | 0.01 | 0.01 | 0.06 | 0.28 | 0.01 | 0.03 | 0.04 | 0.02 | – | 0.01 |
| Netherlands | 1.78 | 1.76 | 2.15 | 1.76 | 1.93 | 1.41 | 1.75 | 2.55 | 1.28 | 1.23 | 3.33 | 1.78 |
| Neth. Antilles | – | – | – | – | – | 0.09 | – | 0.04 | 0.04 | – | – | – |
| New Caledonia | – | – | – | – | – | – | – | – | 0.04 | – | – | – |
| New Zealand | 0.26 | 0.26 | 0.31 | 0.26 | 0.35 | 1.88 | 0.25 | 0.51 | 0.48 | 0.15 | 0.80 | 0.26 |
| Nicaragua | 0.01 | 0.01 | 0.01 | 0.01 | 0.06 | 0.09 | 0.01 | 0.13 | 0.04 | 0.02 | – | 0.01 |

Table 2 *(continued)*

| | UN | ILO | FAO | UNESCO | ICAO | UPU | WHO | ITU | WMO | IMO[b] | WIPO | IAEA |
|---|---|---|---|---|---|---|---|---|---|---|---|---|
| Niger | 0.01 | 0.01 | 0.01 | 0.01 | 0.06 | 0.09 | 0.01 | 0.03 | 0.04 | – | 0.16 | 0.01 |
| Nigeria | 0.19 | 0.19 | 0.23 | 0.19 | 0.23 | 0.94 | 0.19 | 0.51 | 0.25 | 0.16 | 0.30 | 0.19 |
| Norway | 0.51 | 0.50 | 0.62 | 0.50 | 0.48 | 0.94 | 0.50 | 1.27 | 0.61 | 4.32 | 2.22 | 0.51 |
| Oman | 0.01 | – | 0.01 | 0.01 | 0.06 | 0.09 | 0.01 | 0.13 | 0.04 | 0.02 | – | – |
| Pakistan | 0.06 | 0.06 | 0.07 | 0.06 | 0.26 | 1.41 | 0.06 | 0.51 | 0.18 | 0.18 | 0.18 | 0.06 |
| Panama | 0.02 | 0.02 | 0.02 | 0.02 | 0.06 | 0.09 | 0.02 | 0.13 | 0.08 | 7.65 | 0.04 | 0.02 |
| Papua New Guinea | 0.01 | 0.01 | 0.01 | 0.01 | 0.06 | 0.09 | 0.01 | 0.13 | 0.04 | 0.02 | – | – |
| Paraguay | 0.01 | 0.01 | 0.01 | 0.01 | 0.06 | 0.09 | 0.01 | 0.13 | 0.04 | – | – | 0.01 |
| Peru | 0.07 | 0.07 | 0.08 | 0.07 | 0.11 | 0.28 | 0.07 | 0.06 | 0.26 | 0.23 | 0.04 | 0.07 |
| Philippines | 0.09 | 0.09 | 0.11 | 0.09 | 0.28 | 0.09 | 0.09 | 0.25 | 0.33 | 0.71 | 0.48 | 0.09 |
| Poland | 0.72 | 0.71 | 0.87 | 0.71 | 0.49 | 0.94 | 0.71 | 0.51 | 1.16 | 0.90 | 0.68 | 0.72 |
| Portugal | 0.18 | 0.18 | 0.22 | 0.18 | 0.25 | 0.47 | 0.18 | 0.25 | 0.25 | 0.35 | 1.89 | 0.18 |
| Qatar | 0.03 | 0.03 | 0.04 | 0.03 | 0.06 | 0.47 | 0.03 | 0.13 | 0.08 | 0.09 | 0.11 | 0.03 |
| Romania | 0.19 | 0.19 | 0.23 | 0.19 | 0.19 | 0.47 | 0.19 | 0.25 | 0.36 | 0.58 | 0.68 | 0.19 |
| Rwanda | 0.01 | 0.01 | 0.01 | 0.01 | 0.06 | 0.09 | 0.01 | 0.03 | 0.04 | – | – | – |
| St Christopher & Nevis | – | – | 0.01 | 0.01 | – | – | – | – | – | – | – | – |
| St Lucia | 0.01 | 0.01 | 0.01 | 0.01 | 0.06 | 0.09 | 0.01 | – | 0.04 | 0.02 | – | – |
| St Vincent & the Grenadines | 0.01 | – | 0.01 | 0.01 | – | 0.09 | 0.01 | 0.03 | – | 0.04 | – | – |
| Samoa | 0.01 | – | 0.01 | 0.01 | – | – | 0.01 | – | – | – | – | – |
| San Marino | – | 0.01 | – | – | – | 0.09 | 0.01 | 0.06 | – | – | 0.30 | – |
| São Tomé & Principe | 0.01 | 0.01 | 0.01 | 0.01 | 0.06 | 0.09 | 0.01 | 0.03 | 0.04 | – | – | – |
| Saudi Arabia | 0.86 | 0.85 | 1.04 | 0.85 | 0.64 | 2.35 | 0.84 | 2.55 | 0.34 | 1.25 | 0.37 | 0.86 |
| Senegal | 0.01 | 0.01 | 0.01 | 0.01 | 0.06 | 0.09 | 0.01 | 0.25 | 0.04 | 0.02 | 0.28 | 0.01 |
| Seychelles | 0.01 | 0.01 | 0.01 | 0.01 | 0.06 | 0.09 | 0.01 | – | 0.04 | 0.02 | – | – |
| Sierra Leone | 0.01 | 0.01 | 0.01 | 0.01 | 0.06 | 0.09 | 0.01 | 0.03 | 0.04 | 0.02 | – | 0.01 |

| | | | | | | | | | | | | |
|---|---|---|---|---|---|---|---|---|---|---|---|---|
| Singapore | 0.09 | 0.09 | – | 0.09 | 0.59 | 0.09 | 0.09 | 0.25 | 0.09 | 1.60 | – | 0.09 |
| Solomon Islands | 0.01 | – | – | – | – | – | 0.01 | – | – | – | – | – |
| Somalia | 0.01 | – | 0.01 | 0.01 | 0.06 | 0.09 | 0.01 | 0.03 | 0.04 | 0.02 | 0.04 | – |
| South Africa | 0.41 | – | – | – | 0.56 | 0.09 | 0.40 | 0.25 | 0.71 | – | 1.61 | 0.41 |
| Spain | 1.93 | 1.91 | 2.33 | 1.91 | 1.92 | 2.35 | 1.90 | 0.76 | 1.41 | 1.79 | 2.81 | 1.93 |
| Sri Lanka | 0.01 | 0.01 | 0.01 | 0.01 | 0.06 | 0.47 | 0.01 | 0.13 | 0.12 | 0.11 | 0.16 | 0.01 |
| Sudan | 0.01 | 0.01 | 0.01 | 0.01 | 0.06 | 0.09 | 0.01 | 0.03 | 0.09 | 0.05 | 0.04 | 0.01 |
| Suriname | 0.01 | 0.01 | 0.01 | 0.01 | 0.06 | 0.09 | 0.01 | 0.06 | 0.04 | 0.02 | 0.22 | – |
| Swaziland | 0.01 | 0.01 | 0.01 | 0.01 | 0.06 | 0.09 | 0.01 | 0.06 | 0.04 | – | – | – |
| Sweden | 1.32 | 1.31 | 1.59 | 1.30 | 1.12 | 1.41 | 1.30 | 2.55 | 1.37 | 0.90 | 3.33 | 1.32 |
| Switzerland | – | 1.09 | 1.33 | 1.09 | 1.20 | 1.41 | 1.08 | 2.55 | 1.15 | 0.21 | 3.33 | 1.10 |
| Syria | 0.03 | 0.03 | 0.04 | 0.03 | 0.07 | 0.09 | 0.03 | 0.13 | 0.14 | 0.02 | 0.30 | 0.03 |
| Tanzania | 0.01 | 0.01 | 0.01 | 0.01 | 0.06 | 0.09 | 0.01 | 0.03 | 0.04 | 0.04 | 0.10 | 0.01 |
| Thailand | 0.08 | 0.08 | 0.10 | 0.08 | 0.30 | 0.28 | 0.08 | 0.38 | 0.26 | 0.18 | 0.06 | 0.08 |
| Togo | 0.01 | 0.01 | 0.01 | 0.01 | 0.06 | 0.09 | 0.01 | 0.06 | 0.04 | 0.04 | 0.16 | – |
| Tonga | – | – | 0.01 | – | – | 0.09 | 0.01 | 0.03 | – | – | – | – |
| Trinidad & Tobago | 0.03 | 0.03 | 0.04 | 0.03 | 0.08 | 0.09 | 0.03 | 0.25 | 0.08 | 0.02 | 0.30 | – |
| Tunisia | 0.03 | 0.03 | 0.04 | 0.03 | 0.06 | 0.47 | 0.03 | 0.25 | 0.08 | 0.08 | 0.51 | 0.03 |
| Turkey | 0.32 | 0.32 | 0.39 | 0.31 | 0.28 | 0.47 | 0.31 | 0.25 | 0.48 | 0.65 | 0.48 | 0.32 |
| Tuvalu | – | – | – | – | – | 0.09 | – | – | – | – | – | – |
| Uganda | 0.01 | 0.01 | 0.01 | 0.01 | 0.06 | 0.09 | 0.01 | 0.03 | 0.04 | – | 0.10 | 0.01 |
| Ukrainian SSR | 1.32 | 1.31 | – | 1.30 | – | 0.94 | 1.30 | 0.25 | 1.54 | – | 0.04 | 1.32 |
| USSR | 10.54 | 10.45 | – | 10.41 | 9.70 | 2.35 | 10.35 | 7.65 | 10.31 | 6.11 | 4.07 | 10.55 |
| Upper Volta, *see* Burkina Faso | | | | | | | | | | | | |
| United Arab Emirates | 0.16 | 0.16 | 0.19 | 0.16 | 0.18 | 0.09 | 0.16 | 0.25 | – | 0.12 | 0.11 | 0.16 |
| United Kingdom | 4.67 | 4.63 | 5.64 | 4.61 | 5.13 | 4.70 | 4.59 | 7.65 | 5.42 | 4.43 | 5.45 | 4.68 |
| UK Overseas Territories | – | – | – | – | – | 0.47 | – | – | 0.04[d] | – | – | – |
| United States of America | 25.00 | 25.00 | 25.00 | 25.00 | 25.00 | 4.70 | 25.00 | 7.65 | 24.45 | 4.96 | 3.98 | 25.00 |
| Uruguay | 0.04 | 0.04 | 0.05 | 0.04 | 0.06 | 0.28 | 0.04 | 0.13 | 0.23 | 0.07 | 0.16 | 0.04 |

Table 2 (continued)

| | UN | ILO | FAO | UNESCO | ICAO | UPU | WHO | ITU | WMO | IMO[b] | WIPO | IAEA |
|---|---|---|---|---|---|---|---|---|---|---|---|---|
| Vatican City | – | – | – | – | – | – | – | 0.06 | – | – | – | – |
| Vanuatu | 0.01 | – | 0.01 | – | 0.06 | 0.09 | 0.01 | – | 0.04 | – | – | – |
| Venezuela | 0.55 | 0.54 | 0.66 | 0.54 | 0.62 | 0.28 | 0.54 | 0.51 | 0.54 | 0.30 | 0.30 | 0.55 |
| Vietnam | 0.02 | 0.02 | 0.02 | 0.02 | 0.06 | 0.09 | 0.02 | 0.13 | 0.08 | – | 0.10 | 0.02 |
| Yemen | 0.01 | 0.01 | 0.01 | 0.01 | 0.06 | 0.09 | 0.01 | 0.06 | 0.04 | 0.02 | 0.04 | – |
| Yemen (Dem.) | 0.01 | 0.01 | 0.01 | 0.01 | 0.06 | 0.09 | 0.01 | 0.03 | 0.04 | 0.02 | – | – |
| Yugoslavia | 0.46 | 0.46 | 0.56 | 0.45 | 0.46 | 0.47 | 0.45 | 0.25 | 0.52 | 0.65 | 0.52 | 0.46 |
| Zaire | 0.01 | 0.01 | 0.01 | 0.01 | 0.06 | 0.28 | 0.01 | 0.13 | 0.10 | 0.05 | 0.48 | 0.01 |
| Zambia | 0.01 | 0.01 | 0.01 | 0.01 | 0.06 | 0.28 | 0.01 | 0.06 | 0.07 | – | 0.10 | 0.01 |
| Zimbabwe | 0.02 | 0.02 | 0.02 | 0.02 | 0.06 | 0.28 | 0.02 | 0.13 | 0.04 | – | 0.16 | – |

[a] Blank spaces (–) indicate that a state is not a member of the organisation in question, or that its assessment has not been determined.
[b] Assessments for 1984.
[c] French Polynesia.
[d] British Caribbean Territories.

# THE INTERNATIONAL CIVIL SERVICE OF THE UNITED NATIONS 'COMMON SYSTEM' ON SALARIES, ALLOWANCES AND OTHER CONDITIONS OF SERVICE

The work of the United Nations is carried out by the more than 50,000 international civil servants employed by the organisations comprising the UN System (other than the staffs of the IMF, the IBRD and its affiliated organisations). In 1974 the United Nations established the International Civil Service Commission to regulate and co-ordinate the conditions of service of the staff in the 'common system'.

The agreements between the Specialized Agencies and ECOSOC described in Chapter VII in most instances contain provisions regarding the staff and 'recognise that the eventual development of a single unified international civil service is desirable from the standpoint of effective administrative co-ordination'. Most of the agreements also bind the Agencies 'to develop common personnel standards, methods and arrangements designed to avoid serious discrepancies in terms and conditions of employment, to avoid competition in recruitment of personnel, and to facilitate interchange of personnel in order to obtain the maximum benefit from their services'.[1]

The 'common system' is *not* a unified international civil service but a collection of separate services which have attained a degree of administrative uniformity and which apply certain common standards. The principles governing duties and obligations of such staff are mostly contained in a report on the standards of conduct of the international civil service issued in 1954.[2]

At the end of 1984 the 'common system' was composed of 50,544 staff members (see Table 1[3]). These include not only Specialized Agencies but also other organisations which are subsidiaries of the General Assembly or organisations such as the IAEA and the GATT with special status.

In UN nomenclature the grades in the professional categories comprise upper grades of Under and Assistant Secretary-General (UG and D2), a Director category (D1), and a Principal Officer category of five grades numbered P5–P1 (in descending order). Below them are a number of general service grades, the number of which varies from duty station to duty station. Many of these are locally recruited and not subject to 'geographical' spread. There are a number of other grades for specialized staff such as those serving with Peacekeeping missions.

1 The agreements are listed in UN Document E/1983/INF.4.
2 UN Doc. (Co. ord/Civil Service/5).
3 The tables which follow in the Appendix are extracted from Chapter I of John P. Renninger, *Can the Common System be Maintained: The Role of the International Civil Servant*, New York: UN, 1986.

*Appendix B*

Table 1.   STAFF IN THE COMMON SYSTEM

| Organisation | Professional staff | General service staff | Total |
|---|---|---|---|
| UN | 5,597 | 9,884 | 15,481 |
| UNDP | 1,224 | 4,546 | 5,770 |
| UNHCR | 541 | 1,113 | 1,654 |
| UNICEF | 1,134 | 2,076 | 3,210 |
| UNITAR | 19 | 25 | 44 |
| UNRWA | 82 | 10 | 92 |
| ITC | 140 | 129 | 269 |
| ICSC | 24 | 25 | 49 |
| ICJ | 16 | 23 | 39 |
| UNU | 41 | 74 | 115 |
| ILO | 1,278 | 1,306 | 2,584 |
| ICAT | 61 | 123 | 184 |
| FAO | 3,238 | 3,752 | 6,990 |
| UNESCO | 1,338 | 2,021 | 3,359 |
| WHO | 1,454 | 2,995 | 4,449 |
| PAHO | 342 | 538 | 880 |
| ICAO | 599 | 638 | 1,237 |
| UPU | 78 | 81 | 159 |
| ITU | 408 | 467 | 875 |
| WMO | 197 | 193 | 390 |
| IMO | 117 | 167 | 284 |
| WIPO | 89 | 189 | 278 |
| IFAD | 76 | 96 | 172 |
| IAEA | 646 | 1,009 | 1,655 |
| GATT | 136 | 189 | 325 |
| *Total* | 18,875 | 31,669 | 50.544 |

*Source:* Adapted from UN Document ACC/1985/PER/R.34, Table 1, p. 9.

The remuneration of professional and higher categories in determined in grades by what is known as the 'Noblemaire Principle'. This was first laid down in the League of Nations in 1921. It provides that the remuneration of the UN System's officials is to be determined by comparison with that of the officials in the home civil service in what is known as 'the comparator country' with comparable duties. It is high because the essence of the principle is that salaries must be high enough to attract nationals from any member state, including those where pay is highest. The 'comparator country' at present is the United States.

Table 2. LENGTH OF SERVICE OF PROFESSIONAL STAFF IN 'COMMON SYSTEM'

| Organisation | Less than 5 years | 5–10* years | 10–15 years | 15–20 years | 20–25 years | 25 years | Total |
|---|---|---|---|---|---|---|---|
| UN | 2,499 | 1,160 | 803 | 589 | 300 | 246 | 5,597 |
| UNDP | 530 | 239 | 248 | 200 | 5 | 2 | 1,224 |
| UNHCR | 296 | 154 | 38 | 25 | 16 | 12 | 541 |
| UNICEF | 583 | 271 | 121 | 70 | 52 | 37 | 1,134 |
| UNITAR | 14 | 1 | 3 | 1 | 0 | – | 19 |
| UNRWA | 35 | 27 | 9 | 9 | 2 | – | 82 |
| ITC | 55 | 40 | 35 | 8 | 1 | 1 | 140 |
| ICSC | 14 | 4 | 1 | 1 | 2 | 2 | 24 |
| ICJ | 5 | 2 | 3 | 3 | 2 | 1 | 16 |
| UNU | 21 | 15 | 2 | 2 | – | 1 | 41 |
| ILO | 660 | 182 | 143 | 140 | 81 | 72 | 1,278 |
| ICAT | 16 | 11 | 17 | 17 | – | – | 61 |
| FAO | 1,617 | 632 | 327 | 358 | 223 | 81 | 3,238 |
| UNESCO | 546 | 281 | 223 | 144 | 101 | 43 | 1,338 |
| WHO | 548 | 305 | 252 | 165 | 115 | 69 | 1,454 |
| PAHO | 86 | 72 | 84 | 61 | 21 | 18 | 342 |
| ICAO | 380 | 100 | 48 | 38 | 18 | 15 | 599 |
| UPU | 27 | 14 | 9 | 14 | 9 | 5 | 78 |
| ITU | 224 | 63 | 47 | 17 | 27 | 30 | 408 |
| WMO | 113 | 30 | 15 | 23 | 11 | 5 | 197 |
| IMO | 47 | 38 | 23 | 4 | 5 | – | 117 |
| WIPO | 32 | 16 | 19 | 14 | 4 | 4 | 89 |
| IFAD | 46 | 30 | – | – | – | – | 76 |
| IAEA | 364 | 117 | 60 | 39 | 38 | 28 | 646 |
| GATT | 32 | 19 | 29 | 23 | 18 | 15 | 136 |
| Total | 8,790 | 3,823 | 2,559 | 1,965 | 1,051 | 687 | 18,875 |

*Source:* UN Document ACC/1985/PER/R.34, Table 5, p. 16.
* I.e. *Less than* 10 years. The same applies to the other column headings.

Table 3.   GRADE DISTRIBUTION OF PROFESSIONAL STAFF IN THE 'COMMON SYSTEM'

| P-1 | P-2 | P-3 | P-4 | P-5 | D-1 | D-2 | U-G | Total |
|---|---|---|---|---|---|---|---|---|
| 794 | 2,310 | 3,688 | 5,224 | 4,804 | 1,459 | 424 | 172 | 18,875 |

*Source:* UN Document ACC/1985/PER/R.34, adapted from Tables 3-A and 3-B, pp. 11 and 12.

Table 5.   AGE DISTRIBUTION OF PROFESSIONAL STAFF

| Less than: | 30 Years | 30–35* | 35–40 | 40–45 | 45–50 | 50–55 | 55–60 | 60–65 | 65 Years Less Than | Total |
|---|---|---|---|---|---|---|---|---|---|---|
|  | 781 | 1,836 | 2,668 | 3,425 | 3,362 | 3,337 | 2,756 | 630 | 80 | 18,875 |

*Source:* UN Document ACC/1985/PER/R.34, adapted from Tables 7 and 8, pp. 19–20.
* I.e. *less than* 35. The same applies to other column headings.

Table 4. PROFESSIONAL STAFF BY TYPE OF APPOINTMENT

| Organisation | Headquarters & other established offices | | | | Project Staff | | | |
|---|---|---|---|---|---|---|---|---|
| | Without time limit | Fixed term | % expatriate | Total | Without time limit | Fixed term | % expatriate | Total |
| UN | 2,582 | 1,645 | 86 | 4,227 | 12 | 1,358 | 92 | 1,370 |
| UNDP | 594 | 554 | 91 | 1,148 | 2 | 74 | 96 | 76 |
| UNHCR | 199 | 213 | 94 | 412 | 6 | 123 | 91 | 129 |
| UNICEF | 476 | 370 | 56 | 846 | – | 288 | 97 | 288 |
| UNITAR | – | 14 | 85 | 14 | 1 | 4 | 80 | 5 |
| UNRWA | 60 | 22 | 100 | 82 | 1 | – | – | – |
| ITC | 40 | 35 | 90 | 75 | – | 64 | 95 | 65 |
| ICSC | 5 | 19 | 79 | 24 | – | – | – | – |
| ICJ | 14 | 2 | 75 | 16 | – | – | – | – |
| UNU | 2 | 39 | 73 | 41 | – | – | – | – |
| ILO | 417 | 318 | 88 | 735 | – | 543 | 97 | 543 |
| ICAT | 19 | 42 | 62 | 61 | – | – | – | – |
| FAO | 892 | 654 | 88 | 1,546 | 75 | 1,617 | 99 | 1,692 |
| UNESCO | 170 | 961 | 89 | 1,131 | 1 | 206 | 99 | 207 |
| WHO | 90 | 803 | 91 | 893 | 16 | 545 | 95 | 561 |
| PAHO | 35 | 128 | 66 | 163 | 10 | 169 | 84 | 179 |
| ICAO | 159 | 152 | 78 | 311 | 7 | 281 | 96 | 288 |
| UPU | 58 | 14 | 88 | 72 | – | 6 | 100 | 6 |
| ITU | 169 | 74 | 82 | 243 | – | 165 | 96 | 165 |
| WMO | 46 | 88 | 90 | 134 | – | 63 | 100 | 63 |
| IMO | 41 | 42 | 83 | 83 | – | 34 | 94 | 34 |
| WIPO | 43 | 46 | 91 | 89 | – | – | – | – |
| IFAD | – | 76 | 96 | 76 | – | – | – | – |
| IAEA | 44 | 602 | 92 | 646 | – | – | – | – |
| GATT | 111 | 25 | 83 | 136 | – | – | – | – |
| Total | 6,266 | 6,938 | 86 | 13,204 | 131 | 5,540 | 96 | 5,671 |

*Source:* UN Document ACC/1985/PER/R.34, adapted from Table 4, p. 15.

Table 5.   COUNTRIES WITH THE LARGEST NUMBER OF
PROFESSIONAL STAFF IN 'COMMON SYSTEM' ORGANISATIONS

|  | *Staff funded from regular budgets* | *Staff funded from extra-budgetary resources* | *Total* |
|---|---|---|---|
| Belgium | 160 | 337 | 497 |
| Canada | 260 | 244 | 504 |
| Egypt | 212 | 170 | 382 |
| France | 765 | 540 | 1,305 |
| Germany, Fed. Rep. of | 351 | 306 | 657 |
| India | 228 | 466 | 694 |
| Italy | 300 | 332 | 632 |
| Japan | 218 | 193 | 411 |
| Netherlands | 131 | 465 | 596 |
| Spain | 245 | 73 | 318 |
| Sweden | 113 | 232 | 345 |
| Switzerland | 185 | 148 | 333 |
| USSR | 530 | 69 | 599 |
| UK | 629 | 646 | 1,275 |
| USA | 1,136 | 755 | 1,891 |
| Total | 5,463 | 4,976 | 10,439 |

*Source:* Compiled from UN Document ACC/1985/PER/R.34, Tables 11A and 11B, pp. 27–61.

Table 6.   LOCATION OF STAFF BY GEOGRAPHIC REGION

|  | *Professional staff* | *General service staff* | *Total* |
|---|---|---|---|
| Western Europe | 7,080 | 11,690 | 18,770 |
| Africa | 3,957 | 6,191 | 10,153 |
| North America | 3,283 | 4,985 | 8,268 |
| Asia & the Pacific | 2,225 | 4,851 | 7,076 |
| South America (incl. Central America & Caribbean) | 1,453 | 2,101 | 3,554 |
| Middle East | 852 | 1,789 | 2,641 |
| Eastern Europe | 18 | 57 | 75 |
| Unassigned country | 7 | – | 7 |
| *Total* | 18,875 | 31,669 | 50,544 |

*Source:* Compiled from UN Document ACC/1985/PER/R.34, Table 17, pp. 71–102.

# THE NON-GOVERNMENTAL ORGANISATIONS AND THE UNITED NATIONS SYSTEM

## Introduction

The opening words of the Charter declare that *'we the peoples of the United Nations . . .* have resolved to combine our efforts to accomplish' the aims set out in the Charter. In practice, most of the activity which takes place in the United Nations and its System is both initiated and controlled by *Governments*, and reflects their policy. Nevertheless, an important input is provided worldwide by what the Charter recognises as 'non-governmental organisations.' Although still of marginal importance to the System as a whole, the role of non-governmental organisations is growing, despite the many difficulties placed in their way by governments and by some members of both national and international bureaucracies. They have provided a channel for many interest groups to make representations to the United Nations and have given expert advice and political encouragement to many new initiatives by organisations within the UN System (e.g. in the field of human rights, environment and population). Furthermore, in 1984 they not only provided $2.6 billion in grants from private sources to activities in Third World countries, but were also channels through which OECD governments provided a further $1.2 billion. Some 12 per cent of all development funds from OECD countries passed through their hands. How has this come about?

## The origins of IGO/NGO relations

In origin, non-governmental organisations (NGOs) are a largely Western phenomenon. The very concept on which they operate, 'freedom of association', emerged in the nineteenth century from the rise to prominence of the Western bourgeoisie, and the liberal democratic values they professed. Even today, the majority of NGOs have their headquarters in Western cities. Their Western democratic origin has caused dissension about the role that they should play in the UN System, particularly in the case of member governments opposed to the very concept of organisations independent of government control. However, the contention that because NGOs are a Western phenomenon they reflect purely Western concerns and interests is incorrect.

NGOs have their ultimate origin in medieval Christian Europe, when great monastic orders organised across feudal boundaries played such an influential role in the affairs of the secular and spiritual authorities throughout Christendom. The seeds for modern NGOs were sown in the late-

1 This Annex is based on contributions from Mr Arthur Kilgore and from Mr Curtis Roosevelt, who was the Head of the UN Department dealing with Non-Governmental Organisations from 1964 to 1974.

eighteenth and early-nineteenth centuries with the changes in social, political and economic structures that accompanied the democratic and industrial revolutions that spread across Europe and North America; the British and Foreign Anti-Slavery Society, established in 1823, is an early prototype of the modern NGO. But it was the rapid increase of international commerce in the mid-nineteenth century consequent upon the industrial revolution that brought a widespread proliferation of private voluntary associations in the West and their extension to the international arena.

It is more than mere coincidence that since the late nineteenth century the growth in the number of NGOs has been accompanied by a parallel growth in the number of intergovernmental organisations(IGOs). NGOs have focused much of their effort and attention on the activities of IGOs in areas that concern them, and at times NGOs have played an important role in encouraging the creation of new IGOs promoting their concerns. This happened when the Inter-Parliamentary Union contributed to the process of establishing both the League of Nations and the Permanent Court of Justice. Similarly the international labour movement, through the International Federation of Trade Unions and the Second (Socialist) International, was central to the process that led to the creation of the ILO.

Neither of these post-First World War organisations established formal consultative or participatory status for NGOs, but their experience with NGOs influenced NGO/IGO relations in the UN System. The ILO, with its tripartite system of representation for governments, labour and business, was especially susceptible to NGO influence through the non-governmental representatives. Moreover, the work undertaken by the ILO during the inter-war period brought it into such thorough involvement with some NGO spheres of interest that in 1946 the International Co-operative Alliance was granted consultative status under the revised Constitution, while the International Social Security Association emerged in direct response to the Conventions on social insurance adopted by the ILO.

The League Covenant, however, provided no formal machinery for the League and the NGOs; and it was only with Article 71 of the UN Charter, which authorised the Economic and Social Council to accord consultative status to recognised 'non-governmental organisations concerned with matters within its competence', that relations between NGOs and the major universal IGO of the day were formalised. However, Article 71 should be seen as both the codification of practices established under the League and a limitation of them. The non-statutory consultation of NGOs by the League took in the whole range of its activities. In the various committees of the League they were allowed to speak, present reports, initiate discussions, propose resolutions and amendments, and be assigned to sub-committees. The height of NGO contributions to the activities of the League came at the World Disarmament Conference in 1932, at which they were allowed to address a plenary session of government delegates. Under the League, NGOs often enjoyed full participation exclusive of the right to vote, and it is arguable that under the informal relationship with the League they were endowed with greater participatory privileges than they enjoy today, exceeding the consultative rights accorded by Article 71 and more akin to those granted in the UN to the Specialized Agencies. In the later years of the League, the working relationship with NGOs began to deteriorate as the activities of NGO representatives became more circumscribed and their privileges reduced.

By 1945 voluntary organisations were already well known in Western developed countries and were particularly active nationally in North West European countries and North America, although at that time they were less well known elsewhere. It was pressure from supporters of these groups at the San Francisco Conference.in 1945 that obtained the recognised status for voluntary organisations through the UN Charter, with a separate Article devoted to their rights and privileges. NGOs were defeated in their efforts to be statutorily consulted on political questions; but Article 71, which limits them to intervention on economic and social issues, is unprecedented in establishing formal relations between 'interest groups' and an inter-governmental body. In addition, Article 71 provides that ECOSOC may make such arrangements 'with national organisations after consultation with the Member of the United Nations concerned'.

Although the Soviet bloc accuses NGOs of being tools of their governments, in fact Western foreign ministries, including those of the United States and the United Kingdom, were not keen to build into the UN Charter an official access to the governmental process of work in the UN or its Agencies. But because the reluctant United States delegation to the San Francisco Conference in 1945 was strongly influenced by well-known New Dealers, such as James T. Shotwell of the Carnegie Endowment of International Peace and the Committee to Study the Organization of Peace, who were outside government, NGOs were successful in gaining formal recognition. Furthermore, the World Trade Union Congress (WTUC), with the support of the Soviet Union, was pushing to participate in the San Francisco Conference and to be granted special status in the Security Council and ECOSOC. The professional diplomats successfully limited what they saw as the damage by confining the NGOs to the economic and social side of the picture; although these limits are now increasingly blurred as NGOs apply pressure nationally and internationally on issues which governments regard as political such as disarmament, human rights and women's rights, which have substantial political aspects. The tensions between governments and NGOs which were revealed when the Charter was being drafted have in fact continued throughout the decades of the United Nations' existence and will continue in future.

## NGO status in the UN System

*NGOs and the United Nations.* When deciding on arrangements to implement Article 71, the United Nations divided NGOs into three categories according to the interest of the organisation in the work of ECOSOC. Referred to today as Category I, Category II and Roster (initially called Categories A, B and C), the different groups are granted different privileges inside ECOSOC and its subsidiary bodies. Thus Category I NGOs with the greatest privileges are deemed to be 'concerned with most of the activities of the Council', 'have marked and sustained contributions to make to the achievement of the objectives of the United Nations', are 'closely involved with the economic and social life of the peoples of the areas they represent', and have considerable membership that is 'representative of major segments of population in a large number of countries'.[2] Category I privileges include the right to attend meetings of ECOSOC and its subsidiary bodies; to submit written statements to them; to be granted hearings before ECOSOC and its sessional committees; and, most significantly, to propose agenda items for consideration by ECOSOC and its subsidiary bodies. Category II NGOs are those whose competence lies only in a few of the 'fields of activity' covered by ECOSOC, and they possess all the privileges of Category I except the right to propose agenda items. Roster NGOs are those that ECOSOC or the Secretary-General consider 'can make occasional and useful contributions to the work of the Council'. Roster privileges are not only fewer, but much more qualified than those that accrue to Categories I and II. Their only basic rights are to attend meetings and to submit statements. But whereas Categories I and II can attend all meetings of ECOSOC and its subsidiaries, Roster organisations are limited to meetings within their field of competence. As for written statements, Roster NGOs must be invited by the Secretary-General to submit such statements. Moreover, in a shared fate with Category II, written statements from the Roster NGOs must be concise – they must be of 500 words or less, in contrast to the comparatively verbose 2,000 words afforded to Category I.

*NGOs and the Specialized Agencies.* In the Specialized Agencies, relationships with NGOs are usually specified in the constitution of the organisation. The relationships between the other components of the UN System and NGOs either follow the pattern in ECOSOC by dividing consultant NGOs into three categories, or alternatively make no distinction between types of NGOs. The general trend is that organisations involved in a broad range of subjects and activities tend to categorise consultant NGOs, while the more specifically focused technical Agencies do not differentiate between NGOs. Thus ILO, UNESCO and FAO, along with UNHCR, divide consultant NGOs into three groups, while UNIDO, IAEA, WHO, IMO, WMO, ITU, UPU, WIPO and ICAO make no distinction between NGOs that qualify for consultative status in their organisation. The exception is that UNCTAD and UNDP, whose domain of interests and activities are extensive, do not classify NGOs.

## The NGOs and the functioning of the international system

Assessing the role of the NGOs in the UN Agencies and the international system generally is difficult. Much of the evidence about it is anecdotal and conflicting. Many life-time participants in the UN System are almost unaware that NGOs exist and have a role; and if all reference to them were

2 UN ECOSOC Res. 1296(XLIV), 23 May 1968: 'Arrangements for Consultation with Non-Governmental Organisations'.

omitted in a study such as this, many would not notice it. A detailed examination of it by an independent international research team from developed and developing countries could be useful and do much to clarify the place of NGOs in the years ahead, for in the four decades since the UN System was established they have undoubtedly won a place for themselves and will continue to have a role if the System itself survives. Such an investigation could also enlighten governments – many of whom still cannot understand their role and remain suspicious of them – on how they operate and with what purpose. There are five major questions *inter alia* which such an investigation should elucidate.

*How independent are the NGOs?* All NGOs clearly represent interests of one kind or another. Equally clearly, some of these are 'self' interests openly proclaimed as such – e.g. in commerce, shipping or agriculture. Equally clearly, many are often not 'self' interests in the narrow sense but 'public', or philanthropic interests of one kind or another – as concerned, for example, with social problems, the churches, the development of poorer countries, or human rights, women's rights, and the environment. A key question is how independent they are of *governments*, more particularly of Western governments under whose jurisdictions most of them had their origin and many still have their headquarters. Many governments – not merely those of the Socialist bloc countries – have difficulty in believing that any organisation can be active in an area of public policy and not be in some way an agent of the government on whose territory it originates. This is true even when such an organisation is critical of its own government's policies. 'Monolithic' states have genuine difficulties in understanding the operations of more pluralistic societies, and the fact that many NGOs grew up in an age of imperialism and mainly in 'imperialist' countries taints them in the eyes of some elements in countries which formerly were dependent territories. Even when the main purpose of such organisations is to promote the welfare of countries and peoples other than those of their origin, governments still treat them with suspicion – as many international charities have found. There is also the charge that NGOs represent a form of 'cultural imperialism'. Moreover, there was a period in the 1960s when some of these organisations were surreptitiously supported by intelligence organisations such as the CIA as a riposte to the 'front organisations' supported by the Communist bloc. Finally, all governments – especially Western governments – can find it convenient from time to time to use NGOs as 'stalking horses' to float or promote policies which it would be diplomatically inconvenient for them to sponsor openly. However, further investigation would almost certainly show that although NGOs are a manifestation of the cultural values of Western democratic societies, they are not under the control of Western governments, and indeed are frequently an embarrassment to them. This has become more apparent in recent years as development issues have become more important in the United Nations. Some NGOs have provided increasing support to Third World countries by promoting development issues within rich countries and in IGOs. This often leads to the ironic situation whereby NGOs, the alleged purveyors of

Western interests, become a voice 'from within' on behalf of the poor states when Western governments ignore or are resistant to changes of policy on development issues. Some, such as the World Development Movement, see their role as being the promotion of Third World development to the top of the political agenda in developed countries.[3]

There is some evidence that Third World suspicions concerning NGOs are gradually melting as NGOs very openly espouse the interests of developing countries. Significantly, in 1985 India had the headquarters of twenty-five international secretariats stationed on its soil, the Philippines of thirty-three and Mexico of forty-five. With the exception of a few intergovernmental organisations, these were almost exclusively NGOs. Of course, the number of NGOs with headquarters in the Third World remains a small portion of the world total of 4,600 plus, but the more they become involved in matters of concern to the poor countries, the more likely it will be that NGOs become active in UN Agencies and acquire wider international support. For instance, the 1986 FAO 'Development Education Exchange Papers' contain contributions from NGOs in Canada, France, Peru, India, Zaire, the Philippines, Australia and Colombia – thus revealing a trend away from the previous Western domination of this scene.[4]

*How representative are the NGOs?* If part of the *raison d'être* of the NGOs is to be the voice of the 'peoples of the United Nations' as opposed to that of their governments, the question must arise of how representative they are even of the special interest groups for whom they claim to speak. This question will probably prove very difficult to answer. ECOSOC has provided an answer of sorts in dividing them into the three groups described above, but all NGOs are, by their very nature, representative of minorities of activists interested in some special aspect of society. Such minorities, and more especially their dominant groups, tend to be self-perpetuating. They are not usually representative in the sense that they have been endorsed by any form of popular ballot; but they are so in the sense that they do manage to articulate the concerns of large numbers of people – albeit mostly minorities – who would not otherwise be able to make their voices heard in the councils of government at either national or international level. This is a process which all governments at some time or another find unwelcome; it is one which is both essential to good government and at the same time open to abuse. All representatives of 'special' interests can very easily become the defenders of 'vested' interests, however altruistic their original motives. No independent investigation could contribute a final answer to the question 'How representative are the NGOs?' However, it could lead to a better dialogue between the NGOs and the United Nations and its Agencies on the demarcation line between the promotion of special interests and the preservation of vested interests. In other words, what is needed is an examination

---

3  For an account of the role of NGOs in development see Robert Gorman, *Private Voluntary Organizations as Channels for Official Development Assistance* (Boulder, Colo.: Westview Press, 1985).
4  *Yearbook of International Organizations*, 1985/86, vol. II.

of the possible role of NGOs in the processes of peaceful change rather than in the preservation of existing positions.

*What purpose do the NGOs fulfil?* As they have evolved over the years since the UN was founded, the NGOs seem to have acquired four major roles, and an independent investigation could determine how well they are fulfilling those roles and in what ways their performance could be improved.

The first – that of advocacy of special interests of public importance – is an extension of the role which NGOs perform *vis-à-vis* national governments, and it is not necessary to say any more about it here.

The second is that of providing expert knowledge and advice in areas in which governments have an interest but in which their own resources of information are inadequate. This is a function which NGOs perform as much for the governments of developed as for those of developing countries. From anecdotal evidence, however, the quality of their performance in this area differs widely from one NGO to another. It would be useful if it could be evaluated.

Thirdly, NGOs have become executing agents for a number of UN Agencies operating in developing countries. In doing so they have also become competitors for the limited funds such Agencies can spend on development projects, as well as contributors to such funds from their own resources. The need to evaluate their performance is therefore important to secure the best use of limited resources. On the surface, it appears that the experience of some UN Agencies in using NGOs as executive agents on projects must have been better than that of others. For example, UNHCR, UNICEF, WHO and UNEP have made increasing use of them, while the IBRD has encouraged joint operations to such an extent that NGOs now collaborate with the World Bank officially on 5 per cent of its projects in sub-Saharan Africa and unofficially on nearly 20 per cent of them. It is often said that the technical assistance which the Bank can get from NGOs is more efficient and cost-effective than that obtainable from other sources, and there is a proposal for an 'NGO Operational Support Fund' to offer matching grants to NGOs involved in such projects. These moves have met with some opposition both from within the Bank and from other Agencies. It would be useful to establish why there has been this difference in reaction.

Fourthly, NGOs have played an increasing part in publicising the work of the United Nations and its Agencies at a time when these have found it difficult to get anything but adverse publicity in Western media. This public relations function on behalf of the UN organisations has been of great value, particularly in Western countries where 'isolationism' or anti-'internationalism' has been a prominent part of the national politics. For example, it has fallen to the British United Nations Association (UNA), the Council for Education in World Citizenship (CEWC) and similar interested bodies to keep the UNESCO flame burning in Britain since the United Kingdom withdrew from it. At the same time, the CEWC presents the ironic spectacle of a British-based NGO needing and continuing to receive funds from UNESCO for some of its educational programmes after the British withdrawal. It is remarkable that this very useful activity can create friction with many NGOs. They resent the UN and Agency Secretariats assuming, and expecting, that NGOs have an obligation to publicise and promote UN Agencies and their work. Delegates too, when speaking of NGOs' activities, often make this assumption and, thus show, in an irritating fashion, their ignorance of the nature of voluntary organisations and in particular of their independence of governments.

*How effectively do the NGOs operate?* This is a difficult question on which much of the evidence must remain anecdotal. What is clear is that some NGOs have been much more effective than others. Partly this reflects the difference in the competence of individuals. There are, however, a few general trends which would be worth further examination. For example, representatives of the more effective NGOs sometimes attribute the failures of their less successful colleagues to attempts by the latter to 'play delegate' – in other words to ape the manners and methods of government delegates, particularly when it comes to making statements on issues of general policy. This can give the representative concerned a bad reputation of not minding his proper business, and can destroy the effect of his interventions even on issues on which he should be expert. Contacts at Secretariat level behind the scenes are probably more effective, especially if sustained over time. Another lesson which has been learned is that although individual NGOs probably cannot have much influence, a number of them working in coalition can be effective. For example, in the IMO the three environmental NGOs – Friends of the Earth International (FOEI), International Union for the Conservation of Nature (IUCN), and the Advisory Committee on the Pollution of the Sea (ACOPS) – maintain an informal working group during the bi-annual general conference. In this group they designate a division of labour for the monitoring of committees and issues, and during session intervals they meet to exchange information and consult on policy. It may be that, given a high level of skill and good organisation, an NGO coalition can have more impact on an issue under consideration than a weakly represented small state.

An extension of this device is the alternative conference, running parallel to the official conference. Here the Stockholm inter-governmental meeting on environmental questions in 1972 was the milestone. The NGOs demonstrated a power and influence – under the leadership of Barbara Ward (Lady Jackson) and Margaret Mead – that was disconcerting to many governmental representatives (the press knew where the action was and gave full coverage to the NGOs). The pattern of alternative conferences has continued with the succession of UN conferences on population, food, youth, disarmament, water resources and so on, and the conference at Nairobi in 1985 reviewing the Decade for Women.

Expérience is also showing that NGO participation in the Specialized Agencies and programmes of the United Nations varies according to a number of factors. The functions of the Agency are important in determining the role of NGOs. A highly specific, technical agency such as IMO, ICAO or WMO, will often welcome and encourage the participation of NGOs with adequate expertise to make a significant contribution to the proceedings of the organisation. In addition, past experience of governments or international civil servants with NGOs may do much to shape the attitudes towards NGOs within a particular Agency. It is held, for instance, that in the FAO a generally low opinion of NGOs meant that even reputable bodies like the International Federation of Agricultural Producers went unheeded by the Secretariat. However, there are two UN organisations that have always had distinctive relationships with NGOs. At the ILO, representatives of both industry and trade unions function along with government officials in a tripartite arrangement. At UNESCO, certain NGOs are granted direct subventions – rationalised on the basis of UNESCO not having to set up secretariat units in the sectors covered by the activities and representation of these NGOs. These examples have been followed by other Agencies. An independent examination of why different Agencies have reacted in such very different ways to working with NGOs would be illuminating.

One particular factor which might emerge from an independent examination, and on which the public deserves to be informed, is the extent to which internecine strife between the NGOs or simple administrative incompetence has hampered their operations. Shortly before the time of writing, for example, it was alleged that an important organisation in the environment field, while publicly supporting an application from another organisation to be given consultative status, privately tried to induce the sponsoring government to let the application die quietly – on the grounds that the application had been badly prepared. Disputes between NGOs and poor performance can damage their standing in the eyes of Agency secretariats and governments.

*What interest do NGOs have in the reform of the UN System?* It would be useful to all concerned if an independent examination could spell out the nature and extent of NGO interest in the reform of the UN System. Hitherto in discussion of System reform, the role of NGOs has usually been considered in relation to ECOSOC. This is because the main conduit for NGO influence in the United Nations is provided through the forum of ECOSOC or one of its committees. By this means, for example, the International Chamber of Commerce or the World Federation of Trade Unions can comment on the role of transnational corporations. Amnesty International and other major human rights organisations, while certainly not limited to UN forums, find the UN committees useful. The World Council of Churches and other religious organisations find ECOSOC committees a good arena for making pronouncements on political and social issues. The NGOs representing youth, women or environmental issues have provided much of the pressure through similar channels to move the UN organisations to action in these areas. This is co-ordinated through their national branches to persuade their governments to sponsor specific policies. There are also the numerous NGOs that have specific economic interests, organisations representing sectors of trade or commerce. As must be expected, the level of their participation is directly related to the organisations' perception of their constituencies' interests. As the fortunes and authority of ECOSOC have declined, the participation of NGOs has been pushed further to the margins in the United Nations since they have no official participation in the other UN organs (apart from the Agencies). This, not surprisingly, has led to many NGOs expressing open dissatisfaction with their status, and consequently clamouring for greater participation in other UN organs. In particular, improved access to the General Assembly has become a prime goal since it has become the main locus of authority, especially on development issues.

The NGO plight was exemplified in the report issued in 1975 by a group of experts and entitled 'A New United Nations Structure for General Economic Co-operation'. This report represented one of the many unsuccessful attempts to revitalise ECOSOC by recommending that it be assigned a central co-ordinating and policy implementing role in the UN System.[5] The report made no mention of NGOs, which aroused fears that in the recommended streamlining of ECOSOC they might be squeezed out. NGOs in turn brought pressure to bear upon the Ad Hoc Committee that had been established to consider ways of implementing the report. As a result, the Committee's interim report to the General Assembly included the by now obligatory paragraph about strengthening consultation arrangements between ECOSOC and NGOs. Interestingly, a sentence in the draft of the interim report, stating that 'the Council should also consider ways and means of enabling the non-governmental organisations in consultative status to make an effective contribution to the work of the General Assembly', was relegated to an Annex of informal proposals by the time the document was presented to the General Assembly.

Today the United Nations continues to investigate NGO participation in its activities. As acknowledged in the report by the Director-General for Development and International Economic Co-operation on 'Operational Activities of the United Nations System' of May 1986, 'United Nations system operational programmes are benefitting from closer linkages with non-governmental organisations'.[6] In this regard the report recommends that the complementarity of UN resources and NGO contributions 'should be more systematically explored'. Yet it is noteworthy that in a section on women and development, the report speaks of enhancing the involvement of women in UN operational activities without making special mention of NGOs. The 'more meaningful involvement' of women, it seems, will have to come through intergovernmental networks – not always the most propitious way of promoting their interests.

These are just a few of the many aspects of NGO relationships with the UN System which deserve further examination. Despite their many shortcomings and many disappointments, the NGOs have established a role for themselves as sources of organised criticism of the imperfections of international society, as a stimulant to progress, as promoters of new ideas and

5 Chiang, *Non-Governmental Organizations at the United Nations* (New York: Praeger, 1981), pp. 219–20.
6 'Operational Activities of the UN System', 27 May 1986, A/41/350.

programmes, as sources of additional voluntary funds for development, and as channels of publicity for the United Nations and its Agencies. These are valuable functions. NGOs deserve help in performing them more effectively.

# BIBLIOGRAPHY

## Books

Abi-Saab, Georges (ed.), *The Concept of International Organisation*, Paris: UNESCO, 1981.

Ameri, Houshang, *Politics and Process in the Specialized Agencies of the United Nations*, Aldershot, Hants: Gower, 1982.

Ansari, Javed, *The Political Economy of International Economic Organisation*, Boulder, Colorado: Reinner, 1986.

Archer, Clive, *International Organizations*, London: Geo. Allen & Unwin, 1983.

Armstrong, David, *The Rise of International Organisation: A Short History*, London: Macmillan, 1982.

Ayres, Robert, *Banking on the Poor: The World Bank and World Poverty*, Cambridge, Mass.: MIT Press, 1983.

Baehr, Peter, and Leon Gordenker, *The United Nations: Reality and Ideal*, New York: Praeger, 1984.

Bandow, Douglas, *Unquestioned Allegiance*, London: Adam Smith Institute, 1986.

Bennett, A. Leroy, *International Organizations: Principles and Issues* (3rd edn), Englewood Cliffs, NJ: Prentice-Hall, 1984.

Berridge, G., and A. Jennings (eds), *Diplomacy at the UN*, London: Macmillan, 1985.

Bibo, Istran, *The Paralysis on International Institutions and the Remedies*, Hassocks, England: Harvester Press, 1976.

Boardman, Robert, *International Organization and the Conservation of Nature*, London: Macmillan, 1981.

Bowett, D.W., *The Law of International Institutions*, London: Stevens, 1963.

Brown, Christopher, *The Political and Social Economy of Commodity Control*, London: Macmillan, 1980.

Camps, Miriam, with the collaboration of Catherine Irwin, *Collective Management: The Reform of Global Economic Organizations*, New York: McGraw-Hill, 1981.

Cassen, Robert, *Does Aid Work*, Oxford: Clarendon Press, 1986.

Chiang, Pei-heng, *Non-Governmental Organizations at the United Nations: Identity, Role and Function*, New York: Praeger, 1981.

Claude, Inis, *Swords Into Ploughshares: The Problems and Progress of International Organization* (4th edn), New York: Random House, 1971.

Cox, Robert, and H.K. Jacobson (eds), *The Anatomy of Influence: Decision Making in International Organization*, New Haven: Yale University Press, 1973.

Eilan, Arieh, *The General Assembly, Can it be Salvaged?*, Washington, DC: Heritage Foundation, 1984.

Elmandira, Mahdi, *The United Nations System: An Analysis*, London: Faber, 1973.

Erasmus, Marthinus Gerhardus, *The New International Economic Order and International Organisations: Towards a Special Status for 'Developing Countries'?*, Frankfurt: Haag und Harchan, 1979.

Franck, Thomas, *Nation Against Nation: What Happened to the UN Dream and What the U.S. Can Do About It*, Oxford University Press, 1985.

Girling, Robert, *Multinational Institutions and the Third World*, New York: Praeger, 1985.

Goodrich, L.M., E. Hambro and A. Simons, *The Charter of the United Nations: Commentary and Documents* (3rd edn), New York: Columbia University Press, 1969.

Graham, Norman, and Robert Jordan, *The International Civil Service: Changing Role and Concepts*, New York: Pergamon for UNITAR, 1980.

Hill, Martin, *The United Nations System: Coordinating its Economic and Social Work*, Cambridge University Press, 1978.

Hoggart, Richard, *An Idea and its Servants: UNESCO from Within*, London: Chatto & Windus, 1978.

Jutte, Rudiger, and A. Grosse-Jutte (eds), *The Future of International Organization*, London: Frances Pinter, 1981.

Kaufman, Johan, *United Nations Decision Making*, Rockville, MI: Sijthoff & Noordhoff, 1980.

Kelsen, Hans, *The Law of the United Nations*, London: Stevens, 1950.

Kay, D.A. (ed.), *The Changing United Nations*, New York: Academy of Political Science, 1977.

Luard, Evan, *International Agencies: the Emerging Framework of Interdependence*, London: Macmillan, 1977.

——, *The United Nations: How it Works and What it Does*, London: Macmillan, 1979.

——, *A History of the United Nations, vol. I: The Years of Western Domination 1945–55*, London: Macmillan, 1982.

Meron, Theodor, *The United Nations Secretariat*, Lexington, Mass.: D.C. Heath, 1977.

Micholak, Stanley, *The United Nations Conference on Trade and Development: An Organization Betraying Its Mission*, Washington, DC: Heritage Foundation, 1983.

Mitrany, David, *A Working Peace System*, Chicago: Quadrangle Books, 1966.

——, *The Functional Theory of Politics*, London: Martin Robertson, 1975.

Nicholas, H.G., *The United Nations as a Political Institution* (5th edn, reprint), Oxford University Press, 1979.

OECD, *Twenty-five Years of Development Co-operation: A Review*, Paris: OECD, 1985.

Payer, Cheryl, *The World Bank: A Critical Analysis*, New York: Monthly Review Press, 1982.

Pines, Burton Yale (ed.), *A World Without a UN: What Would Happen if the UN Shut Down?*, Washington, DC: Heritage Foundation, 1984.

Rothstein, Robert, *Global Bargaining: UNCTAD and the Quest for a New International Economic Order*, Princeton University Press, 1979.

United Nations, *Some Reflections on Reform of the United Nations* (prepared by Maurice Bertrand for the Joint Inspection Unit), Geneva: United Nations, 1985.
——, *A New United Nations Structure for Global Economic Coordination* (Report of the Group of Experts on the Structure of the United Nations System), New York: United Nations, 1975.
——, *A Study of the Capacity of the United Nations Development System*, 2 vols (The Jackson Report), Geneva: United Nations, 1969.
Van Meerhaege, M.A.G., *A Handbook of International Economic Institutions* (rev. edn), The Hague: Martinus Nijhoff, 1984.
Weiss, Thomas, *Multilateral Development Diplomacy in UNCTAD*, London: Macmillan, 1986.
Williams, G., *Third World Political Organizations*, London: Macmillan, 1981.
Zimmern, Alfred, *The League of Nations and the Rule of Law* (2nd edn), London: Macmillan, 1939.

## Articles

Ascher, W., 'New Development Approaches and the Adaptability of International Agencies: the World Bank', *International Organization*, 37 (1983), 415–40.
Codding, George, 'The Relationship of the League of Nations and the United Nations with the Independent Agencies: A Comparison', *Annals of International Studies*, 1 (1970), 65–87.
Dixon, William, 'The Emerging Image of UN Politics', *World Politics*, 34 (1981), 47–61.
——, 'The Evaluation of Weighted Voting Schemes for the UN General Assembly', *International Studies Quarterly*, 27 (1983), 295–314.
Ewing, A.F., 'Reform of the United Nations', *Journal of World Trade Law*, 20 (1986), 131–41.
Finlayson, J., and M. Zacher, 'The GATT and the Regulation of Trade Barriers: Regime Dynamics and Functions', *International Organization*, 35 (1981), 561–602.
Ghebali, Victor-Yves, 'The Politicisation of UN Specialised Agencies: A Preliminary Analysis', *Millennium: Journal of International Studies*, 14 (Winter, 1985), 317–34.
Gordenker, Leon, 'The United Nations and its Members: Changing Perceptions', *International Journal*, 39 (Spring 1984), 302–23.
Gregg, Robert, 'Negotiating a New International Economic Order: the Issue of Venue' in R. Jutte and A. Grosse-Jutte (eds), *The Future of International Organization* (London: Frances Pinter, 1981), pp. 51–69.
Hocking, Brian, 'Words and Deeds: Why America left UNESCO', *The World Today*, 41 (1985), 75–8.
Hoole, F., 'The Appointment of Executive Heads in UN Treaty-Based Organisations', *International Organization*, 30 (1976), 91–108.
Jacobson, H.K., *et al.*, 'Revolutionaries or Bargainers? Negotiators for a

New International Economic Order', *World Politics*, 35 (April 1983), 335–67.

Krishnamurti, R., 'UNCTAD as a Negotiating Institution', *Journal of World Trade Law* (1981), 3–40.

Luard, Evan, 'Functionalism Revisited: the UN Family in the 1980s', *International Affairs*, 59 (Autumn 1983), 677–92.

McLaren, Robert, 'Mitranian Functionalism: Possible or Impossible?', *Review of International Studies*, 11 (April 1985), 139–52.

Maynes, Charles W., 'The United Nations: Out of Control or Out of Touch?', *Yearbook of World Affairs 1977*, 98–111.

Meltzer, R., 'Restructuring the UN System: Institutional Reform Efforts in the Context of North-South Relations', *International Organization*, 32 (Autumn 1978), 993–1018.

Newcombe, Hanna, 'Alternative Pasts: a Study of Weighted Voting in the United Nations', *International Organization*, 31 (1977), 579–86.

Nicol, Davidson, and John Renninger, 'The Restructuring of the UN Economic and Social System: Background and Analysis', *Third World Quarterly*, 4 (January 1982), 74–92.

Ramsay, P., 'UNCTAD's Failures: the Rich get Richer', *International Organization*, 38 (Spring 1984), 387–97.

Schacter, Oscar, 'Some Reflections on International Officialdom', in J.E.S. Fawcett and Rosalyn Higgins (eds), *International Organization* (London: Oxford University Press for Royal Institute of International Affairs, 1974), 53–63.

Steele, D.B., 'The Case for Global Economic Management and UN System Reform', *International Organization*, 39 (Summer 1985), 561–78.

Underhill, Evi, 'UNESCO and the American Challenge', *Journal of World Trade Law*, 18 (Sept-Oct. 1984), 381–95.

Weiss, Thomas, 'International Bureaucracy: the Myth and Reality of the International Civil Service', *International Affairs*, 58 (1982), 286–306.

Williams, D., 'The Politicization of the Technical Agencies of the UN', paper to the Annual Conference of the British International Studies Association, Oxford, Dec. 1978.

# INDEX

Ad Hoc Committee . . . to Examine the Finances of the UN and its Specialized Agencies, 112

Administrative Committee on Co-ordination (ACC), 16, 22, 24, 51-2, 76, 108-10, 115, 117, 119n, 160, 192, 219, 220

Advisory Committee on Administrative and Budgetary Questions (ACABQ), 21, 23, 108, 112, 226

Advisory Committee on the Application of Science and Technology, 153

African food crisis, 111, 199, 239

agriculture: 111; *see also* FAO

Aid for development (general): 88-9, 90, 126n, 174 & n, 118-9, 203, 209, 224-5; *see also* agencies

apartheid: 12, 58, 66, 69, 70; *see also* South Africa

Arab-Israeli conflict: 12, 56, 57-8, 63-4, 66, 66-7, 69, 70, 97; *see also* Israel

ASEAN, 20, 229

Assembly, *see* General Assembly

Australia, 86, 90

Bertrand Report, 23-4, 87, 89, 97, 181-95, 217

'Big Four/Big Five' agencies: 29, 30-36, 86, 197, 198; *see also* FAO, ILO, WHO, UNESCO, UNIDO

Boerma, Addeke (Director-General, FAO), 156

Brewster, Havelock R., 150

Brandt Report: 146; *see also* North-South questions

Bretton Woods agreements and institutions: 8-9, 13, 14, 28, 39-41, 67-9, 89, 149, 150, 160-6, 193, 198; *see also* World Bank, IDA, IFC, IMF

Budget of United Nations: 95-105, 222; *see also* Finances of agencies

Canada, 86, 90

CARICOM, 202, 230

Charter (of the UN), 17, 59, 75, 99, 106, 117, 128, 129, 182, 217, 220-1, 226, 228, 237, 240

Charter of Economic Rights and Duties of States, 11, 61, 144n

Chernobyl nuclear accident, 39, 233

Chiang Kai-shek, 56, 75

China, 12, 56, 99

CIMMYT, 156

Civil and Political Rights Covenant, 59

Clausen, A.W. (President, World Bank), 164

Colombo Plan, 201

Colonial independence, 6, 7, 8

Committee for Programming and Co-ordination, 219

Commonwealth, 148, 163, 201, 213, 222, 227

Conference on Security and Co-operation in Europe, 81

Congo, 51, 80

consensus decisions, 80-82

Consultative Group for International Agricultural Research (OGIAR), 33, 155-6, 156-7, 158

Co-ordination: 20-1, 23-4, 49, 51-2, 53-4, 89, 94, 106-18, 125-6, 155-9, 167-73, 177-80, 183-4, 191-2, 216-22, 224-5, 231-2, 236-8; *see also* Advisory Committee on Co-ordination; Committee for Programming and Co-ordination; Consultative Group for International Agricultural Research; Enlarged Committee for Programme Co-ordination; Jackson Report; UNDP; World Bank Consultative Groups

Cuba, 63

Developing countries (general), 8-12, 12, 35, 36, 40, 68, 70, 81, 99, 118, 123-5, 130, 143-51, 153-9, 160, 162, 164, 167-80, 186, 188, 190-1, 196, 199, 200, 201, 204, 207-15, 218, 224, 229, 230, 234-6, 239, 240, 241; *see also* North-South question; New International Economic Order

Development Assistance Committee (DAC): 121, 168, 174n, 229; *see also* OECD

Development Decades, 36, 51, 107, 111-2, 144n., 153, 204, 210

Development and International Economic Co-operation, Director-Gen-